MURDER
IN
ATLANTA!

Skyline of Modern Atlanta

The towering skyscrapers of Atlanta in the 1980s reach upward from the remnants of a city that has been almost completely transformed in the years since the first twentieth-century murders shocked its residents.

MURDER
IN
ATLANTA!

SENSATIONAL CRIMES
THAT ROCKED THE NATION

By
James S. Jenkins

ATLANTA
CHEROKEE PUBLISHING COMPANY
1981

ISBN: 978-0-87797-056-9 Hardcover
ISBN: 978-0-87797-327-0 Paper

Jenkins, James S.
    Murder in Atlanta! : sensational crimes that rocked the nation
/ by James S. Jenkins. — Atlanta : Cherokee Pub. Co., 1981.
    xiv, 200 p., [3] p. of plates : ill. ; 24 cm.
    ISBN 0-87797-056-4 : $8.95

    1. Murder Georgia Atlanta History.   2. Murder—Georgia—Atlanta—
Public opinion.   3. Public opinion—Georgia Atlanta.   4. Criminal investiga-
tion Georgia Atlanta History.   5. Atlanta (Ga.) Police.   I. Title.
HV6534.A7J44   81-68541
                      364.1'523'09758231—dc19
                                                      AACR 2   MARC
Library of Congress

Portions of this book appeared originally in a paperback book entitled
Murders and Social Change (1974) under LC Catalog Card No. 73–
91479.

This book is printed on acid-free paper which conforms to the American
National Standard Z39.48-1984 *Permanence of Paper for Printed Library
Materials.* Paper that conforms to this standard's requirements for pH, alka-
line reserve and freedom from groundwood is anticipated to last several
hundred years without significant deterioration under normal library use
and storage conditions.

PRINTED IN THE UNITED STATES OF AMERICA

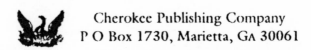

Cherokee Publishing Company
P O Box 1730, Marietta, GA 30061

To
the Memory
of
the Victims

Table of Contents

Illustrations

(For credits, see p. 201)

Introduction

The facts in the case were extremely sketchy. There was little for the investigators to go on. A young man found murdered. No weapon was located at the scene of the crime, but it was believed to be a large rock or boulder—the victim having died from a blow to the head. No eyewitnesses to the homicide came forward. Persons in the vicinity, when questioned, related a story of family rivalry and jealousy. A neighbor told investigators that he was present a few days before during an argument between the victim and his older brother. The older brother accused the victim of conspiring against him with their father to cheat him out of his inheritance. Afterwards, others came forward and related in detail the malice and jealousy of the older brother, who had made threats against his brother. It appeared to the investigators to be an open and shut case. The victim, Abel, had been slain by his older brother, Cain. Motive—jealousy. The accused was condemned, sentenced, and banished away into the land called Nod.

Crimes of violence are the oldest known to mankind. The crime of homicide, the killing of one person by another, is a type of behavior that all cultures tend to condemn regardless of differences in social organization and values. Not only is homicide condemned by most societies but an attempt is made to control such crimes, and the usual method of control is a penalty commensurate with the crime. What should be the punishment for a person who commits the crime of homicide? In the above-mentioned murder the authority passing on the case decided that banishment was the proper punishment. In time, harsher penalties were instituted. Society decided that a person who takes another person's life should be made to pay with his own life. Consequently, society began committing murder as punishment for persons who committed this type of crime. The results of such punishment seemed not to have lessened the crime of homicide, and, if anything, by the violent nature of such a policy, actually contributed to the increase of such crimes. As a result, the punishment of murder in most Western nations has been modified. Now murderers, when tried and convicted, are banished from society. They suffer essentially the same punishment meted out by the Almighty in the case of Cain.

The murder of Abel by Cain has had a profound effect not only on the punishment of people who commit this crime, but an effect upon how investigators of subsequent homicides go about solving them. It was duly noted that Abel was slain because of a family disagreement, or rather a rivalry within the family, which ultimately was resolved by a crime of violence. Investigators still assume that practically all homicides basically follow the Cain-Abel pattern. Abel was murdered by someone known to him, in this case a relative, in most cases by either a relative or a close friend. To find out who committed such a crime the proper procedure for the investigator to follow is to take a close and searching look at relatives and persons known to the victim. There you will usually find the murderer. With all the technological changes and variations in life-styles, this principle in nearly all cases holds true. Today, in practically all instances, a person who becomes a homicide statistic was done in by a relative or close friend.

But not always. The unpredictable.cases which do not follow the Cain-Abel pattern is often what makes detective work harrowing. Some murder cases have become famous due largely to what we might call the investigators falling prey to the Cain-Abel syndrome. In detective work this means that you cannot always follow the Cain-Abel pattern in attempting to solve all murders. Insofar as most homicide victims are murdered by a relative or close acquaintance, and since the police are confronted with this type of crime and see it repeated day in and day out, detectives must be on guard not to assume that a friend or relative is the murderer in a particular homicide case in which there appears to be no quick solution.

The crime of homicide through the years continues to follow the Cain-Abel pattern. Bitter squabbles among members of a family, or close friends, is resolved by a killing. How much or actually how little of this activity goes on is a pretty good index of how civilized a society has become. Throughout his-

tory as a society becomes more technologically advanced, of-
fenses against property (burglary and theft) have risen in the
United States and in other urbanized countries. On the other
hand, crimes of violence (murder, rape, aggravated assault)
have decreased. Even in the decade of the sixties when crimes
in all categories moved upward, the crime of homicide did not
rise at the same rate as crimes against property. This would
seem to indicate that people still usually don't sit down and
plan the death of another. In spite of all the increase in many
areas of crime, the murder of the Cain-Abel pattern seems, if
not to be lessening, at least to be undergoing certain changes.

That is not to say that we do not have an increase in the
homicide rate at the present time. We do. What appears significant, and admittedly is more of an impression than anything else, is that the pattern is changing. The emphasis of
homicides appears to be shifting away from premeditation
and, as the lawyers say, malice aforethought, to an act more
akin to exasperation, unkept promises, and boredom.

The typical homicide today follows the Cain-Abel pattern
to the extent that it is usually committed by a relative or close
friend. The change occurs very subtly as you look over
hundreds of cases. The homicide begins as a matter of assault
triggered by a spur-of-the-moment fit of anger. A cheap .22
caliber pistol is readily at hand. A domestic squabble ensues.
To end the argument the wife or husband ends up snatching
the gun and shooting the other. One or more shots are fired
and the victim, even if hit more than once, often recovers. But
fired at close range, a gun costing less than ten dollars can
readily kill with one bullet. If so, the perpetrator then usually
calls the police and states matter of factly that a homicide has
occurred.

Let's suppose that in the above example the crime was committed by the wife. For this crime the wife receives a ten-year
probated sentence. This is not only a possible sentence but one
which is quite probable. Her only inconvenience is that of
going to court and then living up to the terms of her probation. Hard-liners would insist that if the wife knew she would
get the electric chair she would not have shot at her husband
and would have vented her anger in some less lethal fashion,
such as throwing a plate or coming at him with her rolling
pin like Grandma used to do.

But in our present-day world the rolling pin has been replaced by the handgun, with a resulting rise in the number of homicides. This increase in the number of murders is of great concern to the police, the press, and all persons involved in the fields of crime prevention and social welfare.

This book is a study of several legendary murders which occurred in the Atlanta area. They have been selected for study because of the enormous impact which they had upon the times in which they occurred. These homicides were an essential part of the social fabric of the Atlanta scene and as a result made people more aware of the nature and numbers of homicides then occurring, an awareness which led in some instances to an overall decrease in the homicide rate in the community.

These cases have also been selected for study because they not only illustrate the nature of police practices of the times, but show how in periods of sociological and technological change police methods in attempting to solve murder cases became modified.

MURDER
IN
ATLANTA!

1

A Miscellany of Early Twentieth Century Murders

Crimes of violence tend to increase in periods of social upheaval. In the past homicides have increased in times of economic depression and after wars. The period following World War I was a time notable for social change. In Atlanta, there was an increase in business activity stimulated by the pent-up demand of the war years. New suburbs to the north and east of downtown Atlanta reflected the need for new housing in a growing city. Industry was on the move. The automobile brought about easier transportation and enabled people previously restricted by the confines of quaint, but slow, public transportation to move about the city in their business affairs and to live farther out from town in the mushrooming suburbs. The better means of communication made possible by telephones and modern newspapers brought about a flurry of activity in a city which has always been uninhibited and "on the make." As a rail center in this era of the railroads, trains brought people from everywhere into Atlanta. This brought about an increase in crime.

In the past, criminal activity was hampered by lack of communication and transportation. Lawbreaking among the citizenry was confined to a few kingpins who pretty well governed activity in their neighborhoods. There would be disagreements and fights—and homicides. But these were usually family or gang feuds that were confined to particular areas and had little effect upon life in other sections of the city.

But the boom following World War I, and the enormous advances in technology that followed, changed the crime pattern. The police became more aware and the press began to speak openly about the existence of crime in the city being better organized. Like the city which surrounded it, crime also was being affected by the tremendous shift in living patterns and a rapidly changing society. What came to be called organized crime, which had no doubt been evolving for some time, began to be recognized and identified for what it was.

This doesn't mean that one so-called crime lord came to have sway over all criminal activity, not in Atlanta anyway. What it did mean was that certain persons who carried on illegal activity expanded their operations and became involved in larger and more diversified kinds of crime. It is always the new crime problem that is the most difficult for the police and the public to deal with. Maybe there aren't any new kinds of crime, but there always appear to be people, often very brilliant people, who can constantly come up with endless variations of well-worn schemes that at least give the appearance of a new kind of crime. What they do is refine older forms of criminal activity to meet new and changing conditions. Business, in order to survive in a changing and violatile society, must constantly do this. Somehow the criminal element seems to be ahead not only of the press and the police in this regard, but also the business community. Those persons who originate a new scheme attract countless, less subtle imitators. This leads to conflict between groups, which in turn often leads to homicides. The more usual result, however, is conflict within a certain criminal group that leads to murder. Thus for all the technological advances and what have you, the homicide still follows the Cain-Abel pattern. The players remain the same and only the times and scenery are different.

Some colorful criminal characters flourished in Atlanta in those pivotal years of 1918, 1919, and 1920. People like Walter Clyde Smith, Mark Tillery, Jay "Old Dad" McBride, Abe Powers, Floyd Woodward, and Military Brown were busily engaged in many schemes and rackets outside the law. They talked with their lieutenants over the telephone. They drove fast cars that whipped about the city in defiance of all traffic and safety regulations. In their own gangland world they were the law unto themselves.

Floyd Woodward was the reputed head of the bunco ring in Atlanta during the get-rich-quick days following the end of World War I. The word bunco was a term used to define any of several forms of illegal swindling games or schemes. The bunco business flourished in this period of upheaval and change. Floyd Woodward reportedly devised a scheme that raised the level of the bunco business to a near art form. He understood not only how to take advantage of people but how to bend technological advances to his own criminal ends. His operation was not only organized but took advantage of a new trend in living patterns. During the winters of 1918, 1919, and 1920, Atlanta was crowded with affluent and well-to-do Northerners stopping-over on their way to winter vacations on the Florida coast. This was the beginning of the first Florida land boom and during this time people were flocking southward with legitimate get-rich-quick plans of their own dancing in their heads. As a rail center Atlanta was a connecting point and lay-over stop for these tourists. Many became victims of the bunco ring.

Although the bunco racket as allegedly operated by Woodward and his cohorts had many angles and variations, the best known was the fixed horse race, in which the victim was led to believe he could share in a take on a race that could not possibly go wrong. An elaborate set of props (there was, of course, no actual race) was used in this build-up, and the idea was to let the unsuspecting tourist win a small amount the first time. Greed being what it is among mortals, the would-be tourist decided not to go on to Florida that night on the train, but to stay in town for a few days and play the game again. If the victim bet a small amount the second time, he was allowed to win once more. But ultimately, if he was a real sucker, he would bet that roll of bills intended for a down payment on some choice seacoast acreage on a sure thing, and of course he would lose. His contact would vanish and the sadder but wiser tourist would end up at the police station with a sad tale and empty pockets. Such a racket on a large scale would have a hard time making it in our sophisticated world of today, but in that era the bunco ring was a booming business.

Public, newspaper, and law enforcement scrutiny was cast upon the bunco ring on April 2, 1919. At 8:30 that night, Edward P. Mills, member of an old and respected Atlanta family, was found shot to death on the ninth floor of the Ansley Hotel. Whatever the prominence of his family in Atlanta, Ed Mills was somewhat of a loose branch on the family tree. He was quite a man-about-town, an alleged gambler, and probable associate of Woodward in the capacity of a "steerer" in the bunco ring operation. It was alleged that Mills, a man of debonair appearance and respectable connections, was one of Woodward's men who first made contact with the unsuspecting tourist and steered him toward Woodward and his bevy of con artists. Woodward was no doubt thinking of public relations. He knew his own goons could not approach high-class, honest people successfully; so, he employed someone better suited for this aspect of the job. It would appear from his selection of Mills that Woodward understood not only public relations but also job counseling and the importance of fitting the right man in the right job where he could most effectively serve the organization.

The police, however, were not without some leads in the Mills case. For one thing—all those moaning, sad-eyed, empty-pocketed, winter tourists had given them a clue that something new in the way of swindles had hit the crime market in Atlanta. Officers confided to the press that they were searching for Floyd Woodward for questioning in the case. They had been told that he was a close friend of Mills and that he was in the hotel lobby with Mills a short time before the shooting occurred. Several checks on the body of Mills were examined, one of them for $1,000, a far heftier sum in those days than now. It appeared to Detective Chief A. Lamar Poole that "cards, gambling, and liquor" were responsible for the killing of Mills. A hotel guest who had the room next to Mills was arrested but he vigorously denied that he had any connection with the case. He said that he was from Memphis, had only been in town two weeks, and knew Mills only as someone to drink and play cards with. He certainly didn't kill him. Another hotel guest, a woman from Rome, Georgia, was one of the first people to reach Mills after the shooting and she heard him say before he died: "I have the right kind of nerve to die. I know who shot me, but I won't tell. I'm going to die like a man . . . " A house detective at the hotel told police that Mills was a "known" gambler and had been forbidden to enter the hotel because of his reputation, and he (the house detective) had in fact been on his way up to the ninth floor to evict Mills from the building when four shots rang out. Now there is a conscientious hotel employee for you! Don't let the hotel get a bad name. If someone is murdered on the premises say that you were just planning to throw the bum out. No doubt if Mills had not been shot to death and had continued to pay the bill, he would have remained in residence. Homicide is like the plague; people believe it is infectious.

The police had a lot of information and, as in all such cases, had many reports that turned out to be nothing but gossip. There were no people in town (Had you been fleeced by the bunco ring wouldn't you move on to a friendlier city?) at the time who could identify Mills to the extent of even tying him in with Woodward. Besides, the bunco business was one thing, homicide quite another, and just because the two might have been in business doesn't mean that Woodward shot Mills. Police asked themselves, What was the motive? It was certainly not robbery. Then it must have stemmed from some disagreement. No likely suspects appeared on the scene. The police were making little progress in the case when something very dramatic occurred.

Seventeen hours after the shooting, accompanied by his attorney, Floyd Woodward walked into police headquarters and gave himself up. Twenty-four hours later a coroner's jury was convened to hear the evidence in the case. Woodward testified that he shot Mills in self defense. He stated that Mills had threatened him several times and when the two of them walked into the hotel room Woodward started to leave and Mills followed him out of the room. Mills drew his gun and Woodward shot him first.

Ten minutes after Woodward's testimony the jury returned a verdict: "We, the jurors, find that Edward P. Mills died of wounds inflicted at the hand of Floyd Woodward, the same being a case of justifiable homicide." The coroner was outraged at the hasty verdict.

As a result of the jury's findings, Woodward was set free. On the surface the case might appear to be closed, but the jury's somewhat swift deliverance, and the fact that more questions were unanswered than answered at the inquest, led to widespread public outrage.

A murder within a crime organization very often is the one thing that will lead to public demand that something be done about the crime organization itself. In the eyes of the public Mills was forgotten. Maybe it did happen as Woodward stated. The rumors and talk created as a result of the homicide proved far more interesting to the public than the murder itself. What was all this business about a bunco ring? It was all anybody talked about. An aroused public was demanding to know the facts. The police rushed about in response to public outcry.

In November of 1919, six months after the death of Edward Mills, Solicitor General John A. Boykin and his deputies, in response to public pressure, swung into action. They pulled a surprise raid on a gambling house operated by Woodward on Central Avenue. The raiders were disappointed because they did not snare Woodward in the raid. While the solicitor and his aides placed numerous crap table and poker game players and those in charge of the place under arrest, they failed to find Woodward at the scene. Word had reached him that the raid was in progress and he never showed up at the establishment that night. In fact, Floyd Woodward vanished from the Atlanta scene.

The Central Avenue raid by Solicitor Boykin and his men was but the beginning of a crack-down that eventually put an end to the bunco enterprise in Atlanta. Woodward, who could not be found, was indicted nevertheless on over a dozen counts of larceny after trust, gaming, larceny from the person, and related state charges, in addition to numerous federal charges against him.

The state charged in the murder of Mills that Woodward employed Mills in his bunco operations, and that he had sent Mills to Philadelphia to lure a wealthy merchant to Atlanta to be buncoed. Instead of doing this, the state alleged that Mills went on a spree and Woodward had to send in another steerer to bring the merchant to Atlanta, where he was relieved of between $25,000 and $50,000 in various games and schemes conducted by the Woodward organization. Mills claimed a share of this loot, warning that if he did not receive it he would expose the bunco racket to the authorities. That is why Floyd Woodward killed Edward Mills on the night of April 2, 1919.

Not until twenty years later was Floyd Woodward located by federal authorities at Monrovia, California, where he was living with his second wife and adopted daughter. He was brought back to Atlanta on a federal warrant charging mail fraud, for which he served two years and eight months in the Atlanta Federal Penitentiary.

On April 17, 1943, the old murder indictment was returned and Woodward was placed on trial for the killing of Edward P. Mills 24 years before. The one-time bunco king was given life imprisonment. He was placed on parole by the State Pardons and Paroles Board on June 12, 1947. Returning to California, he died there in 1952 at age 60, known to his neighbors as a kind and gentle man.

THRILL KILLING

On the night of October 20, 1928, Willard H. Smith, a clerk in a drugstore at Boulevard and Tenth streets in Atlanta was shot and killed as he resisted an attempt to rob the store. A few nights later E. L. Meek, clerk in a grocery store at Tenth Street and Hemphill Avenue, was killed in an exchange of gunfire between the store manager and two would-be holdup men. Several days later an unidentified caller to Atlanta Police Headquarters told Chief of Detectives A. Lamar Poole that a student who had attended Oglethorpe College, George Harsh, had been receiving private treatment for a leg wound. The store manager was certain that he had wounded one of the holdup men in the leg during the attempted robbery of the grocery store. George Harsh, the son of wealthy Milwaukee, Wisconsin, parents, was taken into custody by police while on his way to a Georgia Tech football game.

The police rushed Harsh to headquarters, where he was relentlessly questioned for several hours. Ultimately he broke down and confessed to the murder of Willard H. Smith, the drugstore clerk. But he insisted that, although he participated in the gun battle at the grocery store, Meek was actually killed by a bullet from the store manager's pistol. Also in his confession Harsh named his accomplice, Richard G. Gallogly, member of a prominent and well-to-do Atlanta family. Gallogly was arrested and questioned for four hours. He vehemently insisted that he did not participate in the robberies, and only went to the front doors of the two stores in an attempt to prevent Harsh from carrying out his announced intention of robbing them. In his trial Harsh did not deny his guilt, but stated that he committed the crimes under the influence of alcohol. He told the court that he didn't want to commit these crimes, but the alcohol made him do it. He never intended to kill anyone and the whole episode had begun somewhat as a lark. Obviously he did not need the money. His wealthy parents paid for the best legal assistance obtainable to defend him.

Gallogly, who was tried later, was defended in a sensational trial by a battery of prominent Atlanta lawyers. He maintained his innocence throughout the trial, and Harsh, although he had been sentenced to die in the electric chair in his own trial, refused to testify against his former comrade in crime. As a result, the Gallogly trial ended, when the jury was unable to agree, in a mistrial. Gallogly was tried again but this ended in a mistrial. By the time the third trial came around the prosecution had persuaded Harsh to testify against Gallogly, whereupon Gallogly immediately plead guilty and accepted a life sentence. Harsh was then granted a new trial and given a life sentence. Gallogly insisted that he only plead guilty to save Harsh from the electric chair, but few people believed him. In 1939 both Harsh and Gallogly were pardoned by then-Governor Ed Rivers.

At the outset of World War II Harsh joined the Royal Canadian Air Force; he was shot down on a mission over Germany in 1942. As a prisoner-of-war he participated in the heroic but unsuccessful "tunnel escape" from Stalag III German prison camp, which later served as the basis for the movie *The Great Escape*. Afterwards, he wrote a book entitled *A Lonesome Road*, in which he described life on a chain gang and his efforts to redeem himself. In the book he revealed that the downward course of his life began when he became one of five university students who drew straws to pull robberies. He had pulled the short straw when he killed the drugstore clerk. George Harsh died in Toronto, Canada, in 1980 at the age of 72.

This case closely parallels the famous Leopold and Loeb thrill murder in Chicago in 1924. The newspapers at the time referred to Harsh and Gallogly as thrill killers and naturally made the comparison with Leopold and Loeb. The unanswered question remains: Did reading about Leopold and Loeb give Harsh and Gallogly the idea to commit a thrill murder themselves, or rather was it just the trend of the times that brought about these two murders so similar in nature, but occurring in widely different sections of the country? We cannot really know. Gallogly never said, but Harsh stated that he was aware of the Leopold and Loeb case. Both Harsh and Gallogly must have heard over the radio and read in the newspapers about the Leopold and Loeb case. The question is: Would they have committed these thrill murders in Atlanta, four years later, had they never heard or read about the thrill murder in Chicago?

Changes in the level and pattern of criminal activity reflect changes in American life. Just as the unsettled conditions following World War I had an effect on crime, as did the development of technology in the fields of transportation and communication, so did the effects of the Depression.

Hard times and an increase in crime accompany one another. Perhaps spurred on by the example of the kidnapping of wealthy Atlanta banker John K. Ottley, who was held for ransom by two very amateur bandits but escaped unharmed (the case occurring just one year after the much-publicized Lindbergh kidnapping), throughout the early thirties there was an epidemic of ride-rob crimes in Atlanta. Driving at night, or even during daylight hours, often became a hazardous adventure as people without jobs or hope very often turned to banditry. A person would stop at a traffic light in his automobile, and before he realized what was happening a pistol-carrying or knife-wielding bandit was sitting beside him. The bandit would order him to keep quiet and to keep driving. On some lonely road on the outskirts of town, the victims would be robbed, often assaulted, relieved of their cars, and, if lucky enough, spared any further harm. Some were not so lucky.

VICTIM RESISTED

In the early evening of Saturday, September 22, 1934, Max Sjoblom, aged 35, a traveling salesman from Davenport, Iowa, met sudden death at the hands of a ride-rob pair who forced their way into his automobile when he halted for a red light at the intersection of Marietta and Spring streets.

At around midnight that same evening, Detective Lieutenant J. Hiram Davis and his partner answered a call to a downtown hotel where they interviewed Mrs. Max Sjoblom. She was only 23 years old and had been married but a short time. The journey south with her husband on a business trip was also a delayed honeymoon; otherwise she would not have accompanied him on this routine trip. Mrs. Sjoblom was hysterical as she told police of how she and her husband had lunch at the hotel around 1 p.m., and that then her husband had gone out alone to call on some customers. When he did not return for dinner, Mrs. Sjoblom tried to reach her husband at the business address where he had an appointment earlier in the afternoon. She was told by the party there that, yes, Mr. Sjoblom had been at their office earlier in the day, but had departed. No; he did not mention where he was going when he left, but he had been gone for some time and certainly he should have arrived at the hotel by now. Mrs. Sjoblom tried to reach her husband at some other business locations where she thought he might have gone, but failed to do so. She became very worried as evening faded into darkness and notified the police.

Detective Davis and his partner decided, in talking with Mrs. Sjoblom, that Mr. Sjoblom was a devoted husband and not the sort of person who would just stay out all night drinking or playing cards when he had a beautiful wife waiting for him at the hotel. Detective Davis did not realize it just then, but this case would consume his time and energy for the next 35 hours.

The police learned from Mrs. Sjoblom that her husband was a traveling representative of an automobile repair equipment firm and that he traveled in his own car, a business coupe. The officers were then able to determine that the last person to see Sjoblom was the engineer of a local automotive plant about 7:00 that evening. He was alone and had driven off in the direction of his hotel. At this point Detective Davis began to believe that his missing man was the victim of foul play. It followed this new pattern of crime that the police had been plagued with lately—the ride-rob bandits. There was mounting public pressure to put an end to this kind of crime. Just two days earlier a prominent local citizen had been the victim of a pair of ride-rob bandits and had turned up at police headquarters with a black eye and broken nose, the results of having been beaten mercilessly by his two abductors. He wanted something done. He wanted his car returned. He went in to talk with the Chief. Detective Davis knew the pressure was there, and if this case turned out to be what he thought it was, he knew that he had better have all the answers—and quick. Detective Davis started checking the route he presumed Sjoblom took to his hotel, figuring that if he had been abducted it would have been along this route.

The early morning hours of Sunday passed quickly without any break in the case. Lieutenant Davis needed time; he needed a lead before the papers broke the story on Monday.

Then at nightfall a startling development took place. On East Main Street in College Park, an automobile identified as Sjoblom's car was found with blood on the front seat. An identification bureau officer examined the vehicle and found a .38 caliber lead slug embedded in the automobile upholstery. Lt. Davis was fairly certain then that he had not simply another ride-rob case on his hands, but a homicide. This intensified the pressure. Developments came fast.

Police in Fulton and Clayton counties began working with Atlanta police and an intensive search was begun of the area where other ride-rob victims had been put out and assaulted. A man was located who recalled seeing two young men in the College Park area about 10:45 p.m. Saturday. One of the men had his hand bandaged and both men had blood on their trousers. A College Park druggist recalled that two men came into his store about 11 p.m. to use the telephone. One had a bandaged right hand and both had blood on their trousers. They remained in the store until a taxicab came by.

The taxicab driver was found. He told police that he had made a pickup at the drugstore Saturday night but that only one of two young men had entered the taxi—the one with the bandaged right hand. He reported that he drove the man to Kirkwood.

At 7:00 Sunday night Detective Davis received an anonymous tip that a man with a bandaged right hand could be found at an Eleanor Street address in Kirkwood. This was in the vicinity where the taxi driver had let his fare out the night before. Detective Davis went to the address and arrested Robert Riley, white male, aged 20. The taxicab driver immediately identified him as the fare from College Park the night before. His right hand was still bandaged. In a search of the Riley home police found a pair of white flannel trousers spotted with blood stains. At the police station Riley said nothing. In spite of intense police questioning, he stuck doggedly to his story that he had cut his hand in a fight. He had never heard of Max Sjoblom. Detective Davis knew he would have to release Riley unless he found witnesses who had seen him in company with Sjoblom. Even had Riley confessed to Sjoblom's abduction, it would be of little use since Georgia law requires production of the body before a conviction can be obtained in a homicide trial. No body; no homicide. It was as simple as that.

In his interrogation, Riley did give an account of his activities of Saturday night and Sunday. He told police that he and Robert H. Summers had been downtown on Saturday night and met another young man with some girls in their rounds. They had gone for a ride out through College Park. A quarrel occurred and a fight ensued. A door glass was broken and he (Riley) cut his hand. Riley stated that he and Summers were put out of the car and made their way to a drugstore in College Park. When Summers was taken into custody and brought to the police station, he told essentially the same story as Riley. Lt. Davis was convinced that it was a cover that both men had worked out and agreed on beforehand. But he had no proof. The only thing Summers could not explain was why he did not return in the taxicab with Riley to Atlanta, instead of taking the streetcar as he claimed.

There was still no definite connection of the two suspects with Sjoblom's disappearance. Meanwhile a number of Saturday night ride-rob reports had reached the police department, as Lt. Davis had expected. A postal clerk had been waylaid at about 7:30 p.m. by two youthful looking men who leaped onto the running board of his automobile as he was parking at Carnegie Way and Spring Street. They pointed a gun at him; and, when he refused to open one of the car doors, one of the gunmen smashed the window with his fist and fired at him—the bullet grazing his head. Then both bandits fled.

The postal clerk identified Robert Riley in a lineup at headquarters as the man who had broken his car door glass and shot him. Another ride-rob victim, a visitor from Arizona, identified Riley as one of two bandits who had held him up on June 24, taking $50 cash and a .38-caliber revolver. Ballistics tests later showed the bullet found in Sjoblom's car was fired from a .38-caliber weapon.

A drugstore employee identified both Riley and Summers as having entered his business about 8:30 p.m. Saturday. He said Riley's hand was cut, and there was no blood on the clothing of either man. Riley's hand was bandaged in the drugstore.

An anonymous tip to Lt. Davis stated that a relative of Robert Riley had turned a pistol over to a lawyer, and this led to the recovery of the gun. A test bullet fired from the weapon, a .38-caliber revolver which proved to be the one taken from the Arizonian in the robbery weeks previously, compared perfectly with the one found embedded in Sjoblom's abandoned car.

When confronted by Lt. Davis with these findings, Riley

confessed that he shot the salesman when the latter resisted. He also implicated Summers in the Sjoblom case and in numerous other ride-rob jobs during the previous weeks. When asked by Lt. Davis why he had become involved in this ride-rob spree and why he killed Sjoblom he blamed it all on drinking. He said he was under the influence of liquor when he shot Sjoblom. He said that if it had not been for liquor he would never have become involved in all of this. He said that he was glad, in a way, that it was all over.

At 5:45 Monday morning, Riley led detectives to the spot where the Iowan's body had been dumped. The entire investigation had taken from midnight Saturday until early Monday morning. For Detective Davis it was 35 hours of grueling work.

Robert Riley was found guilty and given the death sentence on a murder conviction on September 10, 1934. He was granted several stays of execution, and the death sentence was commuted to life on October 31, 1934 by Governor Eugene Talmadge. He was placed on parole on September 15, 1949, but the parole was revoked on January 19, 1951, and he was confined to prison once again. He was later released.

Robert H. Summers was given a life sentence on a murder conviction in the Sjoblom case. He was paroled on February 17, 1947 and moved to Ohio.

It took a homicide to bring to an end the rash of ride-rob crimes that plagued the city in this time of economic depression. For his swift solution of the Sjoblom case, Lt. Davis received much favorable attention from the press and had a long and respected career with the Atlanta Police Department. He always stoutly maintained that the swift solution and attendant publicity generated in the Sjoblom case deterred other would-be ride-rob bandits and prevented any other innocent persons from suffering a fate similar to that of Max Sjoblom.

THE APPARATUS

Not only the Depression, but the passage of the 18th Amendment to the Constitution, had an effect upon the nature of violent crimes in America in the early thirties. While we usually think of culprits like Al Capone and Dutch Schultz and cops like Elliot Ness, many less well-known individuals were caught up in the crime patterns of the times and became gangster products to a lesser degree than the more famous lawbreakers whom they often imitated. These small-time hoodlums operated in many areas of the country, and Atlanta, unfortunately, had its share of them. Again due to its location as a rail center and stop-over point between North and South, many of these criminals drifted into the city from somewhere else.

Organized crime, like organized business, tends to branch out in order to grow and flourish. To lieutenants of Al Capone's gang in Chicago or Dutch Schultz's Brooklyn waterfront gang passing through Atlanta on their way to the warm sunny beaches of Florida, Atlanta in the thirties often appeared not only a convenient stop-over point but a virgin field where small-time mobsters felt they could become bosses on their own and heads of giant crime syndicates. Although many came, few succeeded in realizing their dreams, and those who did, didn't for long.

Jimmie Rosenfield drifted from New York to Atlanta in the early thirties, allegedly because he had to get out of New York in a hurry and lie low until things there cooled off. Rosenfield was an underling in the Dutch Schultz gang; and it was said at that time that he had shot someone in a holdup in New York, and the police were hot on his trail. In Atlanta he had visions of becoming a big-time gangster in new territory. Ultimately it was discovered that he was involved in gambling activities and he and several associates were responsible for over two dozen burglaries and robberies in the Atlanta area in the years 1934 and 1935.

Rosenfield was clever enough to keep the police from tying him to any of these robberies and burglaries and was well on his way to an increasing life of crime when fate intervened.

Exactly as in the Sjoblom murder, it was a homicide which he committed that ultimately did Rosenfield in. It would appear that society in general was more aroused by murders in those times than today. Perhaps because the murder rate was not as high then, a homicide made a greater impression upon the police and public when one was committed. Certainly a study of crime reports of this time indicates that the criminal was severely weakened and the individual criminal brought to justice and his criminal enterprises smashed most often when, unplanned and for no predictable reason, the criminal committed an act of murder. This really got the press, the public, and the police in high gear.

They strongly believed that the homicide rate more than anything else reflected the true crime index of the community. When a homicide was committed, the reaction was that crime was on the increase. Whether or not the homicide rate is the surest barometer of criminal activity within a community, it is certainly the most dramatic indicator; and then, as now, it received the most attention from the police, press, and public. Whatever, the individual criminal in this era could carry on his criminal activity much better if he refrained from killing. But being gangsters and often lacking subtlety of mind, most never mastered this basic fact. A small-time operator like Jimmie Rosenfield never comprehended it at all.

On Confederate Memorial Day, April 26, 1935, Jimmie Rosenfield, aged 35, and late of Brooklyn, New York, shot and killed Lester V. Stone, Jr., aged 35, of Atlanta, whose mother on that day was presiding at Confederate Memorial Day services. Lester Stone's wife and young son had also gone to the Confederate Memorial Day services. At the last moment Stone changed his mind and decided not to accompany his family. Had he not done so, it would have saved his life. The homicide of Lester V. Stone turned out to be one of the most bizarre crimes of this period.

Lester Stone and his family lived in an apartment building at 572 Parkway Drive, N.E., Atlanta. He had been a star football player in his youth and later became a boxer, but he gave up the career at his mother's insistence. At the time of his death he worked in the radio department of a downtown Atlanta furniture store. A long-time friend and old football mate of Stone's, R. B. Bullock, and his wife, Frances, a beautiful brunette who was the mother of two children by a former marriage, lived in the apartment across the hall from Stone and his family. On the evening of April 26, 1935, Bullock had called Stone to come over to his apartment. When Stone got there, he found his old friend very upset. Bullock told him that his wife had been gone all afternoon, and he did not know where. He told Stone that he was afraid his wife was seeing another man, and he just didn't know what to do.

Soon Mrs. Bullock returned to the apartment, and an argument developed between her and Bullock. Stone got up to leave the apartment, but Bullock urged him to stay. The telephone rang. Mrs. Bullock answered. It was Jimmie Rosenfield wanting to know if she had gotten home all right. She and

Rosenfield had been to a movie earlier, and he was checking to see if she had gotten home safely. Before the conversation was over, Bullock grabbed the phone away from his wife, uttered a remark into the receiver, and then slammed it down. There were more heated words between Bullock and his wife. He accused her of having an affair with another man. The doorbell rang. Bullock went to answer, but Stone restrained him and told him to sit down. Then Stone went to the door, opened it, and stepped out into the hallway and closed the door behind him, without either of the Bullocks seeing who was at the door. Seconds later a shot rang out and Bullock rushed to the door; he found Stone sprawled in the hallway, dead from a bullet in his heart.

Bullock didn't want his wife to leave him. After the murder occurred, she was scared and contrite and promised her husband she would always love him and would never go with another man. They both knew that the murderer was Rosenfield, and they were afraid that if they talked they would get the same treatment that Stone received. Mrs. Bullock told her husband that Rosenfield was tied in with mobsters and recounted frightening stories that Rosenfield had told her of his exploits on the Brooklyn waterfront. Bullock was convinced. If he needed further proof concerning what Rosenfield might do, the body was lying in the hallway in front of the door.

When the police arrived, the Bullocks had their story worked out. They told police they heard an argument in the adjoining apartment and then a shot fired in the hallway. They went out and found Stone. They said they did not see anyone else. They told the police that Stone must have come home and surprised a burglar, who shot him. They could not give any other information.

There was no progress in the case. No one came forward, and of the people the police talked with, none of them linked Rosenfield with Mrs. Bullock. Not until a burglary suspect being routinely questioned supplied them with information did the police get a break in the murder case. The burglar told police that if they would give him a break he would give them some good information.

The burglar related that an associate of his forced him at gun point to drive him to Marietta, Georgia, leaving him with the warning: "I think I have a shot a man . . . don't you put me on the spot . . . " The man's name was Jimmie Rosenfield.

On June 25, 1935, Rosenfield was traced to New York City. Lt. Cal Cates and two other officers went to New York to find him. With the assistance of New York City detectives, and after searching for their suspect for three weeks, Rosenfield was arrested by Lt. Cates as he strolled down Broadway. Lt. Cates testified: "I asked him if he had ever been in Atlanta and he said yes. I asked him if he was the person who had shot and killed Lester Stone, and Rosenfield looked shocked. He told me all the time that he thought he had killed Bullock." It was a mistaken-identity slaying.

Rosenfield was returned to Atlanta to face charges of murder. It was a dramatic trial. Defense attorneys attempted to imply that Mrs. Bullock fired the fatal shot, then passed the gun to Rosenfield. Possibly because of this, the jury, when it found Rosenfield guilty, recommended mercy. Both Mr. and Mrs. Bullock were arrested, and Mrs. Bullock was charged with being an accessory after the fact; but nothing was done about this charge. The gun which killed Stone had been pawned in Chattanooga during Rosenfield's drive north from Atlanta. The pistol was recovered from a prominent physician in Trion, Georgia, who had bought it at the pawn shop. The weapon, a .38-caliber automatic, was taken to Atlanta, where ballistics tests showed it fired the bullet that killed Lester V. Stone, Jr.

On September 9, 1935, Jimmie Rosenfield was sentenced to life imprisonment. On the eve of his retirement from office, Governor Ed Rivers granted Rosenfield a full pardon: January 14, 1941. At this time Rosenfield left the South and returned to New York City, never to be heard from again.

His departure from Atlanta closed the book on the saga of a small-time gangster whose involvement in a mistaken-identity killing spelled the end of his dreams of bigger things.

2

Banker Henry Heinz

In the past crimes of violence have taken on an aura of mystery and intrigue when prominent people have been involved. Homicides of wealthy people then proved more interesting to the general public than homicides of poor people. The more interesting and noteworthy the life, the more absorbing the details if this life ends abruptly in sudden and violent death. Factors enter into such a homicide investigation that are not present in the ordinary case. The victim is not merely known to his family and associates, but well known throughout the larger community. People are interested in the homicide because they are acquainted with the victim or have heard of him. The case receives broad coverage from the news media. The police are under great pressure to apprehend the culprit who committed the murder. People discuss the case and theorize about various motives and angles. Everyone is an amateur sleuth and develops his own ideas about the case from what he has read and heard. The case becomes more than a homicide; it becomes a part of the folklore, as much a part of a town as the waterworks. Such homicides, because of their complexity, are seldom solved to the satisfaction of everybody.

Coca-Cola is an Atlanta institution. The founder of the Coca-Cola Company was an Atlanta druggist, Asa Griggs Candler, a very prominent Atlanta citzen in the early decades of the present century. He was president of the Coca-Cola Company and later chairman of the board. He served as mayor of Atlanta in the period prior to World War I and was active in all aspects of life in the city. In 1908 he had been the moving force behind the development of the Druid Hills neighborhood.

Asa Griggs Candler was the father of four sons and a daughter. In 1943, his only daughter, the former Lucy Candler, lived at 1610 Ponce de Leon Avenue. At this time she was married to Henry C. Heinz, an Atlanta banker. Their beautiful home in Druid Hills was a notable estate in this section of fine homes. Mr. and Mrs. Heinz were charming hosts and entertained often. The Heinz home was one of the showplaces of the city; in the dogwood season the estate was opened to the public, and thousands visited its grounds and gardens. On the night of September 29, 1943, there took place at the Heinz estate not an elegant party, or a tour of the grounds and gardens, but a murder. At approximately 9:50 p.m., Henry Heinz was shot to death in the library of his home.

Officers I. A. Thomas and Ralph Hulsey were patrolling in squad car No. 19 on the north side of the city when they received a call over the police radio to 1610 Ponce de Leon Avenue, signal 4 (burglar in the house.) Though they were the officers who initially received the call to the Heinz home that fateful night, they were not the first officers to reach the scene. But since the call was given to car No. 19 originally, it was the responsibility of the officers in this car to file at police headquarters that night the initial report of the events which transpired at the Heinz home on the night of September 28, 1943. The first report in the Heinz case as submitted by Officers Hulsey and Thomas reads as follows:

We backed car No. 19 up to 1610 Ponce de Leon Avenue on a signal 4 (burglar in the house.) We entered the house and found Mrs. Henry Heinz in a very hysterical condition. She stated to us [that] earlier in the evening she heard a dog barking on the property outside and Mr. Heinz started to go out and investigate. She called him back and told him not to go out. Mrs. Heinz went out to use the telephone, and she could either not reach her party or decided not to call. Mr. Heinz had gone back in the library and she heard him cry out. She went into the library and saw Mr. Heinz scuffling with a Negro man. She went into her bedroom to get a gun, while there she heard two shots. She went back into the library and the Negro man was gone. She described the man as being a large Negro man wearing a blue shirt, brown pants, skull cap and with a handkerchief tied over his face. She said that his back was to her and she could give no other description.

Upon examination the victim, found lying on the divan in the library, had eight bullet holes in his body, and this included both entrances and exits. One bullet entered six inches below the arm pit, another entered at the fifth rib, one entered in the center of the chest, and one entered in the right arm three inches above the elbow. Mr. Heinz was pronounced dead by Dr. J. L. Campbell, a private physician, and the body was removed to Patterson's funeral home. The fingerprint man arrived on the scene and in going over the room, he immediately located three bullet holes in the room. As far as could be determined at the time, there was no property loss at the scene of the crime.

THE ESTATE

The Heinz estate is located on several acres of land at the corner of Ponce de Leon Avenue and Lullwater Road. The house faces Ponce de Leon and sits on a gently rising hill some distance from the street. Although the grounds adjacent to the house are wooded, the front lawn is landscaped, and the house is plainly visible to traffic along Ponce de Leon Avenue. The entrance to the estate is up a driveway that enters the grounds at both the left and the right of the house itself. It is a circular drive which on the left side (facing the house) comes up next to the house, where there is a covered drive-through entryway, screened porch, and side door into the house. A person coming up the drive in an automobile would stop under the entryway, get out of his car, and walk through the porch and side door directly into the library of the house, which is a large corner front room. The driveway does not stop at the entryway, but continues beyond the house and forks; the drive to the left continues in a circular fashion to a three-car garage and storage house located directly behind the main house. Because of tall trees and hollies the garage is practically hidden from the main house. The drive toward the garage is through wooded grounds, and here the land of the estate reaches the crest of the hill and just beyond the drive begins sloping downward to the end of the Heinz property. On the drive, just before one reaches the garage and to the left, there is a children's playhouse built in the style of the estate. Also to the left, and farther down the hill, are a tennis court and a swimming pool. Beyond the garage are greenhouses. The property is planted in azaleas, camellias, hollies, magnolias, and dogwood. The entire Heinz estate, except for the front lawn and the immediate side yards and gardens, is heavily wooded.

A visitor coming up the drive from the street on the left side of the estate would, as stated, drive under the entryway, stop, and enter the house from the side door or else walk around to the front of the house and enter through the front door. Leaving the estate, one would not have to back down the drive, but could continue driving around the house (but would not take the fork to the left to the garage) and would continue driving on the driveway to the right. This drive swings around behind the main house all the way, and bears right and then goes directly toward the street to Ponce de Leon Avenue. The driveway on the right side of the house (facing the house from the street) does not contain an entryway or door, and a person entering the estate up this driveway must go into the house through the front entrance. Therefore to gain access, one must go up the circular drive, entering from the street at either the left or right of the main house. It is an unusual circular driveway in that it circles around behind the house rather than in front of it, in the more ordinary manner. The driveway was constructed in this way to accommodate and be in harmony with the style of architecture of the house.

The house is white stucco with a dark-orange roof and is a replica of a Mediterranean-Spanish villa of the period; and although this type of architecture flourished in Florida and Southern California, in this era it was unique in Druid Hills, where most of the homes tend to be either red brick traditional or English estate limestone. The great charm of the Heinz mansion was certainly due, in part, to its setting on Ponce de Leon and the uniqueness of its architecture in this location.

Flanking each entrance to the driveways are twin white stucco pillars, and suspended above and supported by the pillars there is an ornamental Spanish-design grillwork. In the center of the iron decoration there is an elaborately designed letter "H".

Although the two entrances to the estate are flanked by these pillars, they were placed there for effect and ornamentation, rather than protection, for there was no barrier to entering the grounds of the mansion, either by automobile or on foot. There was no wall or fence enclosing the grounds, or any type of structure to mar the natural beauty and flow of the landscape. Although it was an imposing residence, to the casual visitor it was a home which appeared warm and inviting. The house, even from the outside, reflected the friendliness and old-style Southern charm of the inhabitants. The openness of the Heinz estate is a clue to the character of the people who lived there. It was also an important factor contributing to the tragedy which occurred there one harvest night long ago.

SHOTS IN THE DARK

Officers Marion Blackwell and Bill Miller were not surprised when they heard over the police radio in their squad car the signal 4 to 1610 Ponce de Leon Avenue. It was an address they knew well and a place they had been many times before, for the Heinz estate had been plagued by prowlers in the past several months. At the time the call went out over the radio, the two officers were patrolling in their squad car in the Little Five Points section. Officer Blackwell was at the wheel, and although he was driving along Moreland Avenue from the Druid Hills section when the call came over the radio, Blackwell turned the car around in the middle of the street, driving up over the curb and onto the sidewalk in order to do so. Pressing the accelerator to the floor, Blackwell and Miller roared off as fast as the car would go in the direction of the Heinz mansion, oblivious to all traffic rules.

Blackwell and Miller encountered few cars as they thundered down Moreland Avenue and turned right on Ponce de Leon, the tires squealing as Blackwell negotiated the turn without slowing down. Back then, during World War II, people parked their cars at nightfall because of gasoline rationing and did not drive around on nonessential errands—hoarding their precious gas coupons for work and other important trips. In this era the police, unhampered by traffic congestion, could wheel about the city in their sleek 1941 black-and-white Fords at breakneck speed.

Within minutes after the first call, Blackwell and Miller were roaring up the drive on the left side of the house at 1610 Ponce de Leon Avenue. Blackwell noted that the light was on in the outside entryway, but that otherwise the house appeared dark. As he approached the entryway, Miller leaped out of the patrol car and ran toward the front door. Just as Miller reached the front entrance, he heard a woman's scream from inside the house. It was dark outside in front of the house and there was no moonlight. There were no outside lights with the exception of the lighted porch and entryway around on the left side of the house. Miller tried to enter the front door and found it locked. He tried to enter the tall front windows which reached to the floor, but found that they too were locked. Then there was another scream and Miller managed to squeeze through a small window of the library on the front of the house. The room was dimly lit and as Miller came through the window, he collided headlong with Mrs. Heinz, who had been doing the screaming and now screamed again; but then recognizing Miller as a policeman said: "Thank heaven you have come—I think he is still in the house!!" Miller saw Mr. Heinz lying on the divan in the library. From his experience as a police officer, he immediately knew that the man was dead.

After Miller had leaped out of the car and raced toward the house, Blackwell drove through the entryway and around to the back, whipped the car around, and faced it toward the house, leaving the lights on. His object was to snare the burglar if he was still on the premises or attempted to come out of the house somewhere in the rear. Then Blackwell ran back toward the house, through the lighted entryway and entered through the side door that opened into the library. Blackwell took one look at Heinz and, like Miller, knew at once that the banker was dead. He ran back to the patrol car and placed a lookout for the murder suspect. The only description he could give was that of a large Negro man. He then called for an ambulance and detectives to come to the murder scene. As he returned the police receiver to its place on the dashboard of the car and walked toward the house, a shot rang out, and Blackwell felt the sting of a sliver of concrete graze his cheek as a bullet ricocheted off the stucco abutment of the driveway and sent small pieces of concrete flying. Blackwell thought that the burglar was shooting at him. He wheeled around just as another shot rang out, and from the inky darkness in the shrubbery about half-way down on the side of the drive away from the house, he saw the unmistakable orange glow of pistol fire aimed directly at him. He leaped out of the drive and away from the lighted entryway and took cover behind a tree; grabbing his service revolver and blindly returning the fire toward the orange glow in the darkness. Blackwell called for Miller:

"Here!! He is out here!!! He is shooting at me!!" Inside the house, Miller heard the gunfire and his partner calling out that the slayer was in the yard shooting. Miller ran out through the door of the library and into the porch and lighted entryway. He was in full police uniform and standing there in plain view. Blackwell screamed for him to get down just as the assailant fired toward Miller from his place in the bushes. Blackwell heard the gunfire again and then saw Miller fall off the porch into the dark as though he had been shot. Blackwell thought the murderer had shot and possibly killed his partner. He could not see Miller because of the darkness; his partner had fired once but did not fire again, and he was closer to the slayer than Blackwell. Enraged, Blackwell advanced on his assailant with his service revolver blazing. The gunfire was returned, but even though he drew closer, none of the bullets hit Blackwell. As he advanced, his assailant began moving backward down through the shrubbery toward Ponce de Leon Avenue. At this point, Miller, who had not been shot but had broken his ankle as he leaped off the porch of the entryway to escape the line of fire, managed to make his way painfully down the driveway. This put the assailant almost in a cross fire between the two officers, and, as he turned to fire at Miller, Blackwell ran toward the assailant and fired the last bullet in his gun. Because of the darkness and dense shrubbery, Blackwell was right in front of his assailant before he could actually see him. Miller got within two feet of the person and fired his gun directly at the person's head. The bullet failed to fire properly. With his pistol empty, Blackwell managed to use it to knock the gun out of the assailant's hand. Then, Blackwell grabbed the assailant, leaping upon the back of the man, and began beating him on the head with the butt of his gun. Miller also got into the scuffle. At this point officers Hulsey and Thomas (*remember them*) and Officer Cody arrived on the scene and they joined the fray. Even with five policemen struggling with him, the supposed slayer managed to stay on his feet; and the fight continued furiously until the man was forced to the ground, one of the officers sitting on his chest, another on his stomach. At this point the man shouted:

"I am not the burglar! I am not the burglar!! I have been shot! I am Doctor Vann, Mrs. Heinz's son-in-law." The police backed away in stunned amazement from the darkened form sprawled before them. Officer Blackwell remembers thinking it was all a nightmare: the blazing gun battle, the murder, everything. There in the confusion and darkness it just did not seem real.

SCENE OF CHAOS

While the gun battle was taking place on the grounds, Mrs. Heinz was in the house alone. She thought, too, that the police had cornered the killer before he made a get-away. In the turmoil she had forgotten all about her call to Dr. Vann. When the police came up to the house with Dr. Vann, and Mrs. Heinz learned that the shooting had been not at the slayer, but at her son-in-law, she collapsed.

At this point the situation at the Heinz home was complete chaos. No one was sure exactly what had happened. No more than ten minutes could have elapsed since the original call went out over the police radio; yet at this point one of Atlanta's most prominent citizens was dead and for the moment being ignored, the police were rushing about trying to comfort Mrs. Heinz, and Dr. Vann was thinking he was going to die before anyone came to his aid. Officer Blackwell remembers the oppressive, overwhelming sense of darkness, of trying to get Dr. Vann into the house, of trying to get Miller, who could not walk, into the house, of everybody stumbling over one another and bumping into each other, and of nobody being able to see more than two feet in front of him in the darkness; also, of trying to see by lighting matches, of getting everybody into the house and trying to find the light switches and towels and giving first aid, and all the time the overwhelming sense of frustration bred in the darkness. He also remembers Mrs. Heinz coming around after fainting and rushing about trying to tell them what happened.

Officers Hulsey and Thomas calmed Mrs. Heinz and then examined the body. They sent out several help calls over their police radio. Office Blackwell, as the full impact of what had happened dawned on him, turned his attention to Dr. Vann. To have one of the town's most prominent citizens murdered on your beat was bad enough, but to shoot and possibly kill an in-law at the scene of the crime in a mistaken gun battle had implications almost too frightening to imagine. Blackwell immediately went to Dr. Vann's aid. He determined that Vann had been shot in the right wrist and chest, either from the same bullet or a second bullet. Although understandably in a state of shock, Dr. Vann was coherent. He managed to relate what had happened that night and to explain his presence on the Heinz property.

He stated that his first wife, then deceased, was the daughter of Mrs. Heinz by a previous marriage. Vann lived at 761 Lullwater Road, around the corner from the Heinz home. The backyard of his home backed up to the rear of the Heinz estate. There was a well-worn pathway which both families used to walk back and forth to each other's homes. The path started at the end of Dr. Vann's property and continued uphill by the tennis court and pool and came into the Heinz home at the back entrance. This pathway, easily traveled in daylight hours, was pitch black at night. Dr. Vann stated to Blackwell that he was in his home getting ready for bed when the phone rang. He was tired and disinclined to answer, but the phone kept ringing and he felt that it might be something urgent, possibly a patient (Dr. Vann was a dentist), and that he had better answer. When he answered, Mrs. Heinz began screaming something about a burglar and told him to get a gun and come over to her home at once. Dr. Vann stated that he grabbed his army .45 and loaded it with a full magazine. He started out of the house through the back path but realized that it was so dark that he could not find his way; so he changed his mind and ran out the front of his house, up to the intersection at Ponce de Leon, and entered the Heinz estate from the front.

As he rushed toward the house, he saw Officer Blackwell and thought he was the burglar, about to get away in the car, so he opened fire. When Blackwell returned the fire, his first or second shot hit Vann in the right wrist, thus crippling his firing arm and ruining his aim, for in order to fire the gun after that, Vann had to support his right hand with his left. The wound was very painful, he could not keep his hand steady, and the bullets missed their mark.

At this juncture the ambulance which had been called for Mr. Heinz arrived, and Dr. Vann was quickly placed upon it by the police and attendants. Blackwell noted as Dr. Vann was placed on the stretcher that he was wearing a pajama shirt and a pair of plain khaki trousers of the army uniform type. He wore bedroom shoes and no socks. His mode of dress seemed to match his story.

People were rushing to the estate from everywhere. Senior police officials arrived, summoned by continued calls for assistance and confusion at the Heinz home. As they arrived the police officials encountered Vann being carried out on a stretcher. They realized that the man had been shot, but he did not appear to be in bad shape; certainly he was not a corpse. No doubt the report of a homicide was not accurate. They soon learned otherwise.

Neighbors and curiosity seekers, attracted by the commotion and gunfire, began to invade the estate. A streetcar had been passing in front of the house when the shots were fired, and when the motorman stopped it and ran to investigate, all of his passengers piled out of the car after him to see what had happened. Relatives learned of the tragedy and went from their own homes in Druid Hills to the scene. It would be long after midnight before family and friends, police and press, and the plain curious departed.

After the body was removed from the house, Officer Miller was sent to a hospital. At this point what seemed like a full battalion of Atlanta police officers and investigators was on the scene. Men from the fingerprint and identification sections were going over everything in the house. Four detectives and the chief of the detective bureau were on the scene beginning to unravel the strange goings-on of the evening.

The major portion of the city of Atlanta lies within the boundaries and political and police jurisdiction of Fulton County; however, a portion of the northeast section of the city lies within DeKalb County. 1610 Ponce de Leon Avenue lies within the city of Atlanta but in the county of DeKalb. This jurisdictional anomaly would further confuse and hamper the investigation of the Heinz case.

The sheriff of DeKalb County went to the scene and called for the bloodhounds. The chief of the DeKalb County police was next on the scene. When the dogs were brought there, the officials discussed the possibility of the bloodhounds being able to search for the killer; but it was the unanimous opinion of all the police there that due to the confusion and delay, at that juncture any attempt to use the dogs would be futile.

The police therefore gave their attention to the house and the only person present at the time of the murder—Mrs. Henry C. Heinz. Mrs. Heinz had been taken upstairs and given a sedative by her doctor. Although very distraught and confused, she faced a battery of questions from the police and the press.

She told essentially the same story that is related in the report of officers Hulsey and Thomas. She and Mr. Heinz were alone in the house. They were both sitting in the library awaiting a news broadcast. Mr. Heinz was sitting in a large chair, next to a floor lamp, reading the editorial page of the evening edition of *The Atlanta Journal*, as was his custom before retiring. Earlier they had heard a commotion outside and a dog barking on the left side of the estate, the side on which the library is situated. Mr. Heinz started to investigate, but Mrs. Heinz restrained him. Then Mrs. Heinz stated that she went into another downstairs room to make a phone call, and, before the call was completed, she heard Mr. Heinz cry out. She rushed back to the library and found Mr. Heinz struggling with a Negro man. She stated that it seemed like the struggle went on a long time, and there was gunfire. She could not say exactly what happened after the struggle, but she said she had the impression that the slayer was still in the house when she ran back to the telephone and called Dr. Vann and then the police.

She went back into the library and found her husband lying on the divan. She tried to talk to him, to get him to answer her; but he said nothing, and she stated that she felt sure that he was dead. Mrs. Heinz stated that she had the feeling the slayer was still in the house when the police arrived, but she could not actually say that she saw anyone.

In the library the police inspected an overturned floor lamp and disarranged furniture—the only evidence of a scuffle there. As investigators went over every detail in the library a few meager clues were unearthed. The battered inner workings of a man's wrist watch were found on the library floor. Several relatives and friends stated to police that Mr. Heinz did not wear a wrist watch. An ordinary shirt button was also found on the floor. Three badly smashed bullets were dug out of the library walls. Then the fingerprint man went over the room and lifted prints from furniture, door facings, window sills, and venetian blinds. At this point it was all the available evidence the police had to go on.

Next an attempt was made to determine the route the burglar used in both entering and leaving the house. As you enter the Heinz home through the front door, you step directly into a large reception hall which is a massive room that is two stories high. Standing at the front door, facing the room, there is an enormous fireplace to the left, and to the right a stairway leading to the second floor. Beyond the fireplace, on the left side of the house, is the library—the room in which the murder was committed. To the right, and beyond the stairway, is the dining room. This is the layout of the rooms in the entire front part of the house. There are, of course, other rooms to the rear and bedrooms on the second floor. The only lights burning in the front part of the house that night were in the library and the outside light in the entryway beyond the library. The dining room and reception room were dark. The French windows in the reception room and the front door were locked. Officer Miller had tried to enter the house through all of these entrances and had been unable to do so. There was a small library window on the front of the house which Miller had found opened and through it he entered the house. At this hour, however, Miller was at the hospital, and his partner, Blackwell, was at the police station, making his report concerning the shooting of Dr. Vann. A detective on the scene immediately concluded that this window was too small for a man to enter (he was a very large detective) and that the burglar must have entered the house some other way. A window on the far right corner of the side of the dining room was found raised, and it was thought that the burglar must have entered the house through it. If this were the case, it would mean the killer had to traverse the immense reception hall, both before and after the shooting, which was completely dark. This might account for Mrs. Heinz's impression that the killer was still in the house after the murder, and in the darkness he could have had as much difficulty making his way back to the dining room window as the police had in the darkness outside.

It was also theorized by the police that the floor lamp in the library, when knocked over in the struggle between the intruder and Mr. Heinz, went out. It was not touched by the police until the fingerprint man had been over everything in the room, and it was not burning when the police arrived. Other lights in the room were turned on for light when Dr. Vann and Officer Miller were brought in. The fallen lamp explains why the police found the house in total darkness.

Members of the press, the police, and the curious continued to mill about the house far into the night. Mrs. Heinz left with relatives to escape the confusion and relentless questions. It would be a long while before she returned to the house at 1610 Ponce de Leon.

BACKGROUND

At Atlanta police headquarters investigators began sorting through the meager details they had of the case. The best sources of information were officers Blackwell and Miller. Inasmuch as Miller was at the hospital that night with a broken ankle, it was up to Blackwell to give an account to his superiors and the press concerning the events that evening at the Heinz home.

How was it that he and Miller managed to get to the Heinz home when the original call was given to officers Hulsey and Thomas? It was at this point that some of the background of the case began to emerge.

During the past two or three years burglars had frequented the Heinz home, and Blackwell and Miller had handled those calls. On one occasion, a burglar had entered the Heinz home and stolen a small amount of money, awakening Mr. Heinz in the process. Mr. Heinz had gotten a brief glimpse of the burglar as he fled the house, and when Officers Blackwell and Miller arrived, the banker described him as being a large Negro man. In this same period other homes in the Druid Hills section had been burglarized, and the thief always took only money. Another victim had gotten a glimpse of the burglar and described him as a large Negro man. The press had become aware of the situation in Druid Hills and had written several articles about the robberies. The pattern was always the same. At night, when the victims were either away from home or asleep, someone quietly entered the house and stole money—and sometimes during the daylight hours. Nothing in the houses was ever disturbed or taken, and the burglar or burglars were very careful to enter an unlocked door or window. A fleeting glimpse of a large Negro man was the only clue to the burglaries, and the alleged thief had been dubbed the cat burglar by the press.

After he was robbed the second time, Mr. Heinz decided that enough was enough. He bought a .38-caliber pistol and began target practice in the rear of his estate. He stated to the police that if the burglar came to his house again, he would shoot him.

The police were very concerned about the cat burglar situation in Druid Hills. The most influential people of the community lived there. It was a situation they did not wish to see continue. In attempting to catch the so-called cat burglar, Blackwell and Miller began making nightly checks on several of the estates in Druid Hills that had been visited by the burglar. They made it a practice to drive through the Heinz estate every night between ten and twelve o'clock. They would vary the time of their patrol in order not to establish a pattern for a would-be burglar, thereby allowing him to rob the Heinz home as soon as they departed. If they were not entertaining or up for some special occasion, Mr. and Mrs. Heinz would be in bed by 10 p.m., and all the lights would be out. Blackwell and Miller would ride through the grounds and cruise behind the house, shining the car lights and their police spotlight about the house and grounds. When Mr. Heinz bought that gun, the officers were concerned he might shoot them, thinking they were the cat burglar. Mr. Heinz, a fearless man himself, laughed at this notion and said there was no danger of that. He said he always knew if it was the police, because they shined that spotlight; however, he did caution them never to come onto the grounds without shining the light.

Officer Blackwell was concerned about two things on the Heinz estate: the gun and the total lack of security. He had several conversations with Mr. Heinz about the gun. He pointed out to him that burglars seldom carried guns (we are talking about 40 years ago) and they wished to appear peaceful; and if caught or surprised while on a job, if they had a gun, they might use it. It would be better to face a burglary charge than a murder charge. Mr. Heinz scoffed at this suggestion and continued with his target practice. Blackwell also urged him to take some precautions on the estate. The Heinz place was not enclosed by a wall or fence, and Mr. and Mrs. Heinz owned no dogs. They lived on the estate alone, and the people who worked for them in the daytime left at nightfall. Blackwell stated that when he and Miller drove through the estate on patrol, the grounds were as dark and spooky as a cemetery. They were ready to make their visit to 1610 Ponce de Leon Avenue that night when the call came over the police radio. This explains how Blackwell managed to put a lookout over the police radio for a Negro man in the vicinity, even before talking with Mrs. Heinz.

A second question Blackwell had to answer was the Vann shooting. Members of the press wanted to know, Why did he and Miller shoot Dr. Vann? Blackwell stated that it was all a horrible mistake. They thought Vann was the cat burglar, and he thought they were. But why couldn't Vann see the police car, or see that Miller was in police uniform when he came outside on the lighted entryway? Blackwell stated they would have to ask Dr. Vann that question. When interviewed, Dr. Vann stated that the police fired at him as he entered the grounds and he returned their fire thinking they were the burglars. Upon examination, it was determined that Dr. Vann fired nine times, Blackwell six, and Miller once. Vann stated that when he answered the telephone call from Mrs. Heinz that night, she stated to him in a very frantic voice: "By! By! Come over here this instant! *They* are killing Mr. Heinz!"

"I started to go down the path through the gardens," Dr. Vann continued. "But then I decided that whoever was over there might be outside or have accomplices, so I went down Lullwater Road to Ponce de Leon and up Ponce de Leon to the entrance of the Heinz home."

Blackwell maintained that he could not have fired at Dr. Vann first because he did not know that he was there. Blackwell insisted that he could not see Vann until he was within two feet of him, even after the shooting started. Dr. Vann was not in the drive, but, by his own account, hidden in the bushes; so, how could Blackwell, or Miller, for that matter, know he was there until he opened fire? Blackwell was sure Vann opened fire on him thinking he was the burglar, and he thought this a rather normal reaction considering the hysteria of the moment and the pitch darkness of the setting. In the black night all Vann saw was the form of a man beside the entryway and another darkened silhouette leap from the house. All things considered, it was impossible to tell they were police officers. A man preparing for bed had been thrust into a crazy series of events. Upon reflection, his behavior seems quite normal.

Most Atlantans learned about the Heinz murder the following morning over the radio or by reading the morning edition of *The Atlanta Constitution*. The entire city was shocked and horrified that such a thing could happen in Atlanta. The first news accounts of the events that had transpired at the home the night before painted a rather strange and confusing picture. Needlss to say, on the morning after the shootings the police performance did not come off very well.

Henry C. Heinz was not only a well known but a highly

regarded citizen of the city. Although born in New Haven, Connecticut, on August, 18, 1879, Henry Heinz's father and grandfather had been native Atlantans. Heinz as a young man began a long career in the banking business. He began with the Central Bank and Trust Company, which had been founded by Asa Griggs Candler; and in 1922, when this bank merged with Citizens and Southern, Henry Heinz became a director and vice president of the Citizens and Southern Bank—a position he held at the time of his death. Like other men of wealth of the period, he was very active in civic affairs and devoted much of his time and energy to helping the less fortunate. In 1938 he was a founder of the Atlanta Boy's Club and served this organization as president from then until the time of his death. He took great interest in the work of the Boy's Club, and his desk was cluttered with ashtrays and other artifacts made by members of the club in their projects.

Mr. Heinz was involved in countless civic affairs. He was city chairman of the banking division of the Third War Loan Drive; and he had heard over the radio, just moments before his death, that the drive had reached its goal. Indeed, it was to hear whether the drive had been a success that Mr. Heinz had remained up beyond the time at which he usually retired for the night. Beside Mrs. Heinz, he was survived by a brother, two sisters, and a son and a stepson.

By mid-day all Atlanta knew of the murder, and the police assigned to the Heinz residence had a time of it shooing sight-seers and photographers away. People flocked to the scene of the crime hoping to get a glimpse of Mrs. Heinz. And she was forced to stay away from the home she had built back in 1922. For several days Atlanta was agog over the murder, and even the war in Europe and the Pacific had to take second place to the Heinz case.

The Atlanta Journal headline of Wednesday, September 29, 1943, stated:

GREATEST ATLANTA MANHUNT
LAUNCHED FOR HEINZ KILLER

When Officer Blackwell put out that alert for a large Negro man shortly after the shooting, it had some results. No large Negro man anywhere in the northeast section of the city was safe from either search or seizure. Three suspects had been picked up that night; but by the following morning they had been released, the police satisfied that they were guilty only of being large Negro men.

Following a night of panic, a quiet calm hung over the Druid Hills neighborhood. That night, as news of the murder spread, residents of Druid Hills began to flood the Atlanta police station and DeKalb police station with calls of prowlers on the property and burglars in the house. The police not at the Heinz murder scene were scurrying around all over Druid Hills answering these frantic calls. The residents were gripped by fear. There had never been a murder in the neighborhood before. It was not that kind of neighborhood, and it was in a frenzied atmosphere that the police, in searching the grounds of various homes for reported prowlers, collided with one another—with pistols drawn—in the darkness. It was a replay of the scene at the Heinz home earlier. The miracle of the night of September 28, 1943, is that only one person was murdered.

ENVY SPAWNS RUMORS

As the shock of the murder wore off and the initial reaction of fear ebbed, tongues began to wag. All at once, the city was flooded with a host of wild and unfounded rumors. The case, in that pre-television time, became something to talk about, and as people talked and speculated, fiction very often supplanted fact. Some of the rumors were the result of the dual police investigation of the crime. Some were spread by newspaper writers and radio commentators speculating about the murder, but many of the rumors originated simply from wild imaginations.

Due to the twin police jurisdiction of the case, investigations by two separate police agencies were going on at the same time. The major investigation was being conducted by the Atlanta Police Department, but insofar as the murder occurred in DeKalb County, the police agency there was involved. The chief of the DeKalb County Police stated to the press that he had had several conversations with Mr. Heinz about the burglaries at the Heinz home and had instructed a patrol car from his department to check on the house at various times. The chief's statement strengthened the case against a burglar as the likely murderer.

There were other police detectives assigned to the case who did not agree. Some of them felt the case was more involved;

one detective leaned toward a Cain-Abel theory, and felt that
Mr. Heinz had been killed by someone close to him, that probably his death was the result of some kind of conspiracy. Although he did not actually name the conspirators, Mrs. Heinz
and Dr. Vann were the implied villains in the case. The impression grew and persisted and flowered into full-blown
speculation that Mr. Heinz was killed by Mrs. Heinz and Dr.
Vann because the two of them wished to marry and had to get
rid of Mr. Heinz in order to do so! This rather absurd notion
was given some credence when the press printed what were
supposedly the last words of Heinz:

"Don't shoot me . . . you will get more if you don't shoot me."

This really set the rumor mills to churning for it was inter-
preted to mean that if Vann didn't kill Heinz, Heinz would
give him whatever he wished. The idea persisted that Heinz
was killed because Mrs. Heinz and Vann wished to marry and
wished to "get their hands on the money." Meaning that Mrs.
Heinz would get Vann and all the money too. Many people
believed this was the true motive in regard to the Heinz murder, and that the "facts" never came out because Mrs. Heinz
was a rich woman and the police and press hushed everything
up. For several years afterwards, the press always referred to
the conflicting opinions of various police officials when men-
tioning the Heinz case.

It was exceedingly difficult for investigators to get a complete picture of events because of numerous rumors and false
reports concerning the case. Both Mrs. Heinz and Dr. Vann
were under seige from the police and the press who wished to
question them endlessly concerning what happened. They
grew weary of the ordeal and quit talking to anyone; and
when it appeared in print that Mrs. Heinz was at an undis-
closed location and that Dr. Vann's attorney had told him not
to talk to the press anymore, the "I told you so's" had a field
day.

The Atlanta Police Department issued a directive for all
officers working on the Heinz case not to discuss it with anyone not involved. This order was issued in good faith in an
attempt to cut down on false reports and rumors concerning
the case; however, it was widely regarded as a cover-up.

The first reaction to the Heinz murder had been one of
shock and fear. This could not happen in the city, certainly not
in Druid Hills. People were truly saddened by the violent

death of a fine citizen. But as rumors continued to spread, they began to grow uglier. The viciousness of the attacks on Mrs. Heinz were directed at her because she was a person of wealth.

Soon, strange and threatening letters began to arrive at police headquarters and at editorial offices of the newspapers. Sometimes letters written by near-illiterates, but just as often by people who could write legibly and spell correctly. What they had to say was very clear: Because Mrs. Heinz was a rich woman, a member of the most famous Atlanta family of the era, she could get away with anything, even murder. That is the way it was with rich people: If you had enough money, you could buy your way out of anything; only the poor were ever convicted.

The facts in the Heinz case were swept aside, the police being accused of having been bought out by big money and paid to cover things up. It was a conspiracy which the letter writers felt powerless to do anything about; but the message came across on paper, loud and clear—this terrible hatred and predjudice against the rich. In our present day we are aware of this kind of prejudice existing against certain minority groups within our society, but hatred has not always been so directed. Different times and different conditions create different hates. The era of the Heinz murder was a time when people still lived under the pall and anguish of the Depression. That era of hunger and economic failure had generated a prejudice against the wealthy that even in 1943 had not abated. Strangely enough, it was a homicide that caused this hatred to surface into full view.

PANIC AND FALSE LEADS

The acrimony generated by the Heinz killing severely restricted the murder investigation. The police had become rather sensitive on the subject. They were working very hard for a solution of the case, but they had been accused repeatedly of a sell-out, of treating rich people better than poor people, and any attempt to look for the killer was regarded by many as a mere diversionary tactic to take the heat off Dr. Vann and Mrs. Heinz. But some investigators believed in this Heinz-Vann conspiracy theory and proceeded to try and prove it. This they were unable to accomplish. In fact, about the strongest case against any kind of conspiracy was Dr. Vann's presence on the estate the night of the murder in his pajama top shooting at anything that moved. It would be absurd to believe that people engaged in a conspiracy would behave like that.

A report persisted that because the killer was masked he must have feared recognition and was therefore known to Heinz. An elaboration of this theory held that the man was actually a former employee of Heinz, who was not a Negro man at all, but a white man disguised as a Negro to throw the police off the trail. Very extensive and thorough police investigation could turn up no one who was an enemy of Mr. Heinz. He was the type of man who was beloved by the people who worked for him, and the type of person who would give anyone he knew anything they asked of him. He was constantly coming to the rescue of people who worked for him when they needed money or came upon hard times. If any of these people had any grudge against Henry Heinz, it was not discernable. But Heinz was a man of strong character who did not cotton to being robbed, and it was, with him, as much a matter of principle as of money.

Another theory was that if burglary was the motive the intruder would hardly have gone from the darkness of the dining room into the well-lighted library, especially if he was at the dining room window at the time Mr. and Mrs. Heinz heard the commotion outdoors. Officers Blackwell and Miller felt that the theory that the murderer entered the house through the dining room window did not hold water, and they were convinced that the burglar went in the same front window of the library and entered the house directly into the library as did Officer Miller himself a few minutes later. Others insisted no burglar would enter a well-lighted room with people awake in the house. It was ridiculous! Burglars did not operate in that manner. Never! Only the murderer himself could say what happened that night. Although the search for the so-called cat burglar continued, the quest proved fruitless.

The Druid Hills section of Atlanta was never quite the same after the Heinz murder. Few places are following a homicide. Mrs. Heinz never lived in the house afterwards, and it was closed up and stood empty and forlorn.

Burglaries in Druid Hills did continue, however. Officers received hundreds of calls, but most of them proved to be false. Whereas before the Heinz murder Officers Blackwell and Miller had been handling several prowler calls a week in the Druid Hills neighborhood, after the murder, they were answering dozens of calls a night.

The police thought they had a good break in the Heinz case when they arrested George Arnold, a black male, who fit the description given by Mrs. Heinz. He had been arrested for larceny and burglary in 1936, and for burglary in the northeast section of Atlanta in 1942. The newspapers, too quickly, headlined that a solution to the Heinz murder was imminent. For something more priceless than his own peace of mind, indeed his life, Georgia Arnold had an alibi. He was at work the night of the murder. His white boss stoutly maintained that Arnold was at work loading trucks from 6 p.m. until after midnight on September 28, 1943. Whew! for George Arnold. For the police and the press the speculators had no mercy. A storm of protest from the public followed the Arnold fiasco, and the police and the press became very leery of anything touching upon the Heinz case. Both investigation and reporting of the case came to a near-standstill. It seemed that whatever was done or written about the case created a backlash from the public. The gossips who were saying the case was "too hot to handle" knew more than they thought. Due to the notoriety surrounding the case, nobody wanted any part of it.

Two months after the Heinz murder the police answered a burglary call at a house only two blocks away from the Heinz home. When officers Blackwell and Miller reached the house all the lights were out and a very hysterical lady met them at the front door and in a whisper stated:

"I had turned out the lights in the house and gone to bed and I heard somebody breaking in the back door so I crept downstairs and called the police and waited here by the front door until you got here. He is still in the house."

Blackwell went through the front of the house back to the kitchen where he encountered a large Negro man, who immediately started out the back door and ran right into Miller. The officers had their man. They immediately placed him in the patrol car and began to question him. Upon interrogation, while riding through the Druid Hills area, the suspect confessed and pointed out some 17 homes that he had either prowled around or burglarized. He denied ever burglarizing the Heinz home or being anywhere near it. The suspect was booked at the police station on suspicion of burglary, and the officers were certain that, if not the Heinz killer, they had at least arrested the culprit who was causing them so much havoc in the Druid Hills neighborhood. When the suspect's fingerprints were identified by the FBI in Washington, it developed that the man was from Chattanooga, Tennessee; and upon further questioning and investigation, he revealed that he had arrived in Atlanta for the first time in his life the afternoon before on a Greyhound bus. When asked why he so readily admitted to being a burglar and fabricated such an elaborate but false scenario of his activities in that field, he replied that he was terrified by the obvious eagerness of the officers to implicate him in the Heinz slaying, and felt that if he confessed to something of a lesser nature they would be satisfied with that and not try and pin a murder rap on him. The man had an arrest record of traffic violations and petty theft in Chattanooga and was very frightened by the mess in which he now found himself. When asked why he had come to Atlanta, he stated that he had heard about the Heinz murder and other burglaries in Druid Hills and thought he would come down to Atlanta and do himself some good. When he reached the bus station in Atlanta, he asked for directions to Druid Hills and rode on the streetcar out there. He walked around awhile until it was dark and then entered the first house he could manage to break into, whereupon he found himself quickly in the hands of the police. Blackwell stated that this incident, early in his police career, taught him something about investigative work he never forgot: never put pressure on people to tell you things.

Several days afterwards, Blackwell spent an afternoon talking with Mrs. Heinz. It was three months after the murder, but this was the first time Blackwell had seen Mrs. Heinz since that fateful night. He had some difficulty in locating her, for she still found it necessary to keep where she was staying a secret, to keep from being badgered by the various police from two departments, the press, and the plain curious. Mrs. Heinz had heard the rumors then circulating the city, and they much distressed her. They talked about the case and Mrs. Heinz recounted the facts of the evening once more. They discussed the events in detail, but only one important new fact that Blackwell was previously unaware of emerged from his conversation with Mrs. Heinz. She stated that while she and Mr. Heinz were in the library listening to the news over the radio, and while he had been reading the newspaper, she had been sewing for the Red Cross, and that she carried her sewing in a bright red knit bag. It did not appear significant to Blackwell then, but it was something he had not heard before; and Mrs. Heinz said that in the excitement of that evening she had not recalled it.

The next day Blackwell talked with Dr. and Mrs. Vann for the first time since the murder. Dr. Vann was out of the hospital and recovering from his wounds, but he still appeared dazed by the events of the past few months. The hysterical phone call from Mrs. Heinz that night, the gun battle at the Heinz home, his injuries; and then, the gossip about himself and Mrs. Heinz. It was all a terrible nightmare. He shook his head and wondered out loud about how such things could happen to people. Blackwell wondered how any responsible person could talk with Dr. Vann and then conclude that the man could possibly be involved in the Heinz murder.

CLOSING IN

On Sunday night, January 14, 1945, a year and four months after the Heinz murder, Fulton County police officers, on patrol in the area of north Fulton County, noticed a car driving somewhat erratically with the headlights out. They halted the car, and Officer Thompson got out to investigate. They found a Negro man in the car alone, and they asked him what he was doing in that neighborhood at that time of night, driving around with the lights off.

"I just a railroad nigger trying to get home," the man answered respectfully. "My lights went bad." The officers didn't find this unusual in the third year of World War II when people were finding it difficult to keep cars in good shape or to secure parts for much-needed repairs. The man appeared to be perfectly sober, and nothing else aroused Officer Thompson's suspicions. He told the man to drive on—and get those lights fixed. The Negro man thanked him profusely and drove off. Almost as an afterthought Thompson jotted down the license number of the man's car.

At approximately 8:30 that same night, the wife of prominent Atlanta attorney Hughes Spalding went into the well-lighted bedroom of the Spalding home on Peachtree Road and found a Negro man, gun in hand, his face hidden with a handkerchief, calmly moving about the room. She called to him and demanded to know what he was doing there, but he paid no attention to her, walked over to a closet, removed a pocketbook from the shelf, and then left. When Fulton County police arrived, Mrs. Spalding described the intruder as a large Negro man who walked a short distance from the house and got into a blue car. The police found a bandanna-type handkerchief that the intruder dropped as he left the Spalding home.

When the lookout was placed over the police radio, Officer Thompson felt sure the man involved was the one he had stopped earlier less than a mile from the Spalding home. He immediately called over the police radio and gave the license number of the wanted car.

At 9:40 the same evening, Atlanta police, having been alerted for the wanted man, spotted the car with the license number driving west on Simpson Road. They stopped the car, placed the man under arrest, and took him to the city jail. He offered no resistance. From there he was picked up and taken to the Fulton Tower jail by Fulton County police. He was questioned that night but did not admit entering the Spalding home. Officer Thompson interviewed the suspect and positively identified him as the man driving a blue car with the lights off.

Fulton County police went to the suspect's home and interviewed his wife. She identified the handkerchief found at the Spalding home as the property of her husband. One of their children had given him a set of four for Christmas. When confronted with this, the suspect confessed and took officers to the spot where he had thrown Mrs. Spalding's pocketbook. He admitted also breaking into 14 other houses in the North Atlanta area. In the interrogation the suspect stated that he "didn't have to wait until people went to bed before breaking in." The suspect was booked and held for indictment by the Fulton County grand jury.

The arrest report gave the man's name as Horace Blalock, a black male, of 1986 Simpson Road, Atlanta. He was born in Cobb County, Georgia, on June 26, 1909 and attended school there until he dropped out in the eighth grade. He was a man of large build and was 6'3" tall and weighed 230 pounds. His complexion was described in the report as medium brown. He had a large burn scar on the left arm, inside and above the elbow, and two smaller scars: one on the left side of the forehead and another on the inside right thumb. He was married and the father of three children and had two brothers living in Cobb County. He gave his occupation as porter.

Upon checking, Fulton County police discovered that Blalock had received three citations for traffic violations by Atlanta police over the past three years but had no record of burglary. When he was arrested for burglary of the Spalding home, Horace Blalock was fingerprinted for the first time.

Since the Heinz murder, the fingerprints of all persons arrested for burglary had been compared with the prints found in the Heinz home the night of the murder. When the prints were compared, Fulton County police were amazed at the similarity of the prints taken from the Heinz home and those of Blalock. However, they proceeded with great caution. There had been so much publicity on the Heinz case, so many false leads that in fact led nowhere, that the Fulton County police moved forward warily. But they became the third police agency involved in the case. Blalock was told nothing about the check on fingerprints.

Identification experts of the Georgia Bureau of Investigation, the fourth law enforcement agency to be involved in the case, were called in to examine the prints. Captain Ben Seabrook of the Atlanta I.D. Bureau also studied the prints carefully. It was the unanimous opinion of all these people that the index and small-finger prints taken from the venetian blind in the library of the Heinz home the night of the murder matched those of Horace Blalock. This appeared to make the identification positive. But speculation in the Heinz murder had come in waves in the past year since the homicide, and when the police came upon each speculation they tried feverishly to trace down every possible clue. No case in Atlanta history had ever caused so much unrestrained theorizing. This time officers had to be sure, for if the prints did not match conclusively, then the results would be just more waves of speculation and another dead-end.

Both Blalock's prints and the prints lifted at the Heinz home were sent to Washington for comparison. The FBI, the fifth law enforcement group in the case, was the most respected authority in the country on the subject of prints. The investigators wanted the FBI's evaluation before proceeding any further with their latest lead.

It was an anxious 24 hours for the police connected with the case as they awaited word from Washington. Then, a terse one-line telegram arrived from the FBI:

Latent print identical with print of suspect Blalock.

[signed] Hoover.

Now the police knew that Blalock was at the Heinz home at one time or another, and it would be up to the suspect to provide an explanation of his whereabouts the night of September 28, 1943.

Blalock was being held in Fulton Tower jail for trial on the burglary charge. He had been told nothing about his fingerprints matching with those from the Heinz home. He had not asked to see an attorney.

On Thursday, January 18, 1945, four days after he had been picked up on the burglary charge, Blalock admitted he had burglarized the Heinz home several weeks before the slaying and accompanied officers to the crime scene, showing them how he entered the house (through the library window) and the route he took to Mrs. Heinz's bedroom, where he said he took $80 from a purse on a dressing table. The same afternoon, Mrs. Henry Heinz picked Blalock out of a lineup as the man she saw grappling with her husband the night of the murder.

Blalock was taken into the detective office and questioned extensively by Fulton County police, the chief of the DeKalb County police, and Captain Seabrook of the Atlanta police. Questioned constantly for some 15 hours, Horace Blalock confessed that he murdered Henry Heinz. One of the participants of that session described it later as follows:

Everybody was seated about the office very casual like. We would talk among ourselves about the case. Officers would come in and out on other business, there would be discussion of other cases, of routine police business and then we would begin talking about the Heinz case again. We would ask Blalock questions, mainly about his activities the night of the murder. Blalock was seated at a desk—an ordinary desk there in the office. There were no bright lights or the suspect being subjected to any discomfort, except the questions. Blalock was friendly and agreeable and showed no anger toward any of us. His replys [sic] were always well thought out and intelligent. He was a very likeable person and in the questioning there was none of the seething hostility that often develops in this type of situation. Food and soft drinks were brought in from time to time, and we would not talk about Heinz during these breaks.

Blalock gave the appearance of being very fond of his family. I don't know how to say it exactly except that he was not carefree. In many ways he was different from your ordinary suspect; his manner, his very conservative way of behaving, his politeness, and his intelligence. All this made him different. Talking about his family and children seemed to get to him. We went over again and again all we knew about the case—which was a good deal—and tried to get Blalock to fill in the answers. Bit by bit he began to tell us things we hadn't known before. When he realized this, and this was quickly, he sat quietly for a long time and would not talk to us. We were on the verge of sending him back to his cell and giving it up for the night when he suddenly asked for a paper and pencil. It was handed to him and he began writing vigorously. While he was writing no one in the room said anything, and no one came in to interrupt while he was writing. He took a long time. It was kind of eerie . . . the long silence.

CONFESSION

For the time and the person and the place, Horace Blalock laboriously wrote out in long hand that night a rather remarkable statement. Then, he was writing down a confession to the murder of Henry Heinz; today, it reads more like a commentary, or social document of a by-gone era.

The following statement was written by Horace Blalock on January 19, 1945. Ryburn G. Clay, referred to in the statement, had once employed Blalock for a short time.

On the day of Sept. 14, 1943 I had to go to the hospital for a serious operation on the brest left side and I stay in the hospital until Sept. 18th cause I had a cold. They operated on me on the 18th day of Sept. 1943. I left the hospital on the 23 to go home. I was very weak until the 15 day of Oct. 1943. I began to gain my strain, I need some money. I was get $7.00 a week out of my policy that was not anof and I try to figer out some way to get some more money. I was at home that nite. My wife and myself. So some body came by my house going to Dallas, Ga. to see my sister-in-law. They ask my wife and myself to go with them so I say I am to weak to ride up there so I demand my wife to go ahead so she did but she say will you be allwright. I say sure I will be so when she left I come out of my house and got in my car and left. I went down on out in Druid Hill and

look around. I stop and Mr. Heinzy home on ponde de leon Ave.
I went up there and I look around it was about 7:30 at night so
I spoted them sitting in the side room. They were reading so I
waited until Mrs. Heinzy went into the bedroom then I went to
the winder and walk slower to the side room I thought both of
them was goind to the bed room and I thought I spotted a red
pocketbook on the sofa but it was a sewing bag and I hat a gun
in my pocket when I got there there he was I was sorprised I
turned to run and fell over the tables and he grab me and we
tussle for a few minute he was so strong I could hardly hold
him so he got my gun before I did and point it at me and shoot
my thum half in two, and I got the best of him but I did never
get the gun he had the gun but I twisted the gun point at him
and it was fire every once in awhile. I don't know how many
times it fire I got it in a little while in my hand and I ran out.
Then I saw my finger was bleeding so and I all ready weak I
could hard make it. I went strait home got me some little stick
and did it up. I went to bed it bled all night. I went to the doctor
the next morning and he fix it up. But I have not rested a nite
since it have been worried me so much I could not sleep I say
awake all night if it had not been for my wife and children I
would have done give up. I go to church I could feel right it was
sometime on my mind all the time I am sorrow I don't no what
to do. I bought the gun from a boy on the west side of town. I
dont no who he was. I throw the gun in the river at Marietta
Bridge I was brought up in the church and made to do wright.
My mother and father are dead they made me do wright but
when I got up I staid away from her and his raised. They was
very nice to me I have worked for some very good white people
in Atlanta I work for Mr. Clay for a year or more. I do wont Mr.
Clay to speak for me at my trial gentlemen I need mercy of you
all for my family I have a wife and 3 little children. One 3-8-9
for the sake of my little children I ask mercy of Mrs. Heinzy
please mirm just in order so see my children grow up and not
let the make the same mistake I have made in life I am ask
that you gentlemen please sir, I am so sorrow have mercy on
me for wife and my children. Crime dont pay everbody that is
doing wrong quit it now dont pay. The trial will come off in
Decatur, Ga. High Cort some time in March. I hope you gentlemen will consider my case by that time please sir and please
mirm I am sorrow I turned out to be what I did I married a fine
girl for a wife she is a chrisen woman and not a better one she
beleave in wright and wright a long I hope she will be happier
again someday. She is a mitre sweet girl I will have to give her
critic for my little children that so much of me and there

mother it is hard for me to part from them but the lord says the best of friend must part from one another I wont you all to pray for me and I will pray for me. My time is all mose up but I hope not cose I am so sorrow I dont know what to do please pray for me and my family and children I hope no more of my people dont no crime. So sorrow.

[signed] Horace Blalock

Blalock's statement was printed in the papers and received wide readership. When the trial came up in March, it was very unlikely that anyone on the jury would not have read and been aware of the confession. And the remarkable thing is that is just what Blalock intended, for the confession is not really a confession at all, but a shrewdly worded defense of a man, knowing then that he was fighting for his life. For the person who could reason well and think things through and write it down coherently even to remembering dates without checking, and then slip back into the Negro idiom of the era, indicates that Blalock, from a lifetime of experience, knew well the softer spots in the Southern armor of black-white relationships of the period. Blalock was trying to get the point across that even though he was guilty of stealing money and had unwittingly killed a respected and wealthy white man, and in spite of all these terrible crimes, a person could read the statement and if saying nothing else for the defendant, could conclude that he certainly wasn't uppity. That would be a far worse crime for Blalock to be guilty of than either burglary or homicide. Making himself lowly and being properly humble, Blalock hoped to appeal to the sympathy and prejudice of the incoming jury. That he knew so well how to say not only everything that he knew the white man wanted to hear, and phrase it in a way that he knew the white man wanted it to sound, Blalock probably did himself more good than either of the two attorneys who would ultimately plead his case in court.

When the fifteen-hour session was concluded, Blalock's statement was distributed to the press, which had gotten wind of what was going on and was camped en masse outside the detective office.

The press and photographers were allowed inside to take pictures and interview Blalock, who was totally unperturbed by the mayhem in the rather crowded office and faced the press with quiet composure and unruffled answers to their sometimes-barbed questions and requests for pictures. Blalock had not talked to a lawyer or asked to see a lawyer. It was normal police practice in such cases to get the confession and the case wrapped up before even considering a lawyer for the accused. It was the way all police departments operated then. Had someone suggested that Blalock's rights had been violated, the police would have been incredulous. The police in the case had treated Blalock very fairly, they thought. It had all been very friendly, and Blalock and the police seemed relieved when it was over.

Blalock stated that he earned approximately $200 a month on his railroad job, a good salary for a man at that time. It was certainly deemed sufficient to support his family adequately. Then why did he feel compelled to steal? Blalock told the press that soon after he moved to Atlanta and got a job with the railroad, he began playing the "bug." In no time, he was spending at least $15 a day playing the bug, and most days he would lose; but when he did win, he would put all his winnings on the bug; and as a result he never seemed to get ahead. He stated he wanted to quit playing the bug but that he could not, for it had become a part of him, a part of his everyday life. Blalock stated also to the press in his interview that he took $45 and a billfold from Heinz after killing him.

HEARING

The grand jury of DeKalb County was in session at that time, and, insofar as the Heinz home was located in that county, all facts and data pertinent to the case were turned over to DeKalb County authorities for prosecution. Immediately the grand jury took up the case and called witnesses. The main witness was Mrs. Heinz. She had identified Blalock in a lineup as the man whom she saw grappling with her husband. She had congratulated the officers for finding the slayer and stated to the press how relieved she was that it was all over and that the strain of the past year had at times been more than she could bear. In her sworn statement to the grand jury Mrs. Heinz said in part:

> I was sewing something for the Red Cross. Henry was reading. We were in the library. A few moments before ten p.m. I grew sleepy and decided to go to bed. I laid my sewing bag on a sofa in the library, and went and took a shower. I had just stepped out of the shower when I heard Henry calling:

"Momma, Momma, that devil is in here. Get the gun quick!" I knew who he meant because he said, more than once to me: 'If that devil who has been stealing from us comes back I will kill him with my own hands.' I put a robe on and went rushing around. I do not remember what he said but I heard Henry cry out again and I heard two shots. I went into the library and saw a Negro man struggling with Henry. I went into another room to get a gun, but ran back to the library instead and found Henry on the sofa and the Negro man was gone. I went to the telephone and called Grady Hospital, the police, and Dr. Vann."

The jury heard from the police who had worked on the case and then it indicted Horace Blalock for the murder of Henry Heinz. The case was set for trial in March 1945.

A roar of speculation, gossip, and pure vindictiveness swept the city. Previously friends and relatives had offered a $2500 reward for the solution to the murder of Henry Heinz. There were charges that the police were railroading a Negro man into prison to earn the reward. Some police on the case again speculated about the guilt or innocence of Blalock and the press picked up these rumors. The press often described Heinz as a "rich capitalist" and Mrs. Heinz as the "widow of the rich capitalist"—somewhat inflammatory terms for the era.

The gossip against Mrs. Heinz reached a fever pitch. The rumor-mongers said that of course she was relieved that the case was closed because then the heat would be off to find the real killer, who was someone in league with Mrs. Heinz. At this point Dr. Vann had faded from the picture, for his statements and appearances made it difficult for even the most determined to believe him a villain. Now, it was said, persons unknown who were responsible for the murder were being paid off by the rich to protect Mrs. Heinz. Mrs. Heinz was also criticized for looking too cheerful at the hearing and for not wearing the proper clothes for a truly grieving widow.

THE TRIAL

In March Horace Blalock went on trial in DeKalb County with Judge James C. Davis of the Stone Mountain circuit presiding. Blalock was represented by two lawyers who immediately disavowed the alleged confession and asked the court not to allow it to be placed in evidence. They also asked that the fingerprint evidence not be allowed because it could not be proven beyond a shadow of a doubt that they were Blalock's prints. After hearing from all sides and lengthy deliberation, Judge Davis ruled that both the alleged confession and finger-print evidence was admissible. For the first time in Georgia court history, a projection machine and screen were set up in the courtroom to explain the fingerprint technique to the twelve-man, all-white jury.

Once again, Mrs. Heinz was the principal witness. Visibly shaken by the long ordeal and the attacks made against her, she left a sick bed to testify. In deference to public opinion, she wore a black suit and hat with veil for this appearance in court. Her testimony was essentially the same as that at the inquest. However, following intense cross-examination on the witness stand, she stated that Blalock "looked a lot like" the man in the Heinz home the night of the murder.

The prosecution witnesses were the various police investi-gators who worked on the case and a jeweler, Harold Jacob-son, who testified that he had sold Blalock a watch similar to the one found at the scene of the crime. He could not identify the inner workings of the watch found at the scene as defi-nitely being the watch he sold Blalock because it was an in-expensive watch and did not have a serial number on it. How-ever, two weeks after the murder, Jacobson testified that Blalock had come to him and told him he had lost the inner workings out of his watch and wanted it replaced. The jeweler replaced the inner workings of the watch for him.

Blalock's lawyers alleged that during the fifteen-hour inter-rogation that the police had put some kind of "truth serum" (that was the new thing then) in Blalock's Coca-Cola, and that as a result Blalock was under the influence of drugs when he signed the so-called confession. It appears the lawyers might have erred in their strategy here. The best defense Blalock had was his confession.

THE VERDICT

The case went to the jury after a three-day trial. After six hours there was no decision, and Judge Davis had the jury locked up for the night. They deliberated all the next day and were locked up a second night, spending the night on cots hastily set-up in the court house. After some 50 hours of delib-eration the jury found Blalock guilty—with a recommenda-tion for mercy. Under Georgia law it was automatic that Judge Davis sentence Blalock to life imprisonment. It was re-

liably reported that the jury was split 9 to 3 in favor of giving
Blalock the electric chair. In spite of intense pressure, three
jurors held out to the end for life instead, and rather than
have a mistrial the other nine jurors agreed on life imprisonment for Blalock. It would be interesting to know if the three
jurors who held out were influenced by humanitarian considerations, Blalock's confession, or a belief that Blalock was taking the rap for a murder he did not commit. Maybe it was a
combination of these factors, but it is likely the last consideration was the most overriding.

It was the opinion of many that Blalock took the blame for
higher-ups. No manner of evidence or reasoning could convince some people otherwise. The police were severely stung
by the rumors and accusations in the Heinz case. They felt
that a super-human effort had been made to solve it. However,
many of the rumors developing around the case could be
traced directly to certain police investigators who were influenced by and believed in the conspiracy theory—and became
captives of it, themselves prisoners of the prejudice against
people of wealth. Certainly the possibility of a conspiracy was
thoroughly gone into, for the investigators wanted to find a
basis for their beliefs. But no evidence of a conspiracy was
ever uncovered. The officers closest to the case and best informed from all the police departments involved felt then, and
later, that any implication linking Mrs. Heinz with the murder of her husband was absurd.

Those who attempted the most to make a conspiracy out
of the Heinz case and felt that Blalock had been abused of
his rights by the police and the rich were often those who
thought nothing of insisting that Negroes should go to the
back of the streetcar and take seats behind the white folks,
and if any Negroes were seated and whites got on the streetcar and needed a seat, then the Negroes should stand, as was
the custom. Clearly the prejudice voiced in the case was
against wealth.

Following the events of the night of the murder, Mrs.
Heinz's role in the case was endlessly speculated upon. In a
way, she was also a victim of the case. Some years later when
she remarried, all the innuendoes concerning her role in the
murder were revived once more, and they still linger to this
day. Many people insist that there was "something funny"
about the Heinz murder.

Officer Blackwell managed to interview Blalock prior to the trial. Blalock stated he left the house through the door opening off the library to the entryway. But he also said that he started out of the house through the reception room but changed his mind and doubled back and went out of the house through the side entryway. Blackwell thought that Blalock was probably somewhat disoriented following his fierce struggle with Heinz. It also explains Mrs. Heinz's statement that she felt the slayer was still in the house moments after the struggle. After leaving the house, Blalock stated he went down the path and through the gardens, the same route that Dr. Vann almost took seconds later. Blalock also said his car was parked across the street from Dr. Vann's house on Lullwater Road and that he got into his car, started it up, and as he was approaching the intersection of Lullwater and Ponce de Leon he realized there was a car coming east on Ponce de Leon at breakneck speed. In order to avoid being hit by the speeding car, he came to a complete stop, and the other car roared through the intersection and quickly turned left into the driveway at the Heinz estate. It was Blackwell and Miller in their patrol car.

On May 18, 1955, Horace Blalock, having served ten years of a life sentence for the murder of Henry C. Heinz, was paroled by the Georgia Pardons and Paroles Board. On June 28, 1956, Blalock's wife swore out a warrant in Fulton Superior Court charging him with abandonment. For this he received a twelve-month probationary sentence which was terminated July 1, 1957. Blalock then moved to Vidalia, Georgia, where he worked as a porter for an automobile agency. This was the last the police heard of him. Some years later Mrs. Heinz married Enrico Leide, conductor of the first Atlanta Symphony Orchestra. They were prominent in social and musical circles in Atlanta until Mrs. Leide's death in September 1962.

The Heinz home became the property of a somewhat eccentric lady who lived in the downstairs section of the main house with a bevy of dogs and converted the second story and garage and out-buildings into apartments. People who rented the apartments stated that the place was spooked and that strange things went on there which attracted the attention of occult groups. It was said that on particularly dark nights a person could be heard walking about the grounds, but no one could be seen. It was also said that pistol shots could be heard late at night, like someone target-practicing on the rear of the estate, but no one could be found. People living on the estate began to believe that the ghost of Henry Heinz returned to the scene of the crime periodically. Others moved away, for the darkness, the overgrown estate, and the memories of murder became too much to contend with. The estate was never kept up properly after the murder, and the grounds rapidly deteriorated. Today the house stands vandalized and forlorn. A walk upon the grounds in the dead of night has nothing to recommend it.

Now Ponce de Leon Avenue is a busy thoroughfare for commuters driving into the city from surrounding suburbs. Most of the old estates of another time have been converted into churches or clubs or cleared away to make room for apartments or town houses. The time when this section was regarded as being way out from town has long since passed. Time and the city have caught up with Druid Hills and overgrown it. Busy people driving along gaze at the Heinz home and wonder about its past. Sitting there, on a cloudy misty day, waiting for the developers and earthmovers, its shadow-white stucco makes the house appear like a ghost, and it looks, even to the casual passer-by, like a house with a past.

Just prior to the Civil War a German immigrant came to Atlanta and opened a gun shop. During the war he rendered valiant service to the Confederacy in the manufacture and repair of rifles and small arms. After the war, his son joined him in the business and the firm grew and prospered in the manufacture, repair, and sale of handguns. The firm was a prominent business establishment on Alabama Street in Atlanta. The father died in 1906, but the son continued the business until his own death in 1928, when the business was ended. Obviously the grandson of the founder and the son of the man who operated the business until it closed had no interest in the manufacture or sale of guns, for he took no part in the business. He was a peaceful man, well-liked and highly regarded by everyone who knew him. That man was Henry Heinz.

·

3

Socialite Peggy Refoule

Paul and Peggy Refoule (*Reh´-fo-lā*) moved most of their furnishings into their new home on April 30, 1947. The unusual house on fashionable Howell Mill Road was converted from an old woolen mill dating from the Civil War period, when the area had been a battleground in the Atlanta campaign. The house was located in the sparsely-settled neighborhood of northwest Fulton County, beyond the city limits of Atlanta. The property had a thousand-foot frontage on Howell Mill Road and ran back about 300 feet from the road to the middle of Peachtree Creek, a winding stream in a very wooded tract. There were no close neighbors, and the house sat near the street—all the expanse of property being the wooded area behind the house down to the creek. The old mill part of the house was to be used by Paul, an artist, as a studio. It was a gigantic room 20 by 50 feet with two-feet thick granite walls. It had a beamed ceiling and concrete floors. Several tapestries adorned the walls, and Refoule paintings rested on easels about the room. The studio had an enormous fireplace, with a huge mantel. In the new section of the house which the Refoules had just added to the old mill structure there was a kitchen and small bedroom downstairs, and two bedrooms and two baths upstairs. In the master bedroom upstairs there was a large fireplace. A dry creek bed ran directly behind the home and resembled a moat, and the house from that vantage point looked like a medieval castle, which is exactly the way that Paul Refoule, who was a Frenchman, wanted it to look; for it reminded him of the houses in his hometown of Orleans, France.

On May 5, 1947, the Refoules moved into their new house. The first social gathering which took place there was on the afternoon of Sunday, May 11, 1947, during which time the Refoules were visited by their friends, many of whom brought their children. Among those friends were Dr. and Mrs. Jack Varner, Major and Mrs. William V. Durkin, Mr. and Mrs. Howard Smith, and others. Major and Mrs. Durkin stayed on for dinner that night, and the two couples decided to have dinner together the following night, Monday, at Emile's French restaurant in downtown Atlanta, which they did.

While on his way to Oglethorpe University to teach his art class that afternoon, May 12, 1947, Paul Refoule stopped at the Fulton Hardware Company on Peachtree Road, at the request of Mrs. Refoule, and purchased a cotton clothesline. He asked the clerk in the hardware store for a clothes wire, specifying that his wife wanted one which would not rust, but at the time the store did not have clothes wire in stock; so, the clerk suggested the cotton clothesline instead. In giving Refoule change, the clerk made a mistake of one dollar against Refoule, which the latter called to his attention. Later that same evening, after coming home from Oglethorpe, Paul Refoule attached the clothesline to three small trees on the back of his property near the remains of an old brick retaining wall which runs parallel to Howell Mill Road.

On Tuesday morning, May 13, 1947, Mrs. Refoule drove the family automobile to Buckhead, taking with her soiled clothing of the family which was put through a washing machine at the laundromat in Buckhead. When she returned from the laundromat, Mrs. Refoule hung the clothes on the new clothesline. She told her husband he would have to find a better place for the clothesline, as the pathway leading to and from the line had too steep an incline.

On the morning of May 14, 1947, Mrs. Refoule drove the family automobile, a 1936 Ford Coupe, to Buckhead where she did some shopping. She went to a store which stocked venetian blinds, draperies, shades, etc. and asked one of the owners to send someone to her home that afternoon to make some measurements for draperies. (The man was too busy to go to the Refoule house that afternoon, however.)

Paul Refoule did not notice when his wife left to go to Buckhead or note the time of her return because he was busy doing some cement work about the premises. She must have returned home by 11 or 11:30 a.m., however, for she fixed lunch, which she ate with her husband. Before they had finished eating, two ladies stopped by for a visit and to look at the house. One of these ladies was a lifelong friend of Mrs. Refoule, Mrs.

Cook, and a friend of hers, Mrs. Cason, who met the Refoules for the first time on this occasion. When these two ladies came to the front door, they saw Mr. and Mrs. Refoule at the table finishing lunch. They decided they would go on and not disturb them. Mr. and Mrs. Refoule saw them through the glass front doors, and both came to the front door and insisted that the two ladies come inside. The ladies had coffee with them, and the Refoules showed their guests around the house. While the ladies were there, Refoule made several telephone calls, one of them to a building supply house, and ordered some materials for the house. Refoule said during the course of the conversation that he wanted to go into Buckhead and buy some paint to paint the floor, but Mrs. Cook told him that all the stores in Buckhead closed on Wednesday afternoon. These ladies arrived at approximately 12:30 p.m. and left the Refoule home at 1:45 p.m., at which time Paul Refoule was ready to leave to go to his classes at Oglethorpe University; but he remained until after the departure of the guests. Mrs. Refoule asked him to go by the home of her mother, Mrs. William Ott Alston, Sr., on his way to Oglethorpe, and pick up some of her things which were stored in her mother's basement.

Paul Refoule left his home immediately after the departure of the two guests. He arrived at the home of his mother-in-law a few minutes later, the time of arrival being sometime between 1:50 and 1:55 p.m. He drove into the backyard, parked the car, went to the basement, and began loading into the car some books and other articles which he was to take home after he completed his afternoon's work at Oglethorpe.

At approximately 1:50 p.m. Refoule's mother-in-law returned to her home. She had been out all morning. Just as she came into the house the telephone rang and she had a telephone conversation with her daughter Peggy Refoule.

Mrs. Alston: Hello?

Peggy: Hello, Mother, what are you doing?

Mrs. Alston: Nothing right now. I've just come in. I've been gone all morning and haven't even taken off my hat yet, and it is (looking at the clock) ten minutes until two.

Peggy: Mother! Where have you been?

Mrs. Alston: Oh, I went to my club, then to the stores to try and find some rice for Son (W. O. Alston, Jr., Peggy's brother, who was ill); then to the hospital to see Miss DeGraffenreid.

Peggy: Well . . . why don't you come over to see me? When are you going to help me to do some more sewing?

Mrs. Alston: I'm just not going to sew on that sofa cover in that upstairs room until you can get your window shades in. Have you seen about them yet?

Peggy: Yes. I went to that place in Buckhead this morning, and the man there says he can make the drop curtain the way Paul and I wanted it at first. So he is going to get the measurements for the window this afternoon and make it right away. Don't you think that kind will be all right?

Mrs. Alston: Well . . . it isn't the kind I would want, but I suppose it will be all right if you like it. It is at least the cheapest way to make it.

Peggy: It really will be all right, I think, Mother.

Mrs. Alston: Well, if you are satisfied . . . go ahead and order everything and charge it to me.

Peggy: Thank you, Mother. Oh Mother, is Paul still there?

Mrs. Alston: I think he is downstairs packing.

Peggy: Well; please send me the box of Kotex I left there.

Mrs. Alston: All right. Wait and let me call him before he leaves. (At this point Mrs. Alston went to the stairs and called her son-in-law.)

Paul: Mother?

Mrs. Alston: Paul, come upstairs before you leave. I want to send something to Peggy.

Mrs. Alston: (into the phone) Hello, I got him Peggy.

Peggy: Well now, you be sure to come over. I have a lot of new things to show you. Mrs. Cook and Mrs. Cason came to see us. Mrs. Cason is going to give us a chandelier.

Mrs. Alston: Will it suit the place where you need one?

Peggy: Oh yes, I'm sure it will!

Mrs. Alston: Well, that's fine! People certainly have been nice to you.

Peggy: You haven't seen the new stone steps that Paul just made, have you?

Mrs. Alston: No, I haven't.

Peggy: Well, you have to see them. They are just beautiful. All my new house is beautiful.

Mrs. Alston: Well, I am in a hurry now, Peggy. I must go. Carrie (an old family servant) is here waiting to wash my hair. Maybe I will come over later and bring Carrie. But I must go now and prepare lunch.

When Mrs. Alston said goodby to her daughter she did not hear Mrs. Refoule say goodby or remember hearing any click of the receiver. Mrs. Alston was in a hurry to prepare lunch for her son, who, under doctor's orders, was required to have meals at stated times which were made up of special foods. A few minutes after Mrs. Alston hung up the phone, Paul Refoule came upstairs. She gave him the box of Kotex and talked for a few minutes before he left to return to packing his car.

At 2:10 p.m. Paul Refoule started the motor of his car to drive from his mother-in-law's house to Oglethorpe University. The car had been parked almost immediately underneath a window of the bedroom of William Ott Alston, Jr., which was upstairs. Mr. Alston had been dozing but was awakened by the sound of the car starting, glanced at the clock, and saw that it was 2:10 p.m. He noted the time because he was making a mental calculation as to whether or not Paul would have time to meet his classes at Oglethorpe on schedule.

Art classes at Oglethorpe University were taught by Paul Refoule on Mondays and Wednesdays of each week, commencing at 2:40 p.m. Upon this occasion, as was his custom, Refoule arrived fifteen minutes or more ahead of time, in order to see that everything was in readiness for his art class. He set up a still life of a green vase with honeysuckles in it for the students to draw. At 2:45 p.m. he explained to the students in the class what he wanted them to do. After giving these instructions, he was occupied for the remainder of the afternoon working with individual students as each worked on his painting of the still life.

Upon leaving Oglethorpe University at 5 p.m. or a few minutes thereafter, Paul Refoule drove to a home on Lenox Road to keep an engagement he had previously made to talk with two ladies about the painting of a portrait. Refoule arrived at this home at approximately 5:20 p.m., and he left at approximately 5:55 p.m. The time was noted particularly by one of the women because she was disturbed by the fact that the preparation of dinner was being delayed.

The Refoules' young son, Jon Paul, aged 9, had been taken to school that morning by his father. When he got out of school at 3 p.m., he caught the bus and went over to the Fritz Orr Camp. At 5 p.m. the station wagon of the camp left with young Refoule aboard, and the driver let him out at the Refoule home at approximately 5:30. The driver was later to recall the time because he had been delayed in getting started that day by the time taken up in giving out some awards to the children at the camp for horsemanship. When the driver let young Refoule out of the station wagon, he did not see anyone at the house. It was his practice, when letting children out, to wait and see that they got indoors or if someone met them; but on this day he was already behind schedule and the traffic on Howell Mill Road was brisk, so he drove away quickly.

When Jon Paul got home he tried to go in the front door of the house but found that it was locked. Rather than wait for his mother to come and open the door to let him in, he decided to go around to the back door in order to surprise her. At the back door, he saw muddy footprints on the small back porch, which had a concrete floor, and wondered about them because his mother had always required him and his father to clean their shoes carefully before entering. He did not see any muddy footprints in the kitchen or inside the house. He called for his mother but she did not answer. He looked all over the house but could not find her. The radio was on full. He then went upstairs to his room and read a comic book.

Paul Refoule arrived at his home at approximately 6:10 p.m. He went in the front door, using his key to do so, as the door was locked. He called for Peggy, but she did not answer. He called for his son, and the boy answered him. He asked his son where his mother was, and the boy said that he did not know. He asked him how long he had been there, and young Refoule told him about an hour and that he had come in through the back door, which was unlocked. Refoule unloaded his car and brought the things into the house that he had previously gotten at Mrs. Alston's earlier in the afternoon.

Refoule waited awhile to see if his wife was coming. He called her grandmother and mother, asking if Peggy was at either one of their homes, or if they knew if she was over at Frances', Peggy's sister. They both said that Peggy was not at their house, that they did not know where she was. Refoule thought his wife might be at a neighbor or friend's house and did not worry. He went outside and worked on a ditch by the new retaining wall he was building. He then went inside and made some more calls but received no information concerning his wife's whereabouts. By 7 p.m. Refoule began to worry. Since he had arrived home, he had not left the immediate vi-

cinity of the house because he thought his wife might telephone, and he did not want to leave his son in the house alone.
By now very agitated, he once again called his mother-in-law,
who was very upset when she realized for the first time that
her daughter had not been at home when her grandson arrived from camp. She was convinced that had her daughter
gone out, she would have arranged to return to the house before her son came home, or either arranged for someone else
to be there. Mrs. Alston called her brother, Mr. Douglas
Wright, apprised him of the situation, and asked him to go to
the Refoule home at once.

FAMILY ARRIVES

It was still daylight, about 7:30 p.m., when Douglas Wright,
Peggy's uncle, arrived at the Refoule home. It was just about
dusk when Mrs. Alston arrived at the Refoule home. Shortly,
several other members of the family arrived. Mrs. Alston and
the others searched the house for Peggy or some trace of her.
Mr. Wright and Paul searched outside the house and went as
far on the back of the property as the creek but saw no sign of
Peggy. Now it was nearly dark.

Mrs. Alston and the others in the house were upset; and
when her brother and son-in-law returned to the house and
reported no sign of Peggy anywhere, they became frantic.
Mrs. Alston kept repeating that if something was not wrong
her daughter would have been at home when her grandson
arrived from camp. She insisted that the police be called at
once. A call was placed to the Fulton County Police Department by Mr. Wright at 8:10 p.m.

By 8:20 p.m. there were no less than four police cars at the
Refoule home. Other relatives and friends came to the house.
The large studio in the Refoule home began to fill with people;
soon everyone was standing around, not knowing what to do.
Mrs. Alston requested that the police send for dogs. The police
thought that because of the length of time any trail would be
lost; however, Mrs. Alston begged them to call for the dogs.

When the keeper of the hounds and his helper, an experienced trusty, arrived at the Howell Mill Road home, one
hound was released at a point near the new stone retaining
wall, which is at the side and rear of the home. The hound
first ran a trail down a slope in the direction of the dry creek

bed. One of the policemen told the keeper to call the dog back, as it was the trail of the policeman the dog was following. To call the hound back the keeper fired two shots—which totally shattered the nerves of everyone in the Refoule house, until someone told them that the shots were just for calling the dogs. The police told Refoule and everyone else to remain in the house. By now it was dark.

Upon being called back, the dog picked up another trail which led from the house down into a ravine, to the left side of the Refoule property. The hound was closely followed by the helper this time, and the keeper proceeded along an old dirt road which ran parallel with Peachtree Creek in the rear of the home. When the dog had proceeded for a considerable distance along the ravine, he turned westward into the road at a point approximately 100 feet north of the dead end of the road. He then proceeded southward, to a point just past the dead end of the road, then turned toward the creek. While following the trail he had barked several times. He disappeared into the darkness and was silent.

SHOCKING DISCOVERY

The keeper followed the dog to the edge of the water and looked toward the creek. Standing along the bank of the creek, he allowed his flashlight to play over the shallow, rippling water, then focused on a single spot. There he saw the body of Peggy Alston Refoule.

Lieutenant Cal Cates was one of the first officers at the Refoule home and the first superior officer to view the body. He and two patrolmen started searching the rear of the house as they had been told that Mrs. Refoule was in the habit of picking wild flowers in the woods. When the dog found a track down the creek bank about 200 yards to the rear of the house, Lt. Cates and his men were right behind. There they found a white plastic hairpin, and upon looking further, they found the body lying face up in the creek. Her head was on a rock— her left arm was twisted to her back. She was still limber and not as cold as the water in the creek. Her body was about 300 feet from where they found signs of a scuffle and her pin clasp. The woman's feet had been tied together with her shoe laces and her throat had a mark around it as if it had been corded with a rope or some object used to choke her. One finger had signs of a ring being removed.

Lt. Cates immediately began an examination of the ground in a search for footprints. It was his intention to have the dog undertake to follow the trail away from the point at which the body had been discovered in an effort to find the direction taken by the slayer when he left the scene. Soon after the discovery of the body and before the keeper of the hounds could help Lt. Cates and his men complete an examination of the ground for footprints or resume his work with the dog, a number of persons came to the point at which the body was found. Lt. Cates had observed several footprints in the sandy soil which appeared to him to have been made by someone wearing tennis shoes, the bottoms of which had been worn smooth so that the tracks bore no imprint of grooves or serrated surfaces. The tracks did not contain definite heel prints, but the arrival of the curious in large numbers so confused any trail which the slayer may have left that the keeper of the hounds and Lt. Cates deemed it useless to try and follow the trail, as the dog would have been by that time confronted with a maze of trails. Any footprints that might have proved useful were soon obliterated by the large number of people rushing to the scene.

Paul Refoule from his house saw a car driving up the dirt road that entered his property about 300 yards below the house. He kept inquiring and someone told him that they had found his wife. At this time he went to the front of the house to meet the car when it was coming. He heard one of the policeman say that they needed blankets. He heard a relative say something about blankets and another relative say something about calling Dr. Davison, the family physician; and he gathered from this that Peggy was sick or injured, but alive. He ran out the driveway and on the way saw Peggy's uncle, Douglas Wright, walking slowly up the driveway shaking his head. Refoule asked him what happened to his wife, and her uncle told him that she was dead. Refoule was in a state of shock, and several other relatives came forward and helped him and his son into a car and drove them away from the scene to his mother-in-law's house.

Policemen at the front and rear doors of the Refoule home were attempting to keep the public away from the house and off the property. Some friends of the family arrived, and policemen guarding the front door would not admit them; however, they called to Mr. Wright, and he told the policeman to admit them and anyone else who wished to enter. In a matter of hours, the press and the public were swarming all over the house like bees after honey. Before the night was over, approximately 2,000 people visited the house and property!

After the body was removed from the scene, Assistant Police Chief E. G. Fitzgerald and Detective Captain Fred Bradford attempted to learn from friends and relatives as much as possible about what had happened. They gave up on going over the grounds that night, as it was completely dark by this hour. Missing after the murder were two diamond rings in unusual settings, a plain gold wedding band, a lady's wrist watch, and an inexpensive camera. The two diamond rings cost approximately $1000 apiece at pre-war prices in France. The wrist watch was an ordinary lady's wrist watch and had been purchased in France. Mrs. Refoule's wedding band was missing. She wore the wedding band at all times, except that she sometimes removed it when working around the house. The finger upon which she customarily wore it bore its imprint when the body was discovered, but the ring had been removed. She wore only the other two rings, both heirlooms handed down in the Refoule family, upon special occasions. Before moving to the new home, and while she and Paul were living with her mother, she had been in the habit of keeping the two diamond rings in a small sewing cabinet. When they moved to the new home, this little cabinet, which had several drawers or trays, was placed upon a shelf in one of the closets in the large master bedroom. The cabinet was located by police and relatives, and upon examination the rings were found to be missing. Upon the bed in this same room was Mrs. Refoule's handbag, which was open and contained a few small coins. As she had been in the habit of paying for most of her purchases by check, she would have taken very little money with her to Buckhead that morning.

Since Lt. Cates had been the first officer on the scene, he informed Fitzgerald and Bradford of everything that had happened that evening. Since Cates was a long-time resident of the neighborhood, he had some other interesting comments. Cates told his superiors that there was no evidence or signs that Mrs. Refoule had been dragged through the heavily wooded area that separated the house from the creek. Her body bore no scratches or bruises, and Cates said if she had been carried through the woods it would have been necessary for a man to have carried her on his shoulders. To cross a dry creek bed immediately back of the house and then cross the wooded area with a heavy burden would have been an almost superhuman task. Furthermore, the rear exit, overlooking the woods and creek, was visible from Howell Mill Road, and if Mrs. Refoule had been slain inside the house, the killer would have had difficulty carrying her body outside without being seen by passers-by. Cates said that the dead end road leading to the secluded creek bank was used frequently, and he described it as a perfect lovers rendezvous. He also pointed out that the dirt road was there and being used long before the Refoules started renovating the old mill, and prior to the time they moved into the mill house the lovers' lane road had complete privacy and was secluded day or night. He felt that it might be significant that the Refoules moving into the mill affected the purposes, whatever they might be, of the dirt road. He recalled also many years ago he helped drag the body of a woman from Peachtree Creek near the exact spot where Mrs. Refoule was found. He said the mystery of the woman's death by drowning in the then-higher creek waters was never solved.

Captain Bradford and other detectives searched the Refoule house thoroughly. They did not find any signs of there having been any scuffle or struggle with anyone, and the house had not been ransacked. In the upstairs bedroom, an iron and ironing board were out, and a stack of neatly folded laundry was found nearby. Bradford noted that the position of the ironing board was such that if Mrs. Refoule had been at work there she would have been facing the only door to the second-story room. It would have therefore been difficult for an intruder to come upon her by surprise while she was at work ironing.

Assistant Chief Fitzgerald concluded that Peggy Refoule had surprised a burglar in her home and had been murdered. He thought it followed the pattern of the Heinz case. Fitzgerald had worked on the Heinz case and was instrumental in gathering the evidence against Blalock, who, incidentally, at this juncture was still in prison (although his guilt was still questioned by the public).

At 10 p.m. the feverish activity inside the Refoule home continued. Remnants of the curious wandered about. Relatives talked with the police detail on the scene. The atmosphere at the Alston home was quite different. Everyone sat around in stunned silence or else talked perfunctorily. Paul Refoule sat alone in a room by himself. No one bothered him. Around 1 a.m. the police arrived at the Alston home and asked Paul Refoule if he and Jon Paul would come downtown to headquarters and make a statement.

At 11 p.m. Captain Bradford had left the Refoule home in order to be present at the funeral home when the county coroner arrived there. Preliminary tests of the body by Dr. Jernigan, county coroner, indicated that Peggy Refoule had not been sexually assaulted. A complete autopsy on the body would be performed the following day.

Paul Refoule and his son and a cousin of his wife's arrived at Fulton County Police headquarters at about the same time that Bradford arrived from the funeral home. Assistant Chief Fitzgerald and Captain Bradford questioned Refoule and his son about their activities of the previous afternoon. They both gave written statements to the police and were then returned to the Alston home around 3 a.m. At this point the investigation of the Refoule case rested until later in the day.

Captain Bradford and other detectives went on duty at 8 o'clock on the morning of May 15, 1947. They went directly to the banks of Peachtree Creek below the Refoule house on Howell Mill Road, the scene where Mrs. Refoule was found murdered, to search for any evidence which they might find. It was a beautiful spring morning and on Peachtree Creek the sun shone on the rippling water and birds sang in branches of nearby trees. It did not seem possible that murder could occur in such a setting.

A police detail had closed off the dirt road that ran parallel along the creek, and another police detail was keeping sightseers off the property and out of the area. However, the bridge spanning Peachtree Creek was just below the Refoule property, and people on their way to work downtown the morning afterwards, intrigued by Mrs. Refoule's murder, slowed down and craned their necks as they viewed the police all about the vicinity.

A search of the Peachtree Creek murder scene revealed no new clues, and Bradford, leaving other officers to continue searching, left and drove to Buckhead. There he talked to a man who stated to him that he had seen a torn piece of garment on a branch of a tree about 400 feet from Northside

Drive on the north bank of Peachtree Creek. He added that the torn cloth was not there on Tuesday, May 13, 1947. The man had a distinct recollection of seeing the cloth, and stated that it was his custom to take his dogs down to walk along the creek banks every evening. He said the torn cloth looked like an army jacket or shirt.

While in Buckhead, Bradford talked with a lady who stated that she had passed the Refoule home just a few minutes before and saw there a black coupe automobile with a large rear light flashing on and off. It was parked across the street from the Refoule home. She further stated there was more than one person in the car—a black-haired young man and two women. She did not see the people well enough to be able to identify them later. She thought they looked very suspicious and ought to be investigated by the police. She lectured Captain Bradford for several minutes about how poor the police protection in this area of the county was. She had always said they did not have enough police and now the Refoule murder proved her correct. If the police did not find the murderer, and quick, something would have to be done about the situation. Bradford suggested that the people in the car the lady saw were sightseers. He pointed out that cars would be driving by as people tried to get a look at the murder scene. He said also that sightseers had hampered the investigation of the case. After some more conversation, the irate citizen appeared somewhat mollified and relieved that the police were trying to solve the case.

Bradford then returned to the Refoule home where he conferred with two of his investigators who told him that they had learned that two young men had been down on Peachtree Creek all day May 14, hunting turtles. Bradford and his investigators then went and talked to these two men, and they stated they went to the creek about 10 a.m., where the branch runs into the creek about 300 yards from where the body was found, and went down the creek barefooted toward Moores Mill Road, away from the murder scene. The two men, both of whom worked as gas station attendants, were taken to their homes and agreed to allow investigators to search for the missing Refoule rings, none of which could be found. Reliable witnesses told police the two young men were away from the creek area and at work by 2 o'clock that afternoon. One witness stated that he thought the whole thing was some kind of prank—that some friends of the two men knew they were down by the creek the day of the murder and called the police and told them about it, in a playful effort to upset the men. This appeared to make sense. The two young men were certainly terrified when they realized the police considered them murder suspects. If they had been involved in the murder, it appears unlikely they would have told dozens of people they were going to be in the vicinity of Peachtree Creek.

Bradford then stopped at Marvin Cleaners on Howell Mill Road, and the owner told him that he had seen a car parked about a block and a half away from the Refoule home on Howell Mill Road the day of the murder. The car, a 1941 Ford Club Coupe, was parked under the shade of a tree on the first curve, south of the Refoule home, about 4:45 p.m. with a man and a woman in the car. The man looked to be in his late thirties. Bradford wondered if these people could be considered as suspects or just people out in the springtime afternoon. The Howell Mill-Peachtree Creek area was well known as a place for lovers to go driving. It was spring. The setting was conducive to romance. Many people would be out driving in the afternoon. Bradford had the feeling this could greatly complicate the case.

That afternoon, Captain Bradford talked with Mrs. George Craft at her home. She said that she was a personal friend of Peggy Refoule and that she had started to town and decided to stop by and see Mrs. Refoule. She sent her son, George, Jr., age 5, to the front door of the Refoule home to see if anyone was at home. The front door was locked and she blew the horn on her automobile but there was no response. After waiting a few minutes, she drove away. She stated this was around 4 p.m. on May 14, 1947. She stated that she saw a white man about 50 or 55 years old walking north on Howell Mill Road, wearing a plaid shirt and felt hat. He passed by the house and continued walking south on Howell Mill Road.

Bradford returned to the Refoule home late in the afternoon. The investigators who searched the creek reported that they had found no new evidence or clues in the creek areas. The police detail at the house said they had a difficult time trying to keep the curious off the property and out of the house. The police said some people acted like the Refoule home and grounds had become public property. It was a repeat of what had happened at the Heinz estate three years before.

NO RESPECT FOR GRIEF

Paul Refoule had returned to his home on Howell Mill Road that afternoon. He went into the studio and played the piano softly. He paced about the house smoking. He appeared very remote to friends and relatives who dropped in to offer their condolences. He talked about the murder and paced about, chain-smoking all the time. He asked everyone who came to the house that day, "Who do you think could have committed such a terrible crime?"

Refoule became very upset later in the afternoon when members of the press and the curious tried to enter the house and people stopping in front of the house tried to get a glimpse of those inside. To a friend he muttered:

"In France, they would leave you alone. There people have respect for grief."

Refoule became so upset by all the people about that relatives said it would be impossible for him to have any peace in the house. The police reluctantly agreed. It was therefore decided that Refoule and his son should continue living with his mother-in-law for the time being.

That night, in the studio of the Refoule home, Bradford and his investigators went over everything they had learned about the case thus far. As the two guests who had coffee with the Refoules had not departed until approximately 1:30 or 1:45 p.m. and as Mrs. Refoule talked first with her grandmother, and later with her mother, after the departure of her guests and did not conclude these telephone conversations until approximately 2:05 p.m., and as it was known that no ironing had been done before the arrival of the two guests, it was plain that all of the clothes which were found to have been ironed had been done after the telephone conversation with Mrs. Alston had been concluded. Bradford and the investigators examined the bedroom once more. They examined the number of freshly ironed clothes and estimated that it would have taken approximately 45 minutes for her to have done this ironing. Expiration of 45 minutes after the conclusion of the telephone conversation with her mother would seem to establish that she must have been alive as late as 3 p.m., and thus the fact that Mrs. Alston could not recall her daughter saying goodby or hearing a click of the receiver appeared to have no significance.

Bradford noted that the Refoule home was so constructed that in the absence of curtains a person walking around the house and looking into the windows could see practically all over it. At a right-angle corner formed by a meeting of two brick walls of the house was a water spigot, which was frequently used by a black man, apparently a convict trusty, in carrying drinking water to the convicts who had been engaged in building a sewer line across Howell Mill Road from the Refoule home. Situated near this corner was a narrow but very tall window, which extended from a point about 30 inches above the ground to ceiling height. From this window it was possible to see the upstairs hallway as well as the stairway. It would not have been possible for anyone to have passed from one of the upstairs bedrooms to the other, or to have passed down this stairway, without being in plain view of anyone standing near the water hydrant. This was a temporary hydrant and, instead of having a spout, water had to pass out of the upright pipe, which resulted in some spilling and kept the ground muddy at that point. Bradford thought this might be significant in view of the statement by Refoule's son that he saw muddy footprints upon the back concrete stoop.

Friday, May 17, 1947, two days after the Refoule murder. The first thing that Captain Bradford encountered that morning when he reached police headquarters was the newspaper headline from the morning edition of *The Atlanta Constitution*:

SEX SLAYER INDICATED IN MATRON DEATH

The news account stated that the police thought that burglary was the motive. However, the paper stated also that according to Dr. Herman Jones of the Fulton County Crime Laboratory, Mrs. Refoule had been criminally assaulted. Bradford read this with a start. He had been present on Wednesday night when the coroner first examined the body and told him that the victim had not been assaulted. And yesterday at the inquest Dr. Jernigan, in sworn statement, testified: "After having carefully examined the deceased's body and finding only evidence of an external bruise, located about her neck, having performed an autopsy and having found nothing abnormal, I feel confident that the deceased met her death due to strangulation. There are no signs of drowning. There are no signs that she was raped."

From his own police experience, Bradford surmised that

Mrs. Refoule had not been sexually assaulted. He had seen the bodies of women who had been criminally assaulted and then killed, and it was not an easy memory to forget. He had seen the body of Peggy Refoule, and it did not appear to be a case of sexual assault because, except for the bruise around her neck, where she was choked to death, there was not a mark upon her body. Women who are sexually molested and then killed by a sex slayer do not appear afterward as Mrs. Refoule's body appeared, for there is a struggle until the woman is subdued, and the woman's body always has marks which are a result of the struggle, and there are usually not only severe bruises but broken bones.

Bradford began to have doubts about the case. Things did not appear to add up. Dr. Jernigan stated also at the inquest that it appeared that the victim was strangled with a rope or cord that was a garrot looped around her throat and apparently twisted from the front. He said he thought that from an examination of the body it could be concluded that Mrs. Refoule was killed at the scene rather than carried there later, and that certainly she was not dragged from the house through the wooded area to the creek. He stated that the victim's feet had been tied together by the laces of her shoes.

Next, Bradford got a report from the detectives who had been checking the pawn shops in search of the rings stolen from the Refoule home. One was a plain gold wedding band. One was an heirloom ring with two round diamonds and a square diamond in the center. The third was a platinum ring with a large center saphire and small diamonds on each side. The two diamond rings had been handed down in the Refoule family. The detectives had covered the shops and investigated several tips but had come up with no trace of any of the missing rings.

At 9 a.m. the funeral of Peggy Refoule was held at the Cathedral of Christ the King. Although from an Episcopalian family, Peggy had become a Catholic when she married Paul Refoule. The funeral was held at an early hour in an attempt to keep away curiosity seekers, and with police assistance the funeral was not disturbed.

Peggy Alston Refoule was survived by her son and husband, her mother, and a brother and sister. Her death brought to an end the life of a courageous young woman who had overcome religious barriers, war, starvation, and Nazi occupation to first marry, and then to be with, her French artist husband. All her life a willful fate had doggedly followed Peggy Refoule.

EARLY YEARS

It all began when 19-year-old blonde, blue-eyed Peggy took the grand tour with her mother in the fall of 1935. They traveled to Italy, Switzerland, Belgium, Holland, and France. In the winter of 1936 Peggy became a student at the Sorbonne in Paris. There she met Paul Refoule, an artist. They began dating and soon were very much in love. Paul wanted to marry Peggy at once, but Peggy's family thought she was too young. They considered Paul, although the son of Robert Refoule, Judge Advocate of Orleans, France, where the Refoule family had been prominent for generations, as an artist, a Frenchman and a Catholic, as not the most suitable prospective husband for their daughter. The family prevailed upon Peggy to return to Atlanta in the spring, but the romance continued and in six months time Paul followed Peggy to America, reaching Atlanta by Christmas. Paul and Peggy decided to get married, and the Alston family gave their consent. The couple were married in Atlanta on January 19, 1937, in the chapel where now is located the Cathedral of Christ the King. Atlantans who recall the event say that there was never a more beautiful and radiant bride nor a handsomer groom, for Paul Refoule possessed the dark good looks and magnetic charm which caused people to compare him with actor Charles Boyer.

After their marriage the Refoules lived in Paris, where Paul had a studio at 26 Rue des Plantes. There their son, Jon Paul, was born. While the Refoules were visiting Peggy's seriously ill father in Atlanta, Hitler's invasion of Poland brought war to Europe. Paul returned immediately to France and enlisted in the French Army. Despite pleas from family and friends that she remain in Atlanta, where it was safer, Peggy returned to France with her young son. The Nazis swept into France, and Paul was taken prisoner at Dunkirk. He was held first in Germany, then in Poland. Peggy lived with her son and her husband's family at Orleans, protected from the worst of things by the means of the elder Refoules. Peggy's letters to her mother told of chopping up furniture for kindling and of giving her share of the dwindling food supply to her son. Gradually money became worthless and hunger stalked everyone. There were long silences when there was no news from Peggy at all.

Conditions were so bad in France following the German surrender that the Refoules came to Atlanta to live and to rest after their ordeal. Paul got jobs teaching art at Oglethorpe University and at the High Museum of Art. He also had a private studio in downtown Atlanta. He did the murals of Emile's French Restaurant, the Cox-Carlton Hotel bar, and the then-well-known Mammy's Shanty. At first the Refoules lived with Peggy's mother, who was now widowed. Then they bought the old mill and converted it into a home. It was the only home that the war-weary couple had ever owned. Peggy Refoule would live there only nine days. For her family and old friends, it was impossible to comprehend. That Peggy could have survived the war and suffered its privations—to at last come home—and be murdered, murdered in the wealthy residential neighborhood of northwest Atlanta. It should have been the safest place in the world, and it was not. The family, friends, and neighbors wanted to know: Why?

Captain Bradford spent the morning of Mrs. Refoule's funeral going over the telephone messages that had come into the police department. The pressure on the police was enormous. People were upset about the murder. Housewives in the Refoule neighborhood were greatly alarmed over the slaying and were barricading their doors and putting guns in handy places, lest they had to face an intruder. The newspaper headlines stating that the killer was a "sex-slayer" further terrified the inhabitants of the Buckhead area, and because of the excitement generated by the case and the information that was coming into the police department, the full force of the Fulton County Police Department was thrown into the investigation of the slaying. (In 1947, the areas of Fulton County—including Buckhead—and beyond the old Atlanta city limits were policed by an independent police department.) It was proving to be a difficult job for the department to conduct an orderly investigation of the murder, for the department had few specialists, and it was the practice for officers to work all types of cases—murder, robbery, and larceny. The investigators had no special training for these cases and often had to learn on the job. Up until this point the investigation had been headed by Assistant Chief Fitzgerald and Captain Bradford. The head of the Fulton County Police Department, Chief G. Neal Ellis, was out of town when the murder occurred but would return the following day. Bradford had a lot of loose ends to clear up before then.

Bradford went to the county work camp and talked with the man in charge of the camp. He learned that a black male, Francis Goodman, had been released at noon Monday, May 12, 1947, from the camp, and this man had been working with Loy Reeves, who was in charge of the sewer construction work that the county had been doing in the Howell Mill Road section during the month of April 1947. Bradford was told also that Francis Goodman had been the water boy on this gang. Bradford and another officer then went to Mr. Reeves' home and picked him up and he went with them to the Howell Mill Road section showing them the different roads and the different water plugs that Goodman had been carrying the water from. Reeves stated that Goodman was bad about wandering off and not getting water always from the plugs that he was told. Reeves said that he did not know, but it certainly was possible that Goodman carried water from the Refoule house part of the time the work was being done. Mr. Reeves also told Bradford that in April, when the sewer construction work was being done, that one day a terrific rainstorm came up, and Paul Refoule allowed the workmen to seek refuge from the storm in his then-unfinished house. Refoule, who was there working on his house, also provided hot coffee for the workmen.

Next, the police went to the home of Francis Goodman and questioned him. He stated that he had gone to work at the Atlantic Steel Plant on Wednesday morning, May 14, 1947; he went to work at 7 a.m. and got off from work at 3 p.m. The police found $24 and some change on Goodman, which he told them represented wages that he had coming to him from the steel plant. The police thought it unusual that a man just off the chain gang would have this money coming to him; so, they went to the steel plant and talked with Goodman's supervisor, who told them Goodman was correct, that he did come to work at the steel plant on Wednesday and that he had $25.84 which was back pay that he received that day. Bradford removed Goodman's name from the list of possible suspects in the case.

Bradford and another investigator then interviewed the foreman on the job in building the addition to the Refoule home on Howell Mill Road. They wanted to know if the foreman could account for the whereabouts the day of the murder of the men who worked on the house. The foreman told them that all but two of the workers were with them that day on another job, on the opposite side of town. Upon checking, the police learned that of the two unaccounted-for workers, one was in the city stockade on a drunk charge and the other was home sick the day of the murder. When interviewed, the sick man was deemed by officers to be too old and enfeebled to bother anyone. Bradford struck these two men from the list of possible suspects.

On Friday, Bradford and two other officers returned to the Peachtree Creek murder scene and searched the area but could find no new clues. They went through the house again and searched it. Bradford carefully examined the sashcord that they had first seen the night of the murder. They had found this cord on the tool chest under the kitchen range. Paul Refoule told them it was the excess rope that he had left over from the clothesline. Could this be the rope that strangled Peggy Refoule? The clothesline was still intact. Bradford went upstairs and examined the cord of the electric iron. It was the retractable-type cord. Did the killer strangle Mrs. Refoule with the ironing cord? It did not seem likely, for the cord appeared like new and was not shredded at any point. Neither the sashcord nor the ironing cord appeared to be the murder weapon. Then, was Mrs. Refoule surprised while ironing and strangled in the house and then carried to the creek? The case was a puzzle, and none of the pieces appeared to be fitting together logically.

Saturday, May 17, 1947. The police received a report on a stolen car with a Georgia tag which had been recovered in Austin, Texas. Captain Bradford called the police there and had them question the two occupants of the car concerning their activities the day of the murder. Later in the morning, the police called back from Austin and said that after extensive questioning and a search of the two suspects and of their car and belongings, there appeared to be no link between these two car thieves and the Refoule murder. None of the items stolen from the Refoule home were in their possession. A similar communication was had with the Chattanooga, Tennessee, Police Department concerning another suspect, but it also proved to be fruitless.

G. Neal Ellis, Chief of the Fulton County Police Department, had returned to the city and was conferring with Fitzgerald and Bradford concerning what progress had been made on the case. In the past two days Bradford had checked on a dozen workmen who had labored on the remodeled mill house, hunted an unidentified white man who had been seen loitering May 14 on the Peachtree Creek bridge (found him and cleared him in the case), had checked out the men who had been doing sewer work in the vicinity in the month of April, and had checked out the workers on the Refoule house. A young yard boy had been taken into custody and released.

In spite of all this investigation, Bradford did not have a suspect, and it seemed to Chief Ellis that the department was no nearer solving the case than it was the day of the murder. Some investigators insisted to Chief Ellis that Bradford had done nothing—absolutely nothing—during his four days of investigation!

Ellis, a traffic specialist, had no extensive training as an investigator. Three months before, he had been made chief of the department. Pressure was on him from all sides. He had to rely on what the men in the department reported to him. But he was more aware of certain aspects of the case than others in the department who were working on it.

RUMORS

Ellis asked Fitzgerald and Bradford if they were aware of rumors that Paul and Peggy Refoule were about to divorce? No, they were not. He wanted to know what truth there was to the rumor that Paul Refoule was conducting love affairs with two women and that he planned a flight to Egypt with one of them? The detectives could not say.

The chief made it clear that the information was all just rumors but that he had received several telephone calls. He pointed out also that the information coming to him was from prominent people, *not* crack-pots, and consequently *had* to be treated seriously. The chief implied that his sources were very close to the Alston family.

Bradford insisted that Refoule had an air-tight alibi. Fitzgerald proposed that there could be some kind of conspiracy—that Refoule might have had someone murder his wife. Ellis pointed out sternly that this was merely a theory: How could they prove it? Ellis again made it plain that he was not accusing anyone, but he wanted all the people working on the case not to limit themselves in any way in their investigation and to consider everyone a suspect until proved otherwise. Bradford wanted to know if this included Mrs. Alston, Peggy's mother. Rumors persisted that there was some kind of conspiracy between Refoule and his mother-in-law, and many people felt that her statement concerning the phone call with Peggy the day of the murder was a cover for Refoule. Chief Ellis discounted this entirely, but again, no one was to be ruled out. There were to be no "higher-ups" in this case. Again and again the officers would be cautioned not to spare the higher-ups. The comparison with the Heinz case was already being drawn by the public, and the newspapers were hinting at it. Many people at the time believed the police had protected Mrs. Heinz in that murder and were very vocal in insisting that the Fulton County police not fall into *that* trap in their investigation of the Refoule case. Chief Ellis was determined not to fall into that trap, and probably he and his men were more sensitive to this charge than they, or anyone else at the time, realized. Much of their future action would indicate that this was a factor.

The pressure was building in the Refoule murder. Both Atlanta newspapers had carried the story in its page-one headlines for four consecutive days, something of a record; even more coverage than the Heinz case. The pressure was on to find and punish the guilty party. There was a victim; there had to be a culprit. The police had to locate him—and quick. All other leads in the case had proved futile. Why not look for a Cain-Abel motive in the Refoule case?

Both Bradford and Fitzgerald had little alternative in the matter. Their search for the culprit had proved ineffectual. And there were many details, even discounting all the gossip they had heard, which did not add up.

Two of Bradford's investigators reported on their activity Saturday morning. They had been investigating two former boy friends of the victim. From members of the Alston family, the police had learned that before Peggy married Refoule, she had dated a young man who wanted very much to marry her, but she spurned him. Even so, after her marriage the young man had written her several peculiar letters. The police checked with this man's family and discovered that he was confined to the Shephard-Pratt Hospital in Maryland. He

could not be involved in the murder. They had interviewed
the other man, now a prominent businessman in the city, and
he told them that he had not seen Peggy since before the war.
The police were satisfied with this statement and said this
individual could not be considered a suspect. One investigator
told Bradford that he had heard rumors of marital discord between the Refoules, but no one had had anything derogatory
to say about Peggy Refoule.

Chief Ellis and his men went to the Howell Mill Road home
Saturday afternoon. Ellis suggested that Peggy Refoule was
murdered in her home and then carried by automobile along
the dirt road to the point where her body was dumped in the
creek. This would explain, he stated, why there were no
marks or scratches on the body. But Chief Ellis had not been
on the scene when the murder occurred. He was, in a sense,
second-guessing the case.

How could the slayer surprise Mrs. Refoule at her ironing
since she would have been facing the door to the upstairs bedroom? Well, Chief Ellis told his men, if the slayer was known
to Peggy she would not have been surprised, would she? Ellis
was pretty well convinced that the slayer was someone known
to her, someone who would know where the rings were kept.
An ordinary burglar would not know what in the house was
valuable and would have to search, and as a result make a
mess of things in the process. But the Refoule home was not
ransacked. Little by little, as the investigators talked among
themselves, the idea of a Cain-Abel killing seemed more real,
and they were becoming willing captives of the proposed
theory, participants of the syndrome.

Sunday's papers carried a statement of Chief Ellis saying
that the police were investigating all leads in the case, but
that no one had been accused or arrested for the murder.
When the reporters wanted to know if the investigation included the background of both Mr. and Mrs. Refoule, Ellis
made a strong statement saying that absolutely nothing had
come to the attention of anyone in the police department concerning anything bad about Peggy Refoule and that he was
convinced she was a person of the highest character and was
the victim of a brutal murder; and that his department would
find the killer. Ellis refrained from commenting on Paul
Refoule.

Chief Ellis stated also to the press his theory that Peggy

Refoule was murdered in her home and that then her body was carried in an automobile to Peachtree Creek. When asked by reporters what evidence he had to substantiate this theory, he stated that he thought it was obvious! He stated to the press that the method of tying the feet together as Peggy Refoule's were was taught to servicemen during the war and taught also to first-aid workers, but that he was inclined to believe this crime was committed by a young man and that the slayer was an ex-serviceman. Ellis made public instructions he had issued to the men of his department not to talk about the case to persons with no official interest in its solution. This was an effort to clamp a lid on the wild rumors and false reports circulating that were hampering the efforts of officers dealing with the case. Unknowingly or not, the chief was doing just what he was urging his men not to do by his public statements of unproven theories concerning the case. Gradually Chief Ellis and his department would become total captives of the Cain-Abel theory.

THE CURIOUS

Sunday afternoon was a beautiful spring day with temperatures in the high eighties. Hundreds of people took advantage of the holiday to drive by the scene of the slaying. Others brought picnic lunches and spread their sandwiches and Coca-Cola in the wooded area across the road from the Refoule house. With binoculars they tried to see as much as possible of the house and grounds. The police detail at the Refoule home spent a busy afternoon shooing people away and keeping the traffic moving along Howell Mill Road.

SLAYER OF MRS. REFOULE WAS KNOWN
TO VICTIM, SAYS NEW POLICE THEORY

This was the page-one headline of *The Atlanta Constitution* on Monday, May 19, 1947.

It had been a busy Sunday for the Fulton County police. Chief Ellis had assigned four more investigators to work on the case. The fact that two of these men were beat patrolmen was not considered. This made a total of nine investigators then working on the Refoule case. The renewed activity had brought forth results.

A nineteen-year-old art student had been located and, under questioning, had admitted to having an affair with Paul

Refoule. At 8 o'clock that night, Captain Bradford and other investigators brought the girl and Paul Refoule to the Refoule home on Howell Mill Road. Refoule was now living with his mother-in-law but was brought to his home for the purposes of interrogation. Both the girl and Refoule agreed to come, and neither asked that a lawyer be present. They both stated to police that they wished to cooperate. The questioning was conducted in the room that was to have been the studio, the old mill part of the house. Most of the furniture had been removed. The granite walls gave the room a dungeon-like appearance. The intensive questioning of the girl and Refoule began around 10 p.m. and continued until 3 a.m. on May 20—some six hours.

Captain Bradford was both astonished and pleased with what the grilling of the two suspects produced. He felt that the case had taken such a turn that Chief Ellis should be present; he felt also that the police had gotten their first big break. He telephoned Chief Ellis to come to the Refoule home, and, while they were waiting for the chief to arrive, one of the investigators went out for food, and everyone had a bite to eat. When Ellis arrived, he was briefed privately by Bradford, and then he (Ellis) questioned Elaine, the young art student, and Refoule separately.

At 7 a.m. the former gave a sworn statement to the police.

ELAINE'S STATEMENT

I won a scholarship from Girls High School for three years at the High Museum of Art School, located on Peachtree Street, near Fifteenth Street. I started going to the High Museum of Art in September of 1945, this is my second year. Mr. Paul Refoule was my composition teacher. During that entire year, that is, the first year, he talked to me just as he did any of the other students. It was known to all the students that Paul Refoule was interested in one of the other students, whose name was Pat Sue, who is now married.

I did not know Mr. Refoule except what she told me about their affair. Pat Sue told me that Mr. Refoule told her that he loved her and that he wanted to marry her and that he had made love to her. She told me in class once that Mr. Refoule made love to her beautifully, and that he had kissed every part of her body. We discussed it later in the second year, after I had been with Mr. Refoule.

About two days before school was out in 1946, in May a year

ago, Mr. Paul Refoule asked me if I would like to come to his studio at Wesley Memorial Church Building and paint from a model who posed for him. I told him that I would like to. I had painted with him about 2 or 3 times but never quite finished because I started to work in the advertising department at Rich's, Inc. I became pretty interested in my advertising work but I still wanted to do some painting because I wanted to keep up my interest in fine art. He called me at Rich's. At the time, there was some talk between the two of us about doing some work together, murals, or paintings. I discussed it with the people in the office at Rich's, not very much, but they answered the phone. I told the people in my office that we were planning to do some painting together. About this time, I had my first sexual intercourse with Paul Refoule in his studio at Wesley Memorial Church Building.

This was during my lunch hour when I met him, maybe three times a week. From then on, about three times a week, we would have sexual intercourse. This lasted for about two months. Mr. Paul Refoule told me his life story, about his family in France, his family at home, about how he was not happy at home. He told me that he loved me. I told him not to say it because the word just gave me the cold chills. It was trite. I didn't believe it. I think he could convince himself that he was in love with anyone, any woman, that he was with. The reason I was so sure of this was because of what the other students thought of his relationship with Pat Sue. When he did mention marriage to me, it was because I was airing my views on marriage. I said that I didn't plan to get married. I never had. I wanted a career. After that, he didn't go into very much detail about his trouble with his wife except that it was the same situation, and that I couldn't imagine how miserable he was. At the time I thought it was self-pity. And I wasn't sympathetic enough to encourage him, to talk about it very much. He did tell me that he didn't feel very affectionate towards his wife, and that he didn't love her, and that he never did love her. He married her, he told me, because he thought she was attractive, cute, and felt like getting married. He told me about the way he met her. He further told me that he did not know her at all, but that they weren't together enough because of the war for him to realize this fully until he came back to this country. He told me that he had been planning to divorce her ever since he came back here. I knew this before through Pat Sue. On almost every occasion that we were together he would tell me that he loved me and he thought that I could love him someday, but I always told him that I did not love him, and when he mentioned marriage, it wasn't a definite plan because I had never told him I would marry him, even if he got a divorce.

That was through the summer of 1946 and when school started again, I went on a free lance basis at the store and did my work at home at night. As I got busier with it, I became more interested in my advertising work, so that I lost all interest in Paul Refoule. I told him not to call me either at home or at the office that it was embarrassing to me and I didn't want to see him again. He didn't try to call me after that or see me for six months. I didn't talk to him or see him even on the street because I got busy with my work at Rich's.

It was necessary to stay out of art school a few days to catch up with my work. I had to go to night school at the High Museum, that is, the High Museum School of Art, to make up this time. Paul teaches in the night school and he talked to me there. I told him at first that I didn't want him to give me a ride home because the whole thing might get started again, but then, because I didn't have another ride, I let him carry me home from night school, but we always went straight from the museum to my home. The longest period of time that I was ever out with him after night school was about thirty minutes, sitting in front of my house talking. At night school, I was talking with Bill Gray, a boy who had helped Refoule in the house and had posed for him, for a portrait. I suggested to Paul that he get Bill Gray to come out and pose and that I would come paint him too. This wasn't to get together with Paul, but because I thought Gray was an interesting model and I can't afford to hire my own models. This is how our sketching trip became a plan.

On Sunday, May 4, 1947, Paul came by my house with his little boy and told me that we were coming out here, to his home on Howell Mill Road, to sketch. We came in the house, and he asked me if I would like to see the house. I said yes and he showed me through the house. He asked me if I like it and I told him that I did, but that I thought everything followed his taste exactly and that it wasn't the accepted sort of house in Atlanta. He said that it was a little silly to build the house because he would never live in it, that he would probably sell it. Then he played the piano.

We got our things together, went down by the creek in back of the house. I sketched in one place and he sketched in another place further down this dirt road. Then his little boy came out and told us that lunch was ready and so we came and that is when I met Mrs. Refoule. After lunch, I went back out. He came out and I told him that I thought Mrs. Refoule was very charming and nice, and we talked a few minutes and he went back to the place where he was painting. When we finished our sketches, we came in and he played the piano again. Mrs. Refoule complimented my painting and then they had guests. After the guests left I told them that I had to go home and Paul offered to take me home. Mrs. Refoule was there at the time and she agreed that he should take me home. On the way home, we planned to sketch again on the following Tuesday, May 6, 1947.

I went down to the studio at Wesley Memorial Church about 10 a.m. Then we left immediately and went down to Decatur Street to sketch a store down there. The store was Harry's Loan Office. We went to lunch at the cafe about a half a block from the church. Here we were talking and he talked about how hard he had worked in the house and how everything was going to be all right. The only thing he was unhappy. I told him that I thought he was very lucky to have the studio he had.

We went back to the studio at Wesley Memorial Church to finish our ink and wash drawings and after an hour or so, we had sexual intercourse. This was last Tuesday, a week ago. On the way home I told him that I would never go back to the studio again or any place where any sexual relationship could take place. He agreed to this because it depressed me. I did not go to night school that night or the next Thursday, so the next time I saw him was a week later on Tuesday night, May 13, 1947, the Tuesday night before Mrs. Refoule was killed on Wednesday. The reason I saw him was that I went to night school. It wasn't planned at all. We talked about my work. He mentioned that he loved me and asked me if I even liked him. He made no mention of his wife that night. We went straight home. I talked to him about five or ten minutes, then went into the house. All I know after that was what I heard over the radio and read in the newspapers. According to the newspaper accounts, there was no suspicion cast upon him, so I began wondering how it had affected him. I thought that underneath he had loved his wife very much and that the brutality of it all had probably shocked him out of his mind. I wanted to express my sympathy, so I called him at his mother-in-law's house and told him that I was very sorry and asked him if there was anything I could do to help. He said that there was nothing anyone could do that it was very, very hard to take. Then he said that he was awfully confused and that he didn't know what he was going to do. He said he wasn't going to live in the new house. He said that he was going to live with his mother-in-law and after that he didn't know what he was going to do. It wasn't a

definite plan because I had never told Paul Refoule that I
wanted to marry him, but he suggested that if I ever married
him, ever changed my mind, that we would probably go back to
France, or he went alone after he divorced his wife. He said he
could go to Egypt because he had very good friends there.
When I returned from lunch at school yesterday, there was a
note for me at the High Museum of Art, from Captain Bradford, telling me to meet him at a place down the street from the
school. He asked me about my relationship with Paul Refoule
and I told him the same thing that I am telling you now.

Paul Refoule has told me that he has slept with one or both
of our models. I don't remember their names, but they were the
two models we had at the High Museum last year. He told me
about one relationship, that is a sexual relationship, he had
with a girl who has since gone north. That was during the six
months when I did not see him. I would like to say that although he was interested in me, during this time, Refoule had
told Pat Sue the same things he told me about his home life.
Also, other people around the school. All the students around
the school knew about his affair with Pat Sue and anybody who
talked to him any length of time, would hear about his work,
his family, and his plans. I heard no plans of any murder. All I
know about it is what I read in the paper and heard over the
radio. I know absolutely nothing else about it.

Chief Ellis remained at the Refoule home until Elaine completed her statement, and it had been typed, and she had
signed it. He then left the Refoule home and returned Elaine
to her own home. The time was between 6 and 7 a.m., May 20,
1947.

Captain Bradford then had Paul Refoule make a written
statement.

PAUL REFOULE'S STATEMENT

I met my wife in Paris, I think it was in 1936, probably the
winter of 1935–1936. We had dates and I thought to myself
that someday I would like to marry her. I knew she was in love
with me. I went with her a few months, and saw her once or
twice a week. We would attend movies and other functions together.

In 1936, I arrived in New York in December and came to
Atlanta, Georgia immediately. I had some money which I had
brought from France with me and had enough to live on. We
decided to get married. After we got married, we had a honey-

moon trip to Florida to Daytona Beach and southward. Then we came back to Atlanta. We stayed in Atlanta a very short time and then left and went to Washington, New York, and we sailed from New York on the Hansa, a German boat, and went back to France, and landed at LeHarve probably in February or March, 1937. After I went back to France, I was painting and teaching in Paris.

In 1938, we came back to the states, and to Atlanta, Georgia. We stayed probably about two months and left the states from either Mobile or New Orleans and landed at Cherbourg, France. I went back to painting at the same place. In 1939, my wife came back to the states, and stayed awhile and visited her father who was ill, and then came back to France.

When the war started, I went into the army. I was a liaison officer in the French army, attached to the English army. I was in the army about nine months and was captured in the north of France near Tournei, Belgium. I was sent to Meinz, Germany, where I was held prisoner by the Germans for about four years. I tried to escape many times. I was sent to Poland, where a French doctor gave me an X-ray for someone else and was released as being sick. I went to the south of France, Monein, to be exact. I stayed there until the end of the German occupation. I then came back to Orleans, which is my hometown, and met my wife there, we had met together in the south of France previous to this. I went back to painting and decided to move to this country. During the four years I was a prisoner, I did not see a girl, that is, I did not touch a girl, I saw them from a distance only.

After awhile I came back from the war and had been with my wife, my feeling for her was not the same. I thought that after we came back to this country, everything would straighten out. Instead, it didn't straighten out and my feeling was still not the same I had for her when I first knew her and married her. I had a very deep affection and respect for her, because of the child and because of her.

When we got back to the states, we went to my wife's mother's house. While staying with my mother-in-law, we were not too happy. I tried to have sexual feeling for my wife, but she was unhappy and did not like it.

We bought a place on Howell Mill Road. It was the old mill house. I started building and got a loan from the bank and another from my wife's grandmother. All together, I have a total investment in the place of $28,000, including the lot, remodeling, the addition, everything. The studio was built here and was remodeled from the old mill. During the time I was teaching at the High Museum of Art and also at Oglethorpe University. I had a class of students at both places.

I met a girl named Pat Sue who was a student in the class at the High Museum, and she posed for me privately for portraits and paintings. I went with her and was in love with her for a short while, a very short while. I also had a personal studio located in the Wesley Memorial Church Building in downtown Atlanta. During the time I had this place, Pat Sue came down to the studio to do some posing for me. I thought she was pretty and I tried to make love with her, but she never let me. I tried to sleep with her, and I never did. One day I got to kissing her and she consented and I put my tongue inside her and she did not like it. She wanted to stay a virgin so I did not try to have intercourse with her. This was during the month I worked on the Taj Mahal Bar in the Cox Carlton Hotel. She went to Florida, her home, for Christmas. I went down to see her, and see her mother. I had given her a black leather bag, which I bought down on Peachtree somewhere. It was an inexpensive bag. I wanted to give her a nice present because she had helped me work on the Taj Mahal Bar for no pay. During this time, I had difficult days of temper and humor with my wife and I asked Pat Sue to marry me and she told me no. When I went down to her house I told my wife I was going down to the seashore to draw some sketches and she never knew the difference. I stayed at a hotel, near the seashore. Last year, 1946, I had a student, a very fine art student, named Elaine who was in my class at the High Museum of Art. I never saw her out of class or the school before the end of the school year. She was my best pupil, very talented, and I thought she was very nice. I was interested in her paintings. We got to be better friends. She got a job down at Rich's. I called her several times and I saw her off and on and had lunch together and sometimes we would go back by my studio at Wesley Church, sometimes during the summer. On a lot of occasions we would have sexual intercourse in my studio at Wesley Memorial Church. I probably had sexual intercourse with her on her lunch hour at one time or another. Sometimes she would drop in after school and during paintings and I would have sexual intercourse with her.

I told Elaine my whole life history. After December, 1946, I saw her less and less. I was very fond of Elaine. I told her I loved her. I was very much impressed with her. I told her about my family relations. I asked her to marry me. I told her if she would marry me, I would take her to Paris and that if she didn't want to I would go alone to Egypt where I had friends. She always said no to the idea of getting married. Last Tuesday, two weeks ago, Elaine and I were at the Royal Cafe on Auburn Avenue. I told Elaine that me and my wife were very depressed at home and that we were having trouble again. I asked her what she thought about getting married now. She said no, that she was interested in a career.

From time to time, I gave Elaine presents of a book, a water color painting, some second hand odd books. On her birthday, I went to a florist and sent her flowers. Last Tuesday night, the night before my wife was murdered, I carried Elaine home from school from the High Museum of Art. We left there about 10 p.m. and had a flat tire. I got the tire fixed and carried Elaine on home and probably kissed her goodnight. I told her I loved her and that I cared a lot about her. I was home by 10:30 p.m. During the time I went with Elaine, I told her about my relations with Pat Sue and told her that I had put my tongue in her. I also told her about having an intercourse with one of the nude models, whose last name I never did know, but her first name was Caroline. I had intercourse with Caroline, just as I told her.

Last Sunday, two weeks ago, I called Elaine and asked if she wanted to come out and make some sketches at my home. She came, and I went to pick her up and my son was with me. She got here about 9:30 a.m. We went through the ditch in back of the house and I completed a sketch I had already started and she started a sketch down the dirt road. Elaine met my wife before lunch time. My wife did not like for me to bring Elaine or the other girls in the class, and she did not like it at all. During the week, I had one of my boy students, Bill Gray, over here to do some portraits and other painting. I asked him over here to help me paint the bathroom walls and to make some sketches on the outside. My wife treated him very well. When the girl came she did not like it, that is, my wife did not like for the girl to come here. I showed Elaine through the house when I first got here. She said it was beautiful and very nice, and that it was the home of an artist. I told her maybe I would never live much in it that I could always sell it. I have told other students at the High Museum that I was not happy with my wife.

By the time Refoule had completed making his statement and it had been typed and he had gone over the document and signed each page, it was noon on Tuesday, May 20, 1947. The session had lasted some fifteen hours. Everyone had lunch and Refoule went upstairs to take a nap. By this time the press had learned something was going on at the Refoule

house, and reporters and photographers descended upon the
house and surrounded it. When Chief Ellis learned of this he
was greatly concerned that something in the statements
would be leaked to the press, and he was not ready for that at
this point. He called the editors of both papers and asked
them to call off their boys. He assured the press that nothing
was being kept from them and that the police were merely
going over the details in the case once again. The press retreated from the house but continued to keep the house under
surveillance from their automobiles. In this way they could
see who came out.

For the fifth time, the police on the case walked over the
wooded area and examined the house and grounds carefully.
Since the night following the murder, the police had patrolled
the grounds and kept the public away.

THE POLICE CLOSE IN

In the eyes of the police, the statements of Paul Refoule and
Elaine now made Refoule a suspect in the murder of his wife.
It was a turn of events that the police should have found hard
to believe, but this was not the case. They had not liked Refoule much from the beginning. They wanted to believe he
was guilty of the murder. Since all other avenues of solving
the case appeared to lead nowhere, it was a valid excuse for
blaming Refoule for the murder. At least it seemed so to the
investigators at the time.

Refoule's own words cast the most suspicion upon him, the
investigators thought. The police now felt that it was their job
to either prove Refoule guilty of the crime of which many of
the investigators in their own minds had already found him
guilty or else clear him of any suspicion whatsoever.

The man Refoule had to be thoroughly investigated. With
relish, the police moved in to find out everything they possibly
could about this Frenchman, this artist, this man who would
seduce a young blond girl and then take her to lunch on Auburn Avenue—of all places. It was ghastly. Horrendous! Good
white folks did not behave that way.

For one last attempt, one other suspect in the case was not
overlooked. Robert Griffin, a black male, aged 30, was arrested for burglary in the area of the Refoule home. He was
questioned briefly about his activities on the day of May 14;
but he had an alibi and was then released. This suspect may

have had nothing to do with the murder. He may have. The point is that this suspect was not thoroughly checked as were suspects in the beginning. The police were beginning to zero in on Refoule, and other suspects did not interest them much.

There was other pressure. The newspapers noted that some investigators thought that Griffin might play the same role in the Refoule case that Blalock played in the Heinz case. This caused a rash of telephone calls to come into the police station castigating the police completely for attempting to follow this line. It was just another sell-out. Go after the French artist husband, the callers urged—and his mother-in-law. They both looked pretty suspicious to the general public. Like villains. Such feeling on the part of the public was not lost upon the police. They did not like Refoule. The public was beginning not to like Refoule and the entire family. What the police felt about Refoule, they began to realize, many other people felt the same. It would be a popular thing to prove Refoule guilty. The public would be grateful. Public pressure was pushing at the police dangerously.

On Wednesday, May 20, 1947, the police took into custody a white male, aged 22, who was questioned concerning the slaying. The young man's family hired a lawyer and threatened legal action if the police did not quit questioning this man, who had nothing to do with the case and the police had no evidence whatsoever that he had any connection with the case. This supposed suspect came to the attention of the police because he had been hitchhiking on Howell Mill Road the day of the murder and had been given a ride by a prominent citizen, who, upon reading and reflecting about the murder, decided that his hitchhiking passenger of that day appeared highly nervous. The man was nervous because his car had run out of gas and he was late for work.

Many tips to the police proved to be just this far off base. Hundreds of other tips from persons interested in helping the police solve the case poured into headquarters. Many were the wild notions of people whose neuroses had been turned on by the publicity in the Refoule case. People in the area were jittery and insisted that what was needed were more police to patrol the Peachtree Creek area and that it was not safe for people to be on the streets. Women wrote in to tell the methods they used for protecting themselves while walking in the vicinity. Some of the reports, those which helped the police retrace the activities of the Refoule household the day before and of the murder, were helpful.

Letters and phone calls continued to come into police headquarters stating in essence that Refoule was somehow implicated in the murder of his wife. Even these calls, when coupled with Refoule's own statement of May 19–20, which made the police more suspicious than they were before, were not sufficient evidence to indict Refoule for murder.

In the mail addressed to police headquarters which arrived on May 22, 1947, there was a letter that altered the complexion of the case even further. Written in ink on a plain white sheet of bonded typing paper and placed in a plain envelope with no return address, the letter stated that the police were on the wrong track in the Refoule case. It claimed that Peggy was murdered by her husband Paul. The unsigned letter accused Paul Refoule of being a sexual pervert and said that he gave wild parties at his studio home. The anonymous note alleged that the last wild party was held on Monday, May 12, 1947, two nights before Peggy Refoule was murdered. The letter further stated that Refoule wanted to divorce his wife and go back to France, but he was Catholic, and in the event of a divorce Peggy would never give up Jon Paul. Refoule's parents had written letters urging him not to divorce Peggy and leave America because of the boy. The mystery informant concluded by stating that these letters were in the Refoule studio at the Wesley Memorial Church Building.

Whether it was a combination of factors—the fact that all other leads in the case came to nothing, there were unusual facts of the actual murder scene that did not add up, that there was continuing information coming to the police that the Refoules were on the verge of divorce, that Refoule was French, Catholic, an artist, and now, by accusation, a sexual pervert; or whether it was the continuous demand from the public to "get the higher-ups" the "untouchables"—whatever, from this point onward the police would concentrate all their efforts on proving that Refoule was responsible for the death of his wife. All other considerations in the case were out the window. Attempts to trace the items stolen from the Refoule home were abandoned in the rush to prove Refoule guilty. Other possibilities in the case were forgotten. The police, even if they were not totally convinced of Refoule's guilt, were now hell-bent on proving it.

Friday, May 23, 1947. Captain Bradford and his investigators visited the Refoule studio in downtown Atlanta and
searched the room thoroughly. In a trash can they found letters that had been torn up and thrown away. The letters were
painstakingly pasted together again like a jig-saw puzzle, and
the police discovered that several were from a girl in New
York named Mary, who was a former student of Refoule. They
were, for all intents and purposes, harmless love letters. The
police found the letters from Refoule's parents. They were also
pasted back together again and, because they were in French,
sent out to be translated. When the letters were returned to
the police from the translator, the letters said exactly what
the anonymous note to the police said they contained: that
Refoule wanted to leave Peggy, leave America, but that his
parents urged him to stick it out. The anonymous note proved
its authenticity to the extent that the police realized it was
not from a crackpot—the anonymous note writer knew what
he, or she, was talking about. It was obviously written by
someone who knew Refoule quite well, had been to the studio,
and learned the content of the letters either by reading them
or being told what they contained by Paul Refoule. The
anonymous note was sent to a handwriting expert to try and
determine something about the mysterious author. It became
vital for the police to discover who wrote the note and why.
Was it truth or vengeance? Some personal grudge or a legitimate lead in the case?

NEW EVIDENCE

On Saturday, May 24, 1947, ten days after the Refoule slaying, county convicts, under police supervision, were dragging
and sifting the rocky bottom of Peachtree Creek, once again
going over the area of the slaying in search of clues in the
case. By chance, they came up with a startling discovery.

Eight feet above the spot where Peggy Refoule's barrette
was found swung a noose over the limb of an oak tree. The
six-foot length of rope had spots of blood upon it. It was a sashcord identical with that found on the Refoule tool chest under
the kitchen range. It was knotted exactly as the shoelaces
binding Mrs. Refoule's legs had been knotted, with an extra
turn or loop. After observing the grooves in the tree bark
made by the sashcord, police determined the cord had supported considerable weight.

Chief Ellis was called to the scene. He concluded that "the killer strung up Mrs. Refoule. The welt was high on her jaw because of the upward pull. That is why her feet were tied, to control the action of her legs." This appeared to be an accurate analysis. But then the chief went on: "Maybe the murderer left Mrs. Refoule there two or three hours before he put her in the water." Perhaps the slayer left her there, went to the house and burglarized it, returned to the creek, and, now certain that the victim was dead, placed the body in the creek. But this is not what Chief Ellis had in mind. He did not say so publicly but privately he felt the finding of the rope implicated Refoule more than ever.

Why had not the police discovered the rope before now? The creek area had been gone over many times. All one had to do is look up. In time, there would be talk that the police placed the rope in the tree to implicate Refoule. This possibility appears remote. If the police wished to implicate Refoule, they could have found a better means. The discovery of the rope confused the case more than ever. It certainly was not iron-clad evidence of Refoule's guilt.

Was there some connection between the rope and the anonymous note? Was the same person responsible for both? If Peggy Refoule was hung from a tree, would an ordinary burglar go to such lengths? Not usually. But obviously this was no ordinary case.

Chief Ellis felt it all did not add up. He theorized to the press that Peggy Refoule was strangled in her home, then hung in the tree, and finally placed in the creek much later. Again, by inference, he was strongly pointing at the husband as the murderer. He told the press that the police had eliminated robbery as a motive in the slaying and that an intruder in all probability would have fled the house, leaving the body where it lay—regardless of the fact that previous police investigation had clearly established that the house was burglarized the day of the murder. Ellis said also that the rope in the tree was tied in a distinct navy knot, further implicating Refoule.

The day was full of surprises for the police. They learned also that the will of Peggy Alston Refoule had been filed for probate. The will left her entire estate, estimated at ten thousand dollars or more, to her nine-year-old son and named her uncle, Mr. Douglas Wright, as executor.

On the night of May 24, 1947, Captain Bradford went to the
Alston home and talked with Paul Refoule. He asked him to
come downtown for further questioning. Refoule agreed to do
so. Mrs. Alston and her son, William Ott Alston, Jr., strongly
urged that a lawyer be present during the questioning. Refoule did not want an attorney and said that he could speak
for himself, that he had nothing to hide. Refoule wanted to go
over the details with the police. He appeared eager to do so.
Perhaps he felt that to do otherwise would make him appear
guilty in their eyes. The Alstons felt that Refoule, being
French, had little appreciation for American police procedure
and custom and that in these interrogations with the police
he was in need of legal assistance. On the other hand, Refoule
looked upon the American police in the same way as he did
his German captors during the war—both held the trump
cards, and Refoule wished to escape. In this instance, Refoule
felt that he had the best chance of not being accused of his
wife's murder if he cooperated with the police in every way;
so, Refoule voluntarily went with Bradford to the Hurt Building in downtown Atlanta. When they had gone, Mrs. Alston
and her son discussed the situation, and Mrs. Alston decided
to call an attorney, Hal Lindsay. She told him what was happening and asked him to represent Refoule whether he
wanted a lawyer or not. Mr. Lindsay immediately accepted
the defense of Paul Refoule and drove in his automobile to the
Hurt Building.

Around midnight Chief Ellis arrived at the Hurt Building,
and by this time Assistant Chief Fitzgerald and other detectives who were working on the case were present too. Lindsay
and Ellis went into a private office to discuss the situation.
Lindsay stated that he had been hired as counsel for Paul Refoule and he wished to be present at the questioning of his
client, that this was his practice and custom. But Chief Ellis
abruptlydeclined Lindsay's request. Assistant Chief Fitzgerald then joined them. He told Lindsay that he had just spoken
to Refoule and that Refoule stated to him that he had not employed Mr. Lindsay, that he did not have a lawyer, and that he
did not need a lawyer. Lindsay asked to speak with Refoule.
Ellis denied this request. Fitzgerald told Lindsay that if Refoule requested his presence during the questioning, he would
be summoned. Mr. Lindsay agreed reluctantly. He said that
he would be at his home if his presence was requested by Re-

foule. While at the Hurt Building, neither Chief Ellis nor Mr. Lindsay actually saw or spoke to Refoule directly, his wishes being communicated to them through Fitzgerald.

At 1 a.m. Refoule was taken to the Fulton County Court-house. There he remained from 1:30 a.m., May 25, 1947, until 4:30 a.m., May 26, 1947—a period of some 27 hours! At no time during this questioning in the courthouse did Refoule ask for an attorney or indicate in any way that he desired an attorney, according to all those present at the questioning.

First, the police questioned Refoule about the sashcord that had been found in Peachtree Creek Saturday afternoon. They asked him about the sashcord on the toolbox under the kitchen range. Refoule explained that when they moved to their new house, he strung the cord between two trees for the clothesline. It was much too long. He sawed off a piece and threw it on the toolchest and forgot about it. The police wanted to know if the cord found in the tree was cut from the left-over cord on the tool chest. Refoule said he did not know. He could not remember exactly how much cord was remaining. It could have been from the same cord.

Next, the police put Refoule through extensive and arduous knot-tying tests. Each time, Refoule tied his knots with the extra loop—as the shoelaces and the noose found in the tree had been knotted. The police were jolted. Refoule could tie this intricate knot with ease. They thought this was highly significant. Refoule insisted that it was a simple knot which an ordinary person could, and would, tie—that it required no special talent. The police thought differently. One detective suggested that the knot with the extra loop was a distinc-tively "foreign" knot. But this was only his thought; he could not prove it.

The questioning turned next to the subject of Refoule's sex life. The police wanted to know if he was a sexual pervert. They wanted to know, too, if he had a sex party at his home on the night of May 12, 1947. Refoule denied both assertions. As for Monday night, he and his wife went out to dinner with another couple. They were out late and were seen by many people. But the questioning on these points continued for sev-eral hours. Then, Refoule was questioned again about every-thing concerning the case. He gave essentially the same an-swers as he had given to the police on May 19–20 when he and Elaine were questioned at his home.

While the investigators went over Refoule's statement carefully, the artist took a nap on a couch in a judge's chambers in
the courthouse. While Refoule was asleep, the detectives went
to the home of Bill Gray and brought the art student to the
courthouse for questioning. All the police knew about Gray
was that he was a student and model of Refoule and had
helped Refoule do some work on the mill house. After extensive questioning Gray made the following statement:

> I was discharged from the U.S. Navy at Charleston, S.C., in
> December, 1945 and returned to Atlanta and got a job at Con-
> ley Depot. I worked there six months to the day. I then went to
> work for the National Traffic Guard and worked there one
> month and a half. About three or four months ago through the
> G.I. Bill of Rights handled by the Veterans Administration, I
> started attending the High Museum of Art. I attended school
> two nights a week, Tuesday and Thursday. When I first started
> attending the school Mr. Paul Refoule was my teacher. I at-
> tended his class approximately one month, then went into the
> classes of Mr. Rogers and Mr. Shute in the portrait class and
> saw Mr. Refoule every night that I attended, and started hav-
> ing conversations with him. He told me about his house that
> he was building and his plans of completing it. He told me
> about the studio and his plans of holding a school out there but
> he said there was no bus service that far out. He said that he
> had never run a school like he was planning and he did not
> know if it would pay or not. About this time he told me that
> both he and his wife were unhappy. He stated that his wife was
> not interested in his work anymore. He said that it made him
> very unhappy because she was that way. This conversation
> took place in his car as we were riding to school. I had been
> helping him paint his bathroom upstairs and we talked about
> building a bridge over a big ditch in the back of the house so
> other students could get to the creek to sketch.
> I had supper with the Refoules before we left for school. I
> was out there one other time. I helped him do some painting in
> one of the rooms on the right of the bathroom. I went out there
> about 10:30 a.m. and stayed there until around 6 p.m. that eve-
> ning. While we were eating supper Peggy Refoule said that she
> would like to get someone to rent a room there so she would
> have someone to stay with her at night for protection. On the
> way to school that night Paul told me again that Peggy was
> not happy and neither was he. These were the only two times
> I was ever at the Refoule home. I know absolutely nothing else
> about the case.

Two other male students were brought to the courthouse and gave statements that day, but their testimony added nothing further to the case. Late that afternoon Refoule returned to the Alston home.

GHOULISH CURIOSITY

On Sunday, for the first time since the case broke on May 14, sightseers had the run of the Refoule premises on Howell Mill Road. The police had gone over everything numerous times and no longer kept a guard on the property. The press estimated that some 10,000 persons went through the Refoule home and grounds! The sightseers parked their automobiles and proceeded to conduct their own investigations, retracing the route through tangled underbrush where many thought the slayer had taken his victim. They tramped down the foliage, peered into windows, opened closet doors, and remarked on paintings in the Refoule studio. Various groups got into conversations with others and exchanged theories and gossip about the murder. They voiced their opinion on art and crime. When the police rushed to the scene to clear everyone out of the house, many people were very indignant, and a near-riot ensued between the people and the police. The people felt that they had a perfect right to be there. They considered the Refoule home and crime scene now to be public property, and, if the public wanted to know and see everything concerning the Refoule case, then the police should not deny them. The murder was now public entertainment. If you are prominent and get murdered then you lose certain rights of privacy—like a politician running for office. This was how people felt at the time. For many, the Refoule murder was one of the big events of their lives.

The week of May 26 through May 31 the Fulton County police spent gathering all the evidence possible against Refoule. They went to Oglethorpe University and had all the students in Refoule's art class make notarized statements. The statements were practically all the same.

> I am a student at Oglethorpe University and study art under Paul Refoule. On Wednesday, May 14, I came to class at 2:45 p.m. by the school clock. The class starts at 2:40 p.m. and I was five minutes late. When I got into class at 2:45 p.m., Mr. Refoule was present. He had already set up a still life which we

were supposed to draw. He had already explained what he wanted the class to do. When I came in five minutes late, he explained to me again what the instructions were. My wrist watch is usually ten minutes faster than the school clock. I set up my board and started working on the drawing about 2:50 p.m. About 3:15 p.m. Mr. Refoule checked the roll. I cannot say definitely just when Mr. Refoule left our classroom. Evidently, Mr. Refoule left the classroom between 3:15 and 3:30 p.m. and went into the other classroom, because when I went into the other art classroom to get a bottle of water, I saw Mr. Refoule in the other room. I sat down by him and talked with him for about 15 minutes. I left the classroom about 5 p.m. and Mr. Refoule was still there. The class is rather informal since the students have to go in and out for water and supplies. This is all I know about the case.

All the statements of his students taken together verified that while Refoule was in and out of his own classroom, he did not leave the building at anytime. The statements of the Oglethorpe students tended to firm up Refoule's alibi. It should have been obvious to anyone that Refoule could not have murdered his wife. But the police continued to confine their investigation only to the husband.

Next the police department took on the High Museum of Art. It was not possible that two institutions of the period could have had less in common. Neither understood the other. The police interviewed practically the entire school, faculty and students, and took lengthy statements. Needless to say, the police were operating in a rather unusual environment for them, and what they learned about life among artists in art school was a terrific shock. They thought it deplorable that models posed in the nude. They had never heard of such a thing! They listened wide-eyed to stories about wild sex parties and loose morals. Most of this was just gossip and student pranks to play games with the police, and the murder investigation went rather far afield at this point. A spokesman for the High Museum of Art stated: "High-handed, Gestapo-like, and intimidative methods in questioning art students and models were being used by the Fulton County Police Department." The director of the museum was indignant. But the High Museum depended upon both tax money and civic contributions to stay in operation, and its officials were appalled at what the investigation was doing to the school's reputation.

They wished the police would go away. But the more the police learned about art school, the more they were fascinated and the more active they were in questioning the art students. They requested that the young art student who had written love letters to Refoule from New York and was now back in Atlanta on vacation come and make a statement, and she eagerly did so.

I started going to the High Museum of Art in 1946. I had a class and the instructor was Paul Refoule. I attended his class from February 1946 until May, 1946. All the girls in the class thought Mr. Refoule was very handsome and a good teacher. Mr. Refoule would tell me as an instructor any criticism that he might have of my drawing. I never saw Paul until I started back to the High Museum of Art in October of 1946 and he was my instructor once again. I attended until February, 1947. During my attending this school I posed for Paul privately at his studio located in the Wesley Memorial Church Building located on Auburn Avenue. On two or three other occasions I posed for Paul. On the last occasion I posed for Paul I was still in my posing position and was sitting in a straight or regular chair and Paul kissed me. I enjoyed him kissing me but I reminded him he had a wife and son. I left shortly afterwards because I did not want to get involved with a married man. That was just before I left to go to New York. I was very much in love with Paul at the time and when I came to New York I wrote him everyday and told him about the school I was attending. We corresponded and Paul told me he loved my letters. Before coming to New York, Paul told me of being a prisoner of the Germans. He told me of his plans in painting and of fixing his home. The last time I received a letter from Paul was about two weeks before Mrs. Refoule was murdered. I answered this letter and told him how much I loved him and how I wanted to be with him forever. I was pretty proud of this until I found out you have it [meaning the letter]. I wrote Paul one letter after the murder which was self explanatory. I felt that I was alive and his wife was dead. What I felt like is that he must hate me for what happened. Paul never said to me that he loved me.

This statement indicates that a student was in love with her teacher. What this adds to the murder investigation is hard to say. The police took the statement seriously.

The one student and two models with whom the police really wanted to talk were no longer at the art school and no longer even living in Atlanta. How such individuals could be involved in the murder was hard to comprehend, but they could tell a great deal about Paul Refoule's sex life, which was the main interest of the police now. The murder investigation was fast becoming an investigation into that aspect of the life of an artist and his models. The police maintained this was the key to solving the murder of Peggy Refoule. The evidence thus far did not appear very convincing. On June 3, 1947, the police secured the following statement from former art student Pat Sue.

I started to school at the High Museum of Art in Atlanta, Georgia on September 10, 1945. Mr. Paul Refoule was an instructor in art there at the school. I was a student in the class at which Mr. Refoule was the instructor. A few weeks after I had been in class, Mr. Refoule walked up to me in the hall one day and asked me to do some posing for him in his private studio in downtown Atlanta. He wanted me to pose for a portrait of myself which he was going to paint. I made frequent trips to his studio and posed for the portrait. I did not pose in the nude. I posed wearing my pants and a brassiere.

On the second posing I did for him, in his studio, he kissed me. I posed at first on Thursday, Friday and Saturday. He made love to me at each sitting. After that, I posed on Saturdays for him. Since we belonged to the same church, we would go to mass on Sunday and then go to his studio. Each time we went to the studio, he made love to me. During the time I was posing for Paul Refoule, he asked me to marry him. He told me that he would divorce his wife if I would marry him. He said that if I would marry him, we would travel around Europe doing painting and would probably wind up in Orleans, France. I was very much in love with Paul Refoule, but being realistic, I felt it would never be possible for me to marry him. I had to consider my parents. Other things led me to believe the marriage was not probable. Paul told me on several occasions that his home life with his wife was unhappy.

On one occasion, when I refused to have normal sexual intercourse with him, Paul kissed me all over my body and placed his tongue in my privates. I was partly clothed at the time. He stayed there with his tongue in my privates for approximately three minutes. He asked me if I liked it and I said I didn't think so, not really. He did it again but I was very embarrassed. This was the only time he did this. I posed for him some more after that. He made love to me on another occasion after that incident, in a normal manner. The affair I had with Paul Refoule went on from September, 1945, until sometime in January,

1946. The time Paul Refoule placed his tongue in my privates, we were in his studio at the Wesley Memorial Church. It was sometime during the time he was working on the murals at the Taj Mahal Bar at the Cox-Carlton Hotel, or shortly after he finished working on them. I never knew or had never heard of anyone putting their tongue in anyone else before that time. He did not ask me if he could do it but rather just went ahead and did it. Since that time, and since I have been married, my husband borrowed a book, Rennie McAndrew's *Love and Sex Technique* and I learned that this was done and there was a paragraph in the book which described the whole process. During the time I was having an affair with Paul Refoule he gave me a nice handbag with a handkerchief inside. He gave me some scarfs for my birthday.

Paul Refoule came to Florida and met my mother. I was married in August, 1946, and returned to school in September. My husband is stationed at Ft. Dix, New Jersey. I have seen Paul Refoule just casually since that time, to speak to him and have a casual conversation. He told me that he hoped that I was happy. On May 16, 1947, I received a telegram from my husband stating that he was going overseas and asking me to come to New Jersey. I went to New Jersey and learned that he had sent me the telegram to get me out of Atlanta during the investigation of the death of Mrs. Refoule to keep me from being investigated. He knew about my affair with Paul Refoule. On Thursday morning after Mrs. Refoule was killed on Wednesday, Elaine, a girl friend of mine, came to school and was very nervous and upset. We went out and got in a friend's car and listend to the radio reports of the murder. I have not heard from or seen Paul Refoule since his wife was killed. This is all I know about the case.

The police were anxious to talk with two models at the High Museum of Art who had posed privately for Paul Refoule. One was living in Florida, where on June 10, 1947, Captain Bradford interviewed her.

Question: Did you go to the High Museum of Art?
Answer: I didn't go there. I modeled there.
Q: What kind of modeling did you do?
A: Nude.
Q: What we want to do is a little embarrassing to us and it is more embarrassing after we came down here and found that you are married.
A: Yes. I understand that.
Q: How long did you model at the High Museum of Art?

A: Not more than six weeks.

Q: Did you model at Wesley Memorial for Paul Refoule?

A: Yes.

Q: We want to know the relations he had with you and the other model.

A: I got to know Pat Sue, one of the students at the school. She asked me if Paul Refoule tried to make love to me when I was posing for him and I said yes. I was surprised that he did this, but I went on modeling for him, but it was a struggle all the time. Seems to me like he was a happy-go-lucky fellow but was unhappy with his home life, but since he was a Catholic he could not get a divorce. That is the impression he gave me.

Q: Did the other model, your friend Martha, ever have any conversation with you as to her relations with Paul Refoule?

A: Well, she just had the same trouble that I did. He always messed around and told us all his troubles. She is married now.

Q: In his statement Refoule said he had intercourse with you.

A: Well . . . once.

Q: Did he ever try to do it by mouth—or did he just try to have intercourse?

A: Just the intercourse business.

Q: Your name is Carolyn. The other girl's name is Martha. Did he have the same with Martha?

A: I don't know you will have to ask her.

Q: How many times did Refoule make advances toward you?

A: Every time I went there.

Q: You always went to see Refoule alone?

A: Always. Except that once Pat Sue and I thought it would be fun to go over there together and see if he would make advances to both of us. He thought it was a good joke. We all laughed about it. The next time I went to pose for him he told me how much he loved Pat Sue.

Q: He told you that he was in love with Pat Sue?

A: Yes.

Q: Did he tell you that he had been with Pat Sue in any other way than the natural way? French?

A: He never did say.

Q: Did he ever kiss you down there?

A: Not down there.

Q: To what extent did he work himself up with you?

A: He kissed me all over my body but didn't kiss me down there. He kissed me on the ear.

Q: Did he kiss you on the breast?

A: Yes, and all over, but never down there.

Q: Did you ever meet Mrs. Refoule?

A: I was working at the studio in the nude one day when she came by to see him. His wife didn't seem to think anything about it. I thought she was very gracious.

Q: How old are you?

A: 18.

Q: How many times were you at the studio posing for Refoule before he had this intercourse with you?

A: Gosh, I don't know. Three times, or something like that.

Q: Did he make a pass at you the first time you went over there?

A: Yes.

Q: You just tell us all you can about it.

A: There is not all that much to tell. He made passes at me. I told Martha about it. He asked her to pose for him. She knew what to expect. I told her how he messed around and everything. She told me she had the same experience. He just seemed to like models.

Q: Was it commonly known that Paul Refoule was a sex-pervert?

A: Well . . . the girls seemed to know. I mean Pat Sue and the other girls who modeled for Refoule. There was a lot of talk. You see I bruise very easily so I want to say that one day I went to school with a bruise on my leg and one of the girls came into the restroom when I was dressing and asked me where I got the bruise. I didn't say anything. She said: 'modeling for Mr. Refoule, eh?' So; they all knew.

Q: Did you ever go out to Paul Refoule's house? Ever pass there or see it? Did he ever talk to you about building a new home?

A: I never was at his house. He just told me about his experiences during the war and about how unhappy he was with his wife. He said something about he wished he could build a house but I can't go into any detail. I remember vaguely about a house. The only time I was out with him was the time he took Martha and I out to the Cox Carlton Hotel to see the mural he had done there. He was just talking and talking and seemed to be in heaven to be sitting there between two girls and it didn't seem to matter to him that he was in a public place and that he had painted a mural there and that people probably knew him.

Q: Did you ever model for Refoule at his studio at night?

A: No. We worked in the mornings or afternoons. I remember

Pat Sue saying something about posing for him in the evening. When the dean at the Art School found out he was going to write Pat Sue's mother.

Q: Is posing at night a violation of the school rules?

A: No. Not for models. I wouldn't know about the students. I was not a student. Just a model.

Q: There is something else I want to ask you about. It has come to our attention and is commonly known among several students that we have talked to, and that is the 69 Club. Do you know about the 69 Club at the High Museum of Art?

A: 69 Club? What kind of club is that?

Q: Made up of students and instructors.

A: No, I don't think I ever heard of that.

Q: When did Paul first talk to you? When was the first time he started telling you how unhappy he was?

A: I met him at the High Museum when I was modeling for a painting class and these women in the class were telling me what wonderful workmanship Refoule did and what a wonderful man he was and that kind of thing. I think all the women in the class were kind of taken with Paul, him being French and all. He came into their painting class that day and looked at me and said—'Oh lovely!' So after class I saw him talking to Pat Sue and I heard her mention my name. He came over and asked me if I would like to pose for him. He started telling me when I went out for a sandwich, the first day I posed for him, about what an unhappy marriage he had.

Q: What did he say about his wife?

A: That he was unhappy being married to her, but that he was Catholic and there was the boy.

Q: Did he ever mention of anyway to dispose of her to you?

A: No.

Q: Did he ever tell you that he loved you?

A: Oh yes, several times.

Q: What did he say about it?

A: Oh, he didn't talk in the way of getting married or anything. It was just talk with him. I am sure I am not the only person he told that.

Q: In other words, when he said he loved you he didn't necessarily mean that he wanted to marry you.

A: Yes.

On June 12, 1947, Captain Bradford took a statement from the other model, Martha, in Atlanta.

Caroline, my girl friend and I, came up to Atlanta from Florida in January 1946. When we got to the railroad station, we started calling numbers furnished by the Travel Aid Society for a place to stay. We found a place and rented an apartment on Techwood Drive from Mrs. Hern. She was a widow. Caroline wanted to find work playing the piano and I wanted to find modeling work. I had done some fashion modeling and was interested in that. We went to an agency but the only request for models they had was at the High Museum of Art. We went out there and talked to a man out there about a job. He said they had fashion modeling, bathing suit modeling, and nude modeling. He said the nude modeling paid $2 an hour, considerably more than the others. Caroline went to work but I decided to think about it for a few days. I went out one day to the school and told them that I would do bathing suit modeling. A very nice lady out there told me they needed another model for a life class there at the High Museum. Caroline had told me that no one there paid any attention to the models being nude, that it was very business like, so I accepted the job.

I started modeling nude that day. The class I posed the most for was one for older women, and Mr. Shute's wife was one of them. Mr. Shute was the instructor. Mrs. Charles Nunnally was also in the class. Mr. Shute was the instructor in that class. Paul Refoule never taught that class. Once I was on a break and Paul Refoule came up to me and asked me to pose for him in his private studio. He said he would pay me the same salary as the school. I told him if I had time, I would pose for him. Caroline had posed for him before I did. She had told me that she had a struggle with Refoule when she posed for him and said that I may have one also. She said he would make advances towards her and that she would have to resist him. I went to pose for Paul Refoule for the first time in February, 1946. The first time I posed for him he was very nice. It was very pleasant. The second time I went to pose for him he tried to kiss me. He was strong, although he doesn't look very strong. He kept trying to get me to kiss him. I told him we had better get back to work.

Paul Refoule told me about being overseas in a prison camp. He was painting a watercolor picture of me. The last time I went to the studio he kissed me on the shoulders and neck and on the mouth. I told him that I was very much in love with my husband. He said that he was very unhappy with his wife. He begged me to have sexual intercourse with him. I refused. He was upset, for he was ready for intercourse, but I refused to yield to his advances. I started to leave and he grabbed my

The Fox Theatre

Fulton Tower, Atlanta's Long-time Jail

The Ansley Hotel

Like the grim structure pictured above it, this one-time fashionable hotel has been demolished.

Banker Henry Heinz (*right*) and
Mayor William B. Hartsfield.

Mrs. Henry Heinz
arrives at the Fox
Theatre for a Met-
ropolitan Opera
performance.

Accused killer Horace Blalock
shows investigators where he threw
the gun used in the Heinz murder.

Rainbow Terrace
Curious sightseers descend upon Rainbow Terrace, the palatial residence
of Mr. and Mrs. Henry Heinz.

Judge and Mrs. Robert Refoule (*top*) approach the Federal Building in downtown Atlanta for the hearing of their son's suit in 1947. In happier days, Paul, Peggy, and Jon Paul Refoule (*middle*) are shown assembling a crèche at Christmas 1945. The just-completed Refoule home on Howell Mill Road (*bottom*) is shown shortly after Mrs. Refoule's murder.

WESTERN UNION

AA051 A.LSA60 NL PD=ATLANTA, GA 20=

BARBARA LEVINE=

NATIONAL CONCERT AND ARTISTS CORPORATION 711 FIFTH

AVE NYK=

YOU WILL HAVE ALL TEXTS AND TRANSLATIONS OF GOETHE SONGS
BY MONDAY SORRY FOR THE DELAY REGARDS=

JOHN GARRIS=..

APR 21 REC'D

Telegram sent by opera singer John Garris shortly before he was murdered.

Capt. Cal Cates (*left*) and Supt. E.l. Hilderbrand, who figured prominently in the investigations surrounding Atlanta's most sensational murders.

John Garris in costume for one of his roles in Metropolitan Opera performances.

Terminal Station, the site of which is now occupied by the Richard B. Russell Building, at which the Metropolitan Opera cast arrived in Atlanta and from which all but one of its singers departed on April 21, 1949.

hands and held them and kissed them. He told me that I was beautiful. He told me that I was sweet. Very reluctantly I yielded to his pleadings. But just that once.

I never went back to the studio after that. The only time I was ever out with Paul Refoule was the time he, Caroline, and I went to the Cox Carlton Hotel for a drink. Paul had just completed the murals there. We went down to the bar and had one whiskey sour a piece. He took us on home and as we got out of the car, he kissed us both goodnight. This is all I know about the case.

On Friday, June 13, 1947, one month after the Refoule murder, a man walked into the Tampa, Florida, police station and screamed at the desk sergeant:

"Who am I? Who am I? I have committed a murder!"

The police checked the man out and searched his briefcase. It was crammed with clippings and data concerning the Refoule case. The man turned out to be a mental case.

At 1:30 p.m. Paul Refoule went to Atlanta airport to meet his parents. They had come from France to visit him and their grandson. While at the airport Refoule was taken into custody by Fulton County police officers and arrested on a warrant charging him with committing the act of sodomy. Paul Refoule spoke with his parents briefly after they arrived, and was then wisked away by police officers. The elder Refoules (whose command of the English language was sketchy) were driven to the Alston home by members of the French community in Atlanta. Everyone was in a state of shock. Refoule was interrogated by police officers from Friday afternoon until Saturday night—a period of some thirty hours. The police held Refoule in one room and brought in other people and questioned them separately and together. Bill Gray and two other art students were questioned for ten hours as police tried to persuade them to tell about an alleged all-male party held at the Refoule home on May 12, 1947. The only information the police had on the supposed party came from the anonymous note.

Elaine was questioned and so was Pat Sue. The evidence of the indictment charge of sodomy came from Pat Sue's statement that Refoule had performed an unnatural sex act upon her at his private studio. Assistant Chief Fitzgerald and Captain Bradford brought Refoule and Pat Sue to the same room and questioned them together.

Bradford: I believe this is the girl you had told us about you had been with at the Wesley Memorial Church studio?

Refoule: Yes.

Bradford: This is the girl you knew as Pat Sue; who was an art student and who modeled for you?

Refoule: Yes.

Bradford: This is the girl you said you put your mouth in?

Refoule: Yes.

Bradford: Is Mr. Refoule, here, the one that you have made a statement about going with you in an unnatural way at the studio?

Pat Sue: Yes.

Bradford: On this particular time you stated that Mr. Refoule went with you in an unnatural way by placing his mouth in your privates?

Pat Sue: Yes.

Fitzgerald: Did you do that, Mr. Refoule?

Refoule: I don't remember, but if she says 'Yes,' she is telling the truth.

Bradford: So; you admit going with her in this unnatural way?

Refoule: Yes, that's right.

Bradford: You said that after two or three minutes of this operation that you asked him to stop?

Pat Sue: Yes.

Refoule: (interrupting) I don't think it was that long.

Bradford: The lady said it was two or three minutes.

Pat Sue: It was sort of an incredible short time.

Refoule: Well, I think it was a very short time.

Bradford: I believe you stated that upon another occasion, you gave Miss Pat Sue a nice handbag. Is that correct?

Refoule: Yes, that's right.

Bradford: That was on another occasion, wasn't it? Did you give her anything at the same time you gave her the bag?

Refoule: I think there was a handkerchief in the bag, or something like that.

Bradford: What kind of handkerchief was it?

Refoule: I don't know.

Bradford: Was it a white handkerchief?

Refoule: I think so, but I don't know.

Bradford: What kind of handkerchief was—

Pat Sue: (interrupting) I think this is stupid! What difference does it make what kind of handkerchief it was? (pause) It was a white handkerchief with a little embroidery on the corner of it.

Bradford: Is that right?

Refoule: Yes.

Pat Sue: I still have the handkerchief, that is why I remember.

Fitzgerald: Paul, did you ever ask Miss Pat Sue here to marry you? In any conversation which you had with her?

Refoule: Yes.

Fitzgerald: Paul, just how did you figure on marrying her when you were married to Peggy? How were you planning to marry Pat Sue, if she would have married you?

Refoule: I don't know. That was very vague. I could always divorce.

Fitzgerald: Did you ever in your conversation with Miss Pat Sue say anything about your home life?

Refoule: Yes, I certainly did.

Fitzgerald: Did you tell her it was pleasant or unpleasant?

Refoule: I think I told her sometime it was pleasant, I think I did.

Bradford: What did you say to her, Mr. Refoule?

Refoule: I don't know. It was two years ago.

Fitzgerald: How long did you stay in Florida when you went down to visit Miss Pat Sue?

Refoule: I stayed one night and one morning.

Fitzgerald: Now on that trip down there, did you ask Miss Pat Sue to marry you?

Refoule: I don't know. I guess so.

Fitzgerald: Well, did Miss Pat Sue turn you down flat?

Refoule: Yes.

Bradford: You never did tell your wife you went down there, did you?

Refoule: No.

Bradford: Did you tell your mother-in-law, or any of your in-laws?

Refoule: No.

Bradford: Now then, Paul, at the time you were trying to get Pat Sue to marry you, is that the time you wrote your parents in Orleans, and told them how unhappy you were with Peggy?

Refoule: I think it was about that time.

Bradford: Was it along about the same time that you got a letter from them that stated for you not to leave your son over here?

Refoule: I don't remember. I know sometime I wrote that to my family and I remember once my father said that be very careful and not do anything, to be patient, things would be all right.

Fitzgerald: Paul, how long was it after you were in Florida before you saw Miss Pat Sue again?

Refoule: I think I saw her when she came back from school. It
   was probably January of 1946.
Fitzgerald: Now, did you talk to any of these girls after Pat Sue
   told you she was going to get married to this man in the
   service, did you say anything to any of the other students in
   regard to whether you could keep her from getting married?
Refoule: I don't think so.
Fitzgerald: You don't recall that?
Refoule: No, I didn't know the name.
Pat Sue: Why should he?
Refoule: I didn't even know the name of Pat Sue's husband.
Bradford: You just knew that she was fixing to get married, is
   that correct?
Refoule: No.
Pat Sue: At that time he didn't know.
Refoule: I learned that she was already married.
Bradford: She was already married and you weren't supposed
   to know her?
Pat Sue: What are you trying to get at? Are you trying to mess
   us up or something?
Bradford: No, I am not trying to mess you up.
Pat Sue: Look, I was married last August. Paul didn't know
   about the marriage but he probably learned about it later.

At this point Pat Sue was excused. It should be remembered
that all the girls who had been involved with Refoule, with
the exception of Elaine and the girl from New York, were now
married and were very reluctant to have themselves associated with the case or the police. The police were constantly
assuring all of them that if they would cooperate and give
statements, their names would be kept out of it. Thus, in all
their statements the girls are rather distant toward Refoule
and put all the blame for the affairs upon him, thinking they
were giving the police what they wanted to hear and keeping
themselves out of the investigation as much as possible. It is
interesting that when Pat Sue was confronted face to face
with Refoule, she was much more sympathetic toward him
and that past memories affected her. It becomes rather obvious that the reason none of the girls took Refoule seriously
was that none of them was convinced that *he* was serious; that
he was unhappy at times in his home life but was not really
very likely to part with it. The police viewed the situation in
a similar way but with a different twist, for they were convinced that Refoule would not divorce his wife, mainly be-

cause he was Catholic and because of his son, and they looked upon Refoule as a man in a trap, who to escape from his trap committed murder.

By Friday night everyone was released and sent home except, of course, Refoule, who was under arrest for sodomy, and Elaine and Bill Gray. The police wanted to find out something more concrete from these three, or otherwise they were stuck with a sodomy indictment on the basis of Pat Sue's testimony—which was something against Refoule. In a lengthy talk session the police were to make one final effort to find some link between the murder and Refoule and these two art students. Hours of questioning and going over the same data again and again did not change the statements of anybody.

That night the police made a second trip to Atlanta airport. This time they met a man they had hired from Florida who had an apparatus called a "truth machine" that could, beyond a shadow of a doubt, scientifically determine whether or not a person was telling the truth. This so-called truth machine was what would later be termed a lie detector. Since Atlanta did not have a machine, the Fulton County police hired a Mr. Keen (that was his name, for real) to fly up from Florida with his apparatus. Mr. Keen, dressed in a blue suit, brown shoes, and white socks, got off the plane with his invention under his arm. It was wrapped in brown paper and all tied up with white string. It was heavy, and Mr. Keen puffed along carrying the machine. He would not allow another soul to tamper with it.

On Saturday, June 14, 1947, Elaine, Bill Gray, and Paul Refoule all took lie detector tests. The operator was not satisfied with the first tests, so he administered second tests, and a third series of tests. This went on for hours, until everyone was dead tired. When the test was done, Mr. Keen walked out and held an extensive press conference, somewhat to the consternation of the Fulton County police.

Mr. Keen stated: "I am convinced Paul Refoule was not telling the truth when he answered 'No' to the question: 'were you responsible for the death of your wife'?"

Mr. Keen did not comment on the truth or falsity of the tests administered to the two art students. This would require further study of the tests, he stated. But Mr. Keen did go into great detail with the press about his new machine, and all the reporters hovered over it—this new, infallible machine which could tell the truth from a lie. Since the beginning of time, investigators had wished there was some means by which the police and the courts could separate positively truth from untruth. With this grand machine it was now scientifically possible, or so Mr. Keen claimed. The lie detector was something new. People believed it to be infallible. If the lie detector had suspicions about whether or not Refoule was telling the truth, this was the strongest evidence most people needed that he was not. There are no easy solutions in gathering evidence or easy ways to make people tell the truth. The police in this instance accepted a new, untried invention too readily. In this era it was thought to be the greatest boon to detective work since Sherlock Holmes. But in the Refoule case it was badly misused to make the suspect appear guilty.

The police returned to questioning Refoule—telling him that he had flunked his truth machine test. He might as well confess and tell them that he killed his wife. This line of questioning continued until Saturday afternoon, but Refoule did not change his story. After thirty hours he was allowed to see his attorney, Hal Lindsay, who immediately got Refoule released on bail. The bond was set at $10,000, which was put up by the Alston family.

PAUL REFOULE CHARGED WITH SEX CRIME

That headline appeared in *The Atlanta Constitution* on Sunday, June 15, 1947. It was accompanied by no less than five pictures of Paul Refoule: his being arrested at the airport, entering the Fulton County jail, being fingerprinted, searched, and finally gazing from behind bars. The story was splashed all over both Atlanta newspapers, and in fact it appeared that the two papers were running some kind of contest to see which could write the most compelling headlines. The stories pointed out that Mrs. W. Ott Alston, Refoule's mother-in-law, had put up the $10,000 bond and stated also that she and her mother, Peggy Alston Refoule's grandmother, were offering a $1,500 reward for the solution of Peggy's murder, stating: "We are bereft of police aid and see an effort under way to railroad an innocent man to the electric chair."

On that Sunday afternoon the Alston home suffered the same fate that the Refoule home had suffered on previous Sundays. The ghoulish drove out to stare, and speculate, and walk around. The numbers of people coming to the Alston

home were much fewer than those who had besieged the Refoule house, but they were loud and they hollered from their
cars. The elder Refoules were staying there and did not know
what to think. A reporter stopped Mrs. Alston before she could
get inside the house when she was returning from church and
asked her what she thought about the latest turn in the case.
She replied that "she didn't know what to think."

Members of the French community of Atlanta came to the
Alston home and worked there in shifts: shooing people away,
answering the telephone, and translating developments for
the elder Refoules. The Alston home received a continuous
stream of abusive and obscene phone calls.

The police stated to the press that Refoule's unnatural sex
life was something he admitted during one of the earlier questioning sessions (this referred to the so-called unnatural act
with Pat Sue) but was not brought out previously because
"they were afraid it might cloud over the murder investigation."

Chief Ellis stated to the press that "other persons do not get
away with this, and I see no reason why he should go free." It
became rather obvious that the police, unable to gather sufficient evidence to charge Refoule with the murder of his wife,
were forced to settle for the lesser, gamier charge.

The Georgia legal definition of the charge of sodomy is the
"carnal knowledge and connection against the order of nature, by man with man, or in the same unnatural manner
with woman." The charge of sodomy against Refoule was
based solely on the incident which occurred at his downtown
studio with Pat Sue two years before. The accusation concerning an all-male party at the Refoule home on the night of May
12, 1947, was not part of the indictment but was printed in
the newspaper as though it were a fact—the papers failing to
note that said allegation lacked either substance or proof and
was nothing more than rumors spread by the police when
they received the unsigned note which made the charge. However, those who read the newspaper accounts believed that
the charge of sodomy against Refoule stemmed from the so-
called May 12 party. The police released to the press much of
their gossip gathered in countless interviews. Atlanta matrons were titillated by what they read. None could ever recall
reading about such goings-on in Atlanta before. It was all so
new, so strange, so radical—but *exciting*. Few even knew what

sodomy meant, had never read such a thing in the newspapers before, and asked their embarrassed husbands over dinner to explain it to them.

The aftermath of the Refoule slaying created more public interest than the murder itself. Indeed, the murder and investigation thereof, was forced into the background. The foreigner's love life captured Atlanta's imagination like nothing in years. Amateurs advanced their theories on street corners, on buses, and in barber shops. People spoke of little else.

A virtual orgy of letters inundated the press and the police following the disclosures of June 15. The Fulton County Police Department received 188 letters concerning the Refoule case in the period from June 16 thru June 25.

Why not try the truth machine on Peggy Refoule's mother, Mrs. Alston? She is so all fired sure Refoule isn't guilty. Can she account for her time from 1:30 to 5 p.m. the day of the murder? Maybe there is something between her and Refoule. It smells fishy to me.

We are wondering, as probably thousands of other Georgians are wondering, what has happened to the Refoule case? There are numerous questions in the minds of the public such as: why is Mrs. Alston protecting Refoule in the face of all of the admissions that he has made regarding her daughter? Are the rumors true that Mrs. Refoule was not the real daughter of Mrs. Alston? [*Editor's note:* No.] What age woman is Mrs. Alston? Is it possible that she is infatuated with Refoule? Has Mrs. Alston's home been searched for the missing jewelry? Who is the woman Refoule wanted to marry and take back to France? These are but a few of the questions that people are asking daily. The public feels that the lid has been clamped on tight on this brutal business—but why? [The letter was signed "Georgia taxpayers."]

Have read lots about the Refoule 'murder mystery' and it looks like to me that Mrs. Alston, mother of the murdered Mrs. Refoule, might be mixed up in the affair. Why is she doing so much talking and furnishing bail for her murdered daughter's husband, who is being suspected? Something funny. [Unsigned.]

In spite of the criticism from the family of the late Mrs. Refoule which was announced over the radio today in the latest bulletin on the case, the public congratulates you on the splendid job you are doing.

A civic club in southwest Atlanta wrote the following letter which was signed by a large number of its members:

The people of Atlanta and Fulton County know that Mrs. Refoule's husband murdered her and/or had someone to murder his wife. Why does the mother-in-law take up for this queer French guy if she cares what happened to her daughter? We shudder when we think of the murders in our home city that have never been correctly solved and the murderer given justice. When we think of our good friend Mr. Henry Heinz horrible death, and yet the real murderer was never arrested. A little prowling Negro was railroaded through our courts. If the real murderers were brought to justice and given the electric chair or hanged we would not have so many of these awful murders in our city.

The mayor of Georgia's fifth largest city wrote the following:

I am keeping up with you in this Refoule murder and I am hoping to see everyday that you have solved it. I just want to tell you one thing about this case: the way it was performed just don't look like an American act to me, and you know foreigners do things different in butchering a hog or a human. And too it seems to me that as neat as this job was done it was by a very much of a man or either two people. Keep checking Refoule's friends. They are a sorry lot.

The pastor of one of the largest Baptist churches in the South wrote:

Let me sincerely commend you for the courageous and intelligent way you are prosecuting the Refoule case. We need more policemen like you in Fulton County and in places of public trust.

A Fulton County superior court judge wrote:

I wish to compliment the Fulton County police for their courage and fearlessness in handling the Refoule case. Having been assigned some unpleasant tasks myself, I can sympathize with you. I am glad to know that we have a good police department, when, they see others 'cow-towing' to the untouchables, permits their sense of civic duty and public responsibility outweigh other considerations. The department is to be commended for rendering our community valuable service.

A lawyer wrote:

I want you to know that you and your fellow officers have done a good job so far in the Refoule case. I find most other people feel the same way. My writing this letter was prompted by the statement of the Alston family regarding the work of the police department, which I feel they well know is not true. It makes me wonder—do they have something to cover-up? Keep up the good work in spite of the obstacles.

And a public school teacher:

> We are indeed praying for you. Any traveler in France knows that many of the Catholic men in France practice horrible immoralities with boys as well as women. I know all about the Catholic pressure and the Alston's family pressure to defeat the police investigation and so I say "you all are brave and fine men."

At this point both God and prayer are abandoned and the letters become unprintable: a basketfull of letters written with crayon; words cut from the newspaper and pasted on post cards. The letters continued to pour into police headquarters and into the editorial offices of the newspapers. No letters either to the papers or the police came in support of Refoule. However, a crusty Atlanta physician wrote the following letter to the editor of the *The Atlanta Constitution*. The letter was not printed.

> Even one accustomed to the tabloid tactics of some of our well known Eastern newspapers had to shiver when the Sunday, June 15, 1947, issue of *The Atlanta Constitution* reached his eyes. Since when is the accusation of a man for the "crime" of sodomy fit material for a streamer on the front page of a great Southern liberal newspaper? Is it because Georgia law says sodomy is a crime and carries an automatic life sentence? If that outrage is truly Georgia law, then your writers would have something to crusade against. They would have their work cut out for them, and could spend less time digging into the past of Paul Refoule in the most merciless journalistic crucifixion of recent years. Is it because your writers believe it an important clue in the murder of Paul Refoule's wife? Then they have committed a double sin, that of accusing a man of murder before he is ever [indicted] and of prejudicing the minds of countless readers and future jurors. They have screamed the premises that (1) Mrs. Refoule was killed by a sex fiend, (2) that Paul Refoule is a sex fiend, (3) therefore—they ache to print the obvious conclusion. The only flaw is that the judgment that we are supposed to read between the lines is absolutely invalid conclusion. Or is it that they actually think that sodomy is a sensational and rare piece of news, and that a man

guilty of such a thing is the lowest sort of human being? If that
is the case, then for the sake of truth and fair-play please print
this: In spite of what Georgia law may state, an "abnormal" act
between man and woman is not sodomy. Variations in the relationship between man and woman are exceedingly common,
and are not to be confused with "perversions" which imply such
grossly abnormal acts as sadism and masochism. Let's not fool
ourselves. If we jail everyone who practices "variations" let
alone adultery, we may not have many persons left on the outside. At any rate, the testimony of the woman in the case as to
"unnatural" acts by Refoule, has nothing to do with sodomy.
But if Georgia law insists that it does, why isn't the woman as
guilty as Refoule? Everyone ignorant of the subject should read
Havelock Ellis' *The Psychology of Sex*. This advice especially
applies to newspaper writers who bring such subjects to thousands of readers at random.

On June 18, 1947, the Fulton County Police Department
received a letter from Paris, France. The letter was from a
Prisoner of War Association. The group did not know to whom
to address the letter, so they presented it to the American
Embassy in Paris and requested it be forwarded to the proper
authorities in America.

The Chairman and members of the Committee of the "Ami-
cale de l'Oflag X11 B' [POW's association] beg to draw your
Excellency's attention to the case of their comrade Paul Refoule
who for several years was their fellow prisoner and who was
not repatriated until 1944, after an attempt to escape which
unfortunately failed when he was caught at the Swiss frontier.
We beg to state that while Paul Refoule was in Mainz he always behaved in an honest, loyal and straight forward manner.
He was also an artist of talent, and very fond of his art. He was
in no way addicted to perversion or similar vices. Such vices
could not have passed unnoticed by people who shared Paul
Refoule's room for many months. We should be most thankful
of you if you would forward this letter to the judge who is investigating the case at or near Atlanta, Georgia.

The letter was signed by the eight members of the committee, one of whom was a general. If the letter was ever seen by
Refoule or any members of the press, it is doubtful. It was
never printed in the newspapers; nor were any members of
the French community in Atlanta ever aware of the letter.

The growing animosity between Refoule and the police
which had been building ever since the murder now exploded

in a rash of charges and countercharges. Refoule greatly feared the police. He wanted to cooperate with them in every way, less they think his lack of cooperation concealed guilt. The three separate marathon interrogations lasting 15, 24, and 30 hours must be a record in the annals of police investigation. Obviously such a police procedure could not have been possible without the willing compliance of Refoule. Nevertheless, that the police would even consider such a procedure, and follow it, says a great deal about police practice at the time. But it was a different era and the police could do things then that they cannot do today. Many people insist that the change in police procedure has created a situation where the guilty are not apprehended and crime increases. Doubtless, Paul Refoule would not agree.

Whereas Refoule feared the police and felt uneasy at finding himself in a difficult situation in a strange country, the police, the public, and the press came to hate him. This is an inescapable conclusion. All the fears and terrors of the time found a scapegoat in Paul Refoule. All the ugliness that had submerged in the years since the Heinz killing surfaced once again. People hated in the Heinz case because it involved a person of wealth. People hated in the Refoule case because it involved an individual married to a person of a prominent family, who happened, coincidentally, to be French, Catholic, and an artist. It was just too much for a Southern Protestant community caught up in the shifting social changes and boom years following World War II. People were terrified. The world was changing too fast. They did not know what to think. Somehow hating Paul Refoule made the world appear simpler than it was. It was something to hold onto, this hate. Another rather unusual letter to the police expressed it well:

> Several months ago an article in the Sunday edition of one of the daily papers in the society section told about the Refoule's plan for remodeling the old Howell Mill. It was a full page article, or longer, and included several pictures of the young couple and of the mill. Here was a Frenchman married to a lovely wife, related to a prominent family in the community, with an interesting profession, an established paying position, settling down to security. Following World War I a great many of our soldiers returned with a thorough dislike (in some instances amounting to hatred) of the French; the same opinion, I regret to say, has been expressed following World War II.
>
> I think it would be wise if the police investigated the follow-

ing theory—a disgruntled, frustrated war veteran or student, not necessarily in Refoule's classes, but close enough to have knowledge of his classes and maybe a man unable to secure a home or prevented by circumstances from marrying, as a person who might be involved in the murder. I don't think Mrs. Refoule was the prime object. He was striking at the Frenchman by destroying his home life. I think this crime was planned far enough back that the killer did not think the threads of continuity could be picked up.

The writer of this letter was also anonymous, but he/she was well aware of the bitterness which existed at the time against Frenchmen, a hatred and bitterness that was being proved by events. Whether the letter has any other significance to the case is pure speculation.

On July 3, 1947, *The Atlanta Journal* carried the first in a series of articles with screaming headlines concerning an increase in sex crimes in the city. The articles were accompanied by strong editorials saying that all sexual perverts must go to prison. As it turned out, the so-called sex crime increase was all a myth. The people of the city were gripped by fear and housewives began to suspect every individual walking down the street of being a dirty old man and quickly rushed the kids indoors and called the cops to report the presence of a sexual pervert in the community. The city went on a binge of hysteria. The fear was there, embedded in the era of time and place, but the Refoule case had pinpointed it, brought it to the surface. It was now summer. People get testier and ultimately more violent in hot weather. But the bitterness generated on all sides by the police investigation of the Refoule case was just beginning. It would become more intense as the summer and hot weather continued.

Tuesday, July 8, 1947. Through his attorney, Hal Lindsay, Paul Refoule went into the U. S. District Court in Atlanta and asked the federal court to issue an injunction to prevent further illegal detention or questioning and at the same time entered a $50,000 damage suit against Chief Ellis, Assistant Chief Fitzgerald, Captain Bradford, and three other Fulton County police officers who had been closely involved in the Refoule case. For the first time, Refoule, upon this occasion, issued a public statement.

I have been accused of murder by the police. This charge is not true and the police know it is not true. They know that reliable witnesses have accounted for every minute of my time

on the day of the murder. Instead of accepting this proved fact
and making a real search for the murderer they have resorted
to the old Nazi trick of accusing a person of sexual perversion
if they cannot prove him guilty of some other crime.

The police received an anonymous letter accusing me of sex
perversion. This letter was written by a person who may have
known the layout of my home. Instead of taking fingerprints of
this person from the letter (and he was perhaps the murderer)
they smudge up the letter with their own fingerprints and
broadcast the accusations contained in it. I am not guilty of
murder. I am not guilty of sodomy. I have never confessed to
either. I have never said that I did not love my wife.

The damage suit was based on the due process section of the
14th Amendment of the United States Constitution. Refoule
declared that the police had violated his civil rights as a U. S.
resident. He named 33 points of conspiracy and 60 overt acts
in his charges of brutality of a deliberate police campaign of
slander, of their refusal to let him have either interpreter or
attorney during questioning. He said the police issued false
and fraudulent statements which poisoned the mind of the
public against him while they were conducting a perfunctory
investigation of the murder. Refoule charged that in the May
19 questioning at his Howell Mill Road home he had been
struck in the face by Bradford with the sashcord and forced to
stand under strong electric lights until he collapsed with ex-
haustion. Also on this occasion, he claimed, he was repeatedly
struck, jabbed, stepped on, elbowed, jerked, grabbed, vilified,
cursed, and generally mistreated by his interrogators. He
stated that he was forced to stand while being questioned and
was not allowed to take his coat off, although the weather was
very warm. Refoule maintained that the officers produced pictures of his wife's body and forced him to look at them, all the
time accusing him of the murder and trying to get him to confess. Refoule charged that during the interrogation Captain
Bradford handed a pistol to him and said:

> You have murdered your wife. Why don't you take this and kill
> yourself?

And the Assistant Chief (Fitzgerald) told him that if he would
confess to the murder they would help him to prove that he
was insane and that he could then go back to France. In the
questioning at the courthouse on May 25, Refoule charged
that he was given similar treatment and that the rope which

the police had recovered from the tree on Peachtree Creek that afternoon was put around his neck like a noose and that a police officer twisted the rope around his neck and hit him in the face with the end of the rope. He claimed also that the police told him that if he did not confess to the murder, he would be prosecuted upon a charge of moral perversion, for which he would receive life imprisonment. Refoule also charged in his lawsuit that he was always taken into custody at night, that the police never had a warrant, and that a fake sodomy warrant issued by a justice of the peace was used to threaten him. This police harassment caused him to lose his job at Oglethorpe where he was making $160 a month, $40 a month from the High Museum of Art, and a $100 a month doing paintings and murals on a private contract basis. The Fulton County police officers issued a blanket denial.

JUSTICE DEPARTMENT CITES SEX INDICTMENT: REOPENS REFOULE DEPORTATION PROCEEDINGS

Under that screaming headline on Thursday, July 17, 1947 *The Atlanta Journal* quoted a high justice department "source" which said that because of Refoule's sodomy indictment the department was looking into the possibility of deporting him! The story was somewhat of a hoax. As of yet, Refoule had been convicted of nothing, nor even tried. He had been indicted on a sodomy charge by the Fulton County grand jury, but the case had yet to come to trial. No one appeared to be pushing to bring the case to trial, either.

Due to a continuous stream of vicious and obscene telephone calls, Mrs. Alston had her telephone disconnected. Other relatives and friends came forward to add to the reward to apprehend the killer of Peggy Refoule, and the reward reached a total of $2500, the same as in the Heinz case. The reward was never paid.

The hearing in federal court was set for July 21. The case was put off until July 29 when the defense in the case asked for more time. Spectators had waited in line at the court building most of the night and were already filing into seats in the spectators gallery when the case was postponed.

Wednesday, July 30, 1947. The temperature in Atlanta that day reached 95 degrees by afternoon. In the unairconditioned court room, the temperature was not any cooler. Hundreds of spectators crowded into the building and, those who could make it, into the courtroom. Everybody came—housewives with babies, summer school students playing hooky, young matrons wearing big straw hats, and a scattering of farmers in overalls looking for a place to spit tobacco juice.

Refoule and his lawyer entered the building by a side entrance and managed to elude the crowd outside. Inside they had to go up in the regular elevator, and there they were besiged by a crowd of screaming teenage girls. Wherever Refoule went, hordes of young girls would follow, much as though Refoule were some kind of teenage idol or Hollywood celebrity. Getting off the elevator, a young girl ran up and touched Refoule on the arm, swooned, and then ran off hollering excitedly: "I touched him! I touched him!!"

The elder Refoules, Paul Refoule's parents, appeared at the trial. They were not as fortunate as their son in arriving at the court building for there was some mix-up by the driver of the car which was bringing them, and for some reason they were let out in front of the court building instead of at the side entrance; consequently they had to fight their way through the crowd of eyeballers clustered in front of the court building. The Refoules were dressed in black and were very somber and dignified. Mrs. Refoule wore a big black hat and black shoes and black gloves, and Judge Refoule walked stiffly with a cane, having suffered a leg injury in France in World War I. They were a striking couple, and their regal appearance mollified the mob sufficiently for the crowd to move back and make room to form a path that allowed the Refoules to enter the building. But there were catcalls and the ever-present photographers. The Refoules were very much alone. It was an ordeal for them to have to endure, particularly Mrs. Refoule, who spoke practically no English. She glared at the hollerers and jumpers in the crowd which surrounded her and wondered, no doubt, if she had arrived in the land of Oz.

Inside the courtroom, Judge Refoule was introduced to the court and bowed stiffly before the judge. The presiding judge had warned the spectators they had better keep quiet, he would brook no outbursts; so many had to supress their giggles as Judge Refoule bowed to the court. Paul Refoule and his parents sat at one table with Paul's attorney; the police officers sat at a table opposite with their attorneys.

Procedure took up the activities for most of the first day. Both sides had many long affidavits that had to be included in the record. In the afternoon the defense called many witnesses—practically everyone who had been interviewed by the police in the Refoule murder investigation. Refoule was suing the Fulton County police for damages and also the bonding companies which had put up bonds for the police. The bonding companies were practically hysterical. The one insuring Captain Bradford wrote him the following letter:

> At your special insistance and request, Maryland Casualty Company executed your official bond as Fulton County police officer effective August 1, 1946 in the penalty of $1,000. As a result of the execution of this bond, Maryland Casualty Company has been sued by Paul Refoule in the District Court of the United States for the Northern District of Georgia for damages in the penalty of our bond. This is to advise you that we are expecting you to hold Maryland Casualty Company harmless for any loss, cost or expenses as a result of the execution of this bond. This is to advise you that in the event any judgment is rendered against Maryland Casualty Company in this case, we will expect you to pay the same.

The motto of this company, as stated on their letterhead, was: "Protect Yourself Against Unforseen Events." Although it was an out-of-state company, the bond was executed through the branch office located in Atlanta. After all the letters from the public telling the police to hang Refoule and what a great job they were doing, this letter to Captain Bradford came as something of a jolt.

Refoule's lawsuit was certainly no joke, and the police did not take it as such. In light of all that had occurred in the Refoule case, the lawsuit had to be looked upon as more than a mere harassment suit. The county attorney and his assistant vigorously defended the five Fulton County police officers accused by Refoule.

Judge Refoule had enough after the first day in court and caught a train for New York that night, and from New York immediately sailed back to France. He had pressing business at home for France was beset with strikes and shortages and a constant change of governments. He wished also to leave the scene of the trial and the oppressive Southern heat. All this together had been too much for the courtly old gentleman. His only comment to the press upon leaving was, "This is a foreign country to me. It has foreign habits and strange customs. I don't know what to think."

The trial continued for several days. The presiding judge in the beginning ruled out testimony on Refoule's love life and sternly told the tittering crowd in the courtroom, "You may now be excused if you so desire. I don't think the proceedings will be of much interest to you from here on out."

Elaine had already told how she had been relentlessly questioned and how the police promised her she would be let off if she would testify against Refoule. Bill Gray testified that the police threatened him and held him incommunicado demanding that he confess to being a sexual pervert. He testified also that the police went to the home of his estranged wife and told her that he (Gray) was a homosexual and tried to force her to make a statement detailing his sex perversions. The allegation in the anonymous note to the police concerning a sex party at the Refoule home on the night of Monday, May 12, 1947, was refuted by Major Durkin, who stated to the court that he and his wife had dinner with the Refoules that night and there could not possibly have been any such party. Many of the art students who testified at the trial stated that the police constantly referred to Refoule as being a man as "guilty as hell" and that they "were going to see that he did not get away with anything."

As the trial in the suit reached its last day, the tide began to turn. The protest and the hate-Refoule mail began to diminish. By the last day the courtroom spectators and reporters had all but vanished. The passions aroused over the Refoule case had about ebbed. Now the police found themselves getting the brunt of public ire. The trial pointed out that indeed the police had overstepped their bounds in their relentless investigation of Refoule. Public pressure and journalistic sensationalism had no doubt pushed the police into excesses that they would have not otherwise fallen prey to in the ordinary murder case and then deserted them. It is very poor policy for the police to bend to public prejudice. It always backfires, and it was doing so now in the Refoule case.

Refoule's attorney had a good case and he presented it well. The legal system created sympathizers for Refoule when the police and press had not. The press, beginning to sniff the change in opinion, began to back off from its former militant stand and began to chide the police for the behavior of their investigators in the case. During the trial, *The Atlanta Constitution* carried an editorial abhoring the behavior of spectators and the carnival-like atmosphere outside the court building and the rather harsh treatment afforded the Refoule parents on opening day. But the newspapers in their zeal had undoubtedly helped create this climate of opinion, this appalling behavior.

The police were not well represented in the courtroom. The county attorneys did their best, but they were so outraged by Refoule that their legal judgment was blinded and they had a difficult time being rational as they presented their defense.

What was the true picture of police practice in the Refoule case? Was Refoule subjected to the treatment he maintained in the suit, or was his affidavit somewhat exaggerated?

All the files and recordings of the case are still available. And they are mountainous. From a close study of these files it appears doubtful that Refoule was actually subjected to any physical threat or harm; that he was constantly subjected and intimidated by oral threats, there can be no doubt. The investigators in the case tape-recorded (the use of tapes was another police *first* in the Refoule case) many of the sessions they held with Refoule and the others. They did this in the hopes of building a murder case against Refoule, but the tapes today do quite the opposite, for they record in exact detail the voices, the words, and the statements of all involved. The eerie sound quality of nearly forty years ago is there on the twirling reels, and there can be no doubt that the police practice in the case was just as Refoule stated. Upon this point, there can be no doubt.

The important point about the police investigation here is that the police and the suspect began to hate each other. Their positions became rigid and polarized, and from two extreme points of view there was no retreat. Neither could really think rationally after awhile nor communicate, and both retreated into armed camps of hate. We see such things happen today. Among groups and among some police there grows and ferments an abiding hatred that can only lead to excesses on the part of both and to the detriment of each. It is not today, nor was it at the time of the Refoule case, a situation which pits the good guys against the bad guys. A retreat to such positions is disastrous.

Most thoughtful people today with knowledge of the Refoule case believe that Refoule was relentlessly persecuted by the police. While this is certainly true, we believe this study of the case creates more understanding of why the police acted as they did—at the same time fully aware it does not excuse such action.

The particular police department involved in the Refoule

case lacked the personnel and experience to handle the case. They were under enormous pressure from the press and the public to reach a quick solution of the case and bent much too easily to the pressure of both. They let their dislike of the suspect influence their investigation of the suspect's involvement with the murder.

Paul Refoule's behavior was influenced by the fact that he considered himself to be guilty of the murder of his wife. Certainly not in the physical sense, but more in a moral or religious sense. Probably Elaine described it best in her statement when she said that "underneath Paul loved his wife and the brutality of it all shocked him out of his mind." This appears to be a very clear observation. Here was a marriage that was undergoing some rough times. The husband was unhappy and had affairs with other women and thought about a divorce—but before anything is resolved one way or the other the wife is brutally murdered. It is a harrowing situation. The husband is overcome with shock and grief—and then guilt, a guilt that grows as what happened begins to sink in. This Catholic Frenchman attempts to purge himself of this guilt by confessing over and over again everything about his life, but which certainly does not include murder.

The problem was that Refoule was confessing to a policeman and not a priest. This made quite a difference in the South of 1947. But it is true, too, that Refoule had to tell the police everything to keep from becoming the prime suspect. But the police did not know who murdered Peggy Refoule, nor did Refoule know who murdered his wife. Neither did anyone else, it would seem.

In October of 1947, Paul Refoule had some good news for a change. The federal judge issued an injunction forbidding the Fulton County police from questioning Refoule further about the case unless he was placed under arrest for murder. It was a moot point, however; the police had not bothered Refoule since he filed the suit against them.

In November of 1947, Paul Refoule had some bad news. At the request of Solicitor General Paul Webb, who said he was unable to bring a key witness to Atlanta (the art student, Pat Sue), the morals charged against Paul Refoule was *nolle prossed* by the Fulton County superior court. Pat Sue had left the state to join her husband, who was still in the service, and refused to come back to Atlanta to testify; and the court was reluctant to force her to do so. After all the hue and cry this testimony of Pat Sue's was the only evidence against Refoule on the sodomy charge, and there was nothing the authorities could do but drop the case. They were secretly relieved for they had no case and the last thing they wanted was to go to trial. Refoule issued the following statement:

During the bereavement, humiliation, mental, and physical suffering which I have striven uncomplainingly to endure since the death of my dear wife on May 14, 1947, her mother, and grandmother and other members of my wife's family have stood loyally by me. Knowing that at the time of my wife's death I was teaching my art class at Oglethorpe University miles away and that I could not and would not have done the murder, they employed counsel for me. Each promptly made and signed statements of such pertinent facts as were within his or her knowledge. Many other persons, some of whom were friends, others acquaintances and still others who had been strangers to me until that time, did likewise. Motivated solely by a desire to see justice done, they have remained unshaken in their adherence to truth and doubt as to my innocence of the murder now exists only in the minds of those to whom the facts have not been made available, or who will not take the trouble to inform themselves.

This morning the sodomy charge against me was dismissed upon motion of the solicitor general over the objection of my counsel and in the face of my demand for trial which has been on file for many weeks. While I appreciate this action by the solicitor, my demand for trial stands and upon expiration of the present and next succeeding terms of Fulton Superior Court, my counsel will ask for the judgment of acquittal to which I shall be entitled under the law. In his statement to the court, when he presented his motion for dismissal of the charge against me, the solicitor stated that law enforcement officers have my confession in their files. Anyone familiar with methods then in vogue in interrogations by the police, but since, I am told, much modified and improved by court actions, will understand that, when threats and physical violence are employed, there is no such thing as a confession and no statement so obtained can be used in evidence. Had this absurd charge been tried before a jury, I feel confident that there would have been a speedy acquittal.

To those who, at personal sacrifice of time and often their own expense, have lent their assistance, to those who have written and spoken their words of cheer and confidence, to *The Atlanta Journal*, which had endeavored to present the facts fairly and accurately, my father, my mother, my small son, and I give thanks. To us, these are America.

One of those whom Refoule was thanking for lending assistance was Atlanta author Margaret Mitchell. She had spoken out publicly on Refoule's behalf and had pleaded with her former colleagues at *The Atlanta Journal* to report the Refoule case less sensationally.

The authorities had the last say. Since they knew they had no chance of conviction, they refused to bring the case to trial. In the minds of many people Refoule was still guilty. He had been denied the right to prove himself innocent.

At this point, Refoule was too ill for further protest. Shortly thereafter he entered the hospital and underwent two operations for kidney stones and hernia. While he was in the hospital, doctors discovered that he had a cancerous lung and removed it. Two weeks later he was suffering from pneumonia.

RELEASE

On February 13, 1948, Paul Refoule went into a coma and died. It was but one day from being nine months after the death of his wife. Thus ended a troubled life of adventure and story-book romance set amid a background of war and its aftermath. Paul Refoule was a man of the era. He was a victim of the times in which he lived.

People who knew Refoule felt that he was so weakened by all that he endured at the hands of the police that nothing could have saved him. At the time of his death, the suit for $50,000 against the Fulton County Police Department was still pending.

There was much bitterness engendered by the Refoule case. For many, even death did not free Refoule from public denunciation, and there was widespread comment that Refoule's priest should be made to take a lie detector test, to prove Refoule guilty! For minds so encased in prejudice, Refoule *had* to be guilty of this crime. They could never believe otherwise. The bitterness toward the Alston family and their friends, of Refoule's friends, and of the artistic and intellectual community in Atlanta was just as intense. The aftermath of the case remained a part of the Atlanta scene.

But very quickly times move on and things change. Two years after the Refoule case, the two Atlanta newspapers were merged into a single corporation. This altered reporting procedure in such cases. There was no longer the keen competition between two papers to see which could get the more sensational stories. Reporting of such crimes became more balanced, and this helped a great deal in future cases. The Refoule case had an enormous effect upon police procedure in the community and was one of the principal reasons that the Fulton County Police Department was dismantled upon implementation of the Plan of Improvement in 1952.

This leads us back to where we began: Who murdered Peggy Alston Refoule? To this day most Atlantans don't really know what to make of the murder of Peggy Refoule. It was, and remains, one of Atlanta's most baffling murder mysteries. Even when all the sensationalism regarding the investigation of Refoule and the attendant publicity is discounted, the case itself is certainly not your run-of-the-mill homicide. There are several theories concerning the case.

SUMMATION

First of all, some people still believe that Refoule was somehow implicated in his wife's death, and that if he was not the actual killer he was engaged in a conspiracy to murder his wife. After a prolonged and extensive review of the case—which involved interviewing countless numbers of people—there remains no evidence linking Refoule with any kind of conspiracy; and any impartial investigator must conclude that those who still insist on implicating Refoule will not or cannot separate in their minds the act of murder from what is, to them, a peculiar life-style and/or profession, and probably for some the two can never be really separated. The fact is that there is no evidence linking Paul Refoule with the murder.

Secondly, many people feel that the murder of Peggy Refoule was committed by someone who was unknown to either her or her husband, and that the motive was burglary, as in the Heinz case. They point out that had the police spent as much time looking for this person or tracking down the items stolen from the Refoule home as they did in investigating Paul Refoule's sex life, they would have come up with the murderer. This is a legitimate point. However, we believe it can be said for the police that they did not exclusively limit their number of suspects to Refoule. Every person who could have possibly been considered a likely suspect was investigated by the police in the beginning or after the death of Refoule. As late as 1957 investigators of the solicitor general's office traveled to Philadelphia, Pennsylvania, to interview a person who might be considered a suspect. But critics point out that when the police started investigating Refoule they turned their attention away from a search for the missing jewelry—which was the best evidence in the case. If the motive for the murder was burglary, the murderer would have tried to sell the stolen items eventually. It is true the rings were very distinctive. But it is also true that many police departments were on the lookout for the missing rings and none ever turned up. Maybe the murderer was so frightened by the uproar of the case that he hid them away somewhere and never tried to get rid of them.

Critics lambast the police for failing to search the house for fingerprints, as was done by Atlanta police in the Heinz case. The police answer to this was that the house was so overrun by people that such an effort would have been futile.

A very strong case can be made for the burglar theory. It has been supposed that Mrs. Refoule finished her ironing and went outdoors, returned, and surprised the burglar and he killed her because she could identify him. An extension of this theory is that the murderer had the house under surveillance for a long time and that when the guests left that day and Refoule departed, the killer knew that Mrs. Refoule was alone, entered the house and killed her, and then burglarized the house. The house was so constructed that a person looking in the windows could see practically everything. The Refoules had moved into an area frequented by lovers along the dirt road in back of the house. It should be pointed out that although the dirt road along the creek was used as a lovers' lane, there were no reports to the police of anyone being molested or attacked in the area either before or after the Refoule murder.

Most investigators do not believe that Peggy Refoule was murdered in the house but that she finished her ironing, decided to go for a stroll along the creek bank, and was waylaid and then strangled to death by being hung from the tree. Since the body was found in the creek, it is far more likely she was killed near the creek. It just does not seem probable that she could be murdered in the house and then removed from it. Certainly she was not dragged from the house. And if she was murdered there and removed by automobile, then it would have been a very risky thing for the murderer not to be observed. But if she was murdered along the creek bank, then the slayer had to come up to the house afterwards (probably while the victim was hanging from the tree branch) and burglarize the residence. Then, how did he get the sashcord? If it was a part of the left-over clothesline, it means he had to have been in the house before the murder. Maybe he had stolen the items from the house prior to the murder and had returned to the scene for some reason. Could the reason be to lie in wait near the creek and surprise and sexually assault the owner of the rings? This does not appear likely, for although the victim's underpants were removed, she was not raped.

Thirdly, some people believe that the person who wrote the anonymous letter accusing Refoule of being a sexual pervert killed Peggy Refoule. An elaboration of this theory is that the murderer hung the clothesline in the tree after the slaying to make Refoule appear guilty. If an examination of the case reveals nothing else, it makes plain that the Frenchman was hated. The question is: Was he hated enough by one person so much that this person killed Peggy and then tried to frame Refoule for the murder? This seems a rather bizarre assumption. The fact remains that the murder was committed on May 14 and the rope was not found until May 24, ten days later. During that time many police officers had gone over the area but the rope was not discovered, even though it was hanging from a tree branch over the area only eight feet from the ground.

Was Peggy Refoule killed by hanging? Even if we knew the answer it probably would not solve the case. Most investigators think the rope was the real murder weapon, that the victim was strangled by being hanged from the limb of the tree. This conclusion is based on the evidence that the tree limb showed that it supported considerable weight and that the mark on the victim's neck indicated upward pull.

Some people believed that the person who wrote the anonymous letter was somehow a member or in-law of the Alston family. This certainly is not very likely. There were many rumors circulated that Peggy's brother and mother were somehow involved with Refoule. This absurdity doesn't bear even repeating, except that it was discovered in investigating the case that many people still firmly believe it.

If anyone, indeed probably the only person closely involved in the case, emerges nearly 40 years later as a heroine, it would have to be Peggy's mother, Mrs. Alston; for regardless of the most vicious public opinion and police pressure, she refused to be swayed or intimidated; and if she had not believed in Refoule's innocence, it is doubtful that anyone in Atlanta would have. It is also an inescapable conclusion that (1) had Peggy Refoule's mother not believed in Refoule's innocence and spoken up for him and (2) had not Refoule been teaching at the time of the murder and had an airtight alibi, he would probably have been lynched. Not to consider lynching a possibility is to inaccurately read the signs of the times and to underestimate the fear and hatred generated by the Refoule case.

Finally, can we rule out the writer of the anonymous note as being the murderer? Quite frankly, we cannot. We can say only that it is not probable. Most likely the person who wrote the note was a person, like countless others of the time, who was swept up in the hysteria which surrounded everything concerning Refoule. It is even possible that the note writer sincerely believed in what the note said, i.e., he honestly thought or had heard that Refoule was a sexual pervert and that being such probably killed his wife. If the note, taken in context, can therefore be considered honest and not a ploy of some nature, then, as far as the murder is concerned, it becomes unimportant.

Unfortunately a review of the Refoule case raised more questions than it answers. One would think that after nearly 40 years, an impartial investigation of the facts and an interview of people involved would turn up a generally agreed upon chain of events.

It is logical to assume that Peggy Refoule was murdered incidental to and preceding or following a burglary of her home. Whether she was murdered in her home or along the creek bank becomes beside the point, for it was not a Cain-Abel homicide but a murder committed because the victim could identify the burglar. If this is what occurred, then all the other doubts in the case must arise from the temper of the times—that is within the life and times of Paul and Peggy Refoule—and the foreign, Catholic background of the main person involved. It is interesting that of all the people in the neighborhood the hand of fate reached down and touched the artist and his wife. To put it simply: If Mr. Refoule had been Mr. Rice, a bank executive, who was a traditional Southern Protestant who lived in a typical house of the time with venetian blinds and lace curtains, his wife would have had less chance of being murdered; but he was not, and he chose to live in an unconventional house (for the time and place) and to follow a different line of work; so, in this context, his life and work probably did contribute to this tragedy. Whether or not it was because of this or was premeditated, remains a mystery to this day. Whatever, the killer is still unknown.

The Refoule home suffered the same fate as the Heinz house. Nobody wanted to live in the murder house. The Alston family, anxious to be rid of it, had a difficult time disposing of it. The home changed hands several times and suffered much personal and architectural abuse. Some twenty years after the murder, a very lovely lady, herself an artist, gained possession of the house and restored it in a way fitting the plan and design that Paul Refoule had in mind. The present owner wonders if the young couple who once had a vision of converting an old woolen mill into a home, should they come back to the present day, would they be pleased with the house? Probably so, very much.

It is not a fallacy to conclude that because Paul and Peggy Refoule were people very much ahead of their time their lives were plagued by tragedy, and the Refoule case is an absorbing revelation of how much our institutions and Atlanta has changed in the years since. At the time of the Refoule murder, Atlanta was little more than a small town in the heartland of the Bible belt.

The atmosphere of Atlanta is quite different today. Paul and Peggy Refoule would feel very much at home. Living in their old mill house, which is now engulfed by suburbia, they would be, but for another day, a charming middle-aged couple who would no doubt find the Atlanta of the 1980s a very exciting place in which to live, for they were a part of all that is now present-day Atlanta many years ago.

1947. The Refoule case. These were the times that we look back to nostalgically and fondly recall as the good old days. It comes as something of a shock to realize that the rose garden was not without its thorns.

4

Farm Wife Jeanette Reyman

The homicide rate in Atlanta and the nation reached all-time highs in the years immediately following World War II. In 1946 Georgia had one of the highest homicide rates of any state in the nation. In 1947 Atlanta led the nation in having more murders per capita than any other United States city. On the outskirts of town, along lonely streets, and in placid neighborhoods, women no longer went out unescorted and carefully kept their windows locked and their doors bolted, day and night. In Buckhead, the hardware store that sold the clothesline to Paul Refoule was now selling guns to many of his neighbors. Two lurid murders had terrorized Atlanta and made people afraid. The first of these murders was the strangulation death of Peggy Refoule and the second was the bludgeoning to death of Jeanette Reyman.

In February of 1947, Mr. and Mrs. Raleigh M. Reyman had moved from their home in Winchester, Indiana, and settled in Bogart, Georgia, a small town some 60 miles from Atlanta on the highway from Athens to Atlanta. They had bought an old farm and were in the process of erecting on a part of it a tourist court, which was a modest predecessor of today's motels. At 8 o'clock on the morning of June 25, 1947, the attractive, blonde Jeanette Reyman got into the family pickup truck and drove to Atlanta. Her errand was to purchase supplies for the restaurant and motor court she and her husband were building in Oconee County.

Jeanette Reyman had a busy shopping day in mind as she drove to Atlanta, but awaiting her in the city was a bizarre death, a brutal slaying that would erupt into one of the state's most sensational murder trials, and yet remain a clouded mystery to this very day. The death of Jeanette Reyman was all the more shocking because it followed by only six weeks the slaying of Peggy Refoule. Investigators would find many strange parallels in the Peachtree Creek murder and the death of Mrs. Reyman.

Both women were slain on Wednesday afternoons, both women were the same age and rather similar in appearance, and both women had one young son of approximately the same age. Peggy Refoule died from stangulation and Jeanette Reyman by bludgeoning. The feet of both victims were bound together, Mrs. Refoule's by her shoelaces and Mrs. Reyman by one-half-inch hemp rope. In addition, Mrs. Reyman's wrists were bound together behind her back with rubber insulated wire. A portion of both women's underwear was missing when the bodies were found, and Jeanette Reyman had been raped. The slayers of both women were bold to the point of being foolhardy. Perhaps the most pronounced similarity in the two cases is that both murders remain unsolved.

At 10 o'clock on the morning of June 25th, Jeanette Reyman reached Atlanta. She made purchases at various stores and then had lunch. She was last seen at 2:30 p.m. at the Sears store on Ponce de Leon Avenue, where she made a purchase in the housewares department. When Jeanette Reyman did not return to Bogart that night, her husband and brother went to Atlanta searching for her.

At 5 o'clock on the afternoon of the 25th, a black pickup truck pulled up in front of the Standard Coffee Company at 247 Moreland Avenue—just as the employees of the company were leaving for the day. Two employees noticed the truck and thought it might be someone making a delivery to the coffee company. They noticed a heavyset man of medium height get out of the truck and walk around to the rear of the truck, adjust and tighten some ropes, then walk away. About a half an hour later two more employees of the coffee company left the building and noticed the truck. One man said he saw blood coming out of the end of the truck but that his companion only laughed and said that it was just red paint and that he had been reading too much about murder in the newspaper lately. When these same employees returned to work the next day and found the same truck parked in front of their building, they grew suspicious and began to investigate. In the rear of the truck, they discovered the body of Jeanette Reyman.

When police arrived on the scene, they discovered that Mrs. Reyman's body had been wrapped in a green quilt, which was now blood soaked. The restaurant stools she had purchased the day before had been piled on top of the body. The keys to the trunk (a large traveling trunk in the back of the truck) were missing, as was Mrs. Reyman's pocketbook. She had left Bogart the day before with $85 in cash, two blank checks, and a $15 money order. The checks were used to buy supplies for the restaurant, but she should have had most of the cash with her. It appeared as though robbery might possibly be a motive for the slaying. The police went over the truck carefully for fingerprints, but were ultimately unable to produce anything that was significant.

Since the victim's pocketbook was missing, there was no way to identify the body. All the police had to go on was the truck with an Indiana license plate. The husband and brother of the victim were having breakfast at a diner on the highway from Athens. They had spent most of the night searching for Mrs. Reyman, and then returned to Bogart about daylight to see if she had returned. When they discovered she had not, the two men drove again to Atlanta. After stopping for breakfast, they heard over the radio that the body of an unidentified woman had been found in Atlanta near the Sears store. They knew that Jeanette had been in that vicinity the day before. They drove rapidly to the police station in Atlanta. At the morgue, Raleigh Reyman identified the body as being that of his wife.

The Reyman slaying was the first big case to break within the city limits of Atlanta after Herbert Jenkins had become chief of the Atlanta Police Department. Coming on the heels of the much-publicized Refoule case, the murder had wide press coverage.

A reorganization of the detective department within the Atlanta Police Department was one of the first official acts of the new chief. Under the reorganization, the detective force was divided into five squads or specialties—all under the overall direction of Detective Superintendent E. I. Hilderbrand. The number one squad was the homicide group under command of Lieutenant Coppenger, a veteran homicide expert. It was he who was in charge of the investigation of the Reyman case.

It was quickly determined that Jeanette Reyman was not killed where the body was found, but that the truck had been merely parked there after the murder had been committed. The first thing the police tried to do was locate the murder scene. Miles of area, stretching over two counties, were covered by detectives and police officers who rode in cars and walked on foot in an attempt to discover the spot where Mrs. Reyman met her death. But to no avail. Detectives fanned out over the city and talked with everyone who saw Mrs. Reyman that day. They determined that she knew no one in Atlanta except business acquaintances. The police questioned people in both Bogart and Athens in an attempt to find out something about the Reymans. All the reports indicated that the couple was well liked and had a fine reputation in the community where they lived—although they had been in the area only a short time.

An autopsy upon the body of Jeanette Reyman indicated that death was caused by a blow to the head that completely crushed the left side of the skull. The medical examination also bore out the fact that Mrs. Reyman had been sexually assaulted.

A man reported to the police that he saw a pickup truck similar to Mrs. Reyman's turn off Ponce de Leon Avenue into a side road described as a perfect lovers' lane. The man reported this happened late Wednesday afternoon. A search by police of the area failed to turn up the murder site. A Marietta, Georgia, man, in town on business the day of the 25th, told police that he had seen a heavyset man driving a truck bearing an Indiana tag around 5 o'clock on Wednesday afternoon. He said he noticed the truck had an Indiana license plate and that it looked very much like one he had sold about a year ago. The man was alone in the truck driving along Forrest Road near Sears. Scores of Atlanta police and detectives joined in searching the wooded area in the vicinity, and casts were made of tire tracks found in the area for matching against the tire tracks of the death truck. But once again, these efforts were to no avail. The police were unable to pinpoint the crime scene.

A clerk at the Sears store, the last person known by police to have seen Mrs. Reyman alive, insisted that she was accompanied by a heavyset man who advised her regarding several purchases. He said the two people were together and left his department together.

Police determined that Mrs. Reyman had been married once before, and that her son was born of that earlier union. The police began a search for her former husband, who turned

up in California, where he was then living. It was determined
that he had never been in Atlanta.

SUSPECTS QUESTIONED

A twenty-year-old dishonorably discharged army man was
arrested for an attempted assault upon a young female employee of Western Union. She was going home on the streetcar
late at night when the man followed her off the streetcar and
stuck a gun in her back and tried to force her into an alley.
She cooly replied that she knew a better place, and as they
walked along they were soon in front of the young woman's
home. The young lady began screaming at the top of her voice
and kicking her would-be assailant in the shins, and the man
quickly fled. The young woman's brother came running out of
the house and the two of them jumped into his automobile.
They pursued the assailant for several blocks and then leaped
from the car and tackled him. The two sat on top of their prey
while someone sent for the police; then they awaited the blue-
coats' arrival and took the man into custody. The young lady
stated she was tired of women being assaulted and murdered,
and she was determined it was not going to happen to her. It
just made her mad, she stated. Upon investigation by police it
was determined that the former service man had nothing to
do with either the Reyman or Refoule murders.

Police questioned a heavyset man concerning the Reyman
slaying. The police had received a tip that such a person had
been seen driving the Reyman pickup truck the day of the
murder. The suspect was located and taken in for questioning
on Thursday, July 3, 1947. On Friday, he was questioned in a
14-hour session by police. During the course of the questioning, officers were able to place the man within four blocks of
the spot where the body was found—within an hour after the
pickup truck was abandoned.

The man was identified as William Autry, a white male,
aged 43, a cook in a local bakery. On Thursday he had been
identified by the Marietta businessman as the person seen
driving the pickup truck with an Indiana license tag. The
Marietta man had picked Autry out of a lineup at the police
station. He was not entirely sure of the man's identity from
the full-face view of the lineup, and the Mariettan asked officers to have the man turn so he could get a profile view. As

soon as this was done, he made his identification, sure that Autry was the man. Another witness viewed Autry in the lineup, and he told police that he was sure that Autry was the man he had seen driving the Reyman truck the day of the murder.

The police had a murder warrant drawn up against Autry but did not charge him with the murder—mainly because they had no other evidence except the identification by the two witnesses to link Autry with the murder. Police determined that Autry had been married twice, for the second time just recently, and members of his first wife's family said he frequently visited her home after the divorce over her protests. They supplied police with information they said was brought out in the divorce suit charging that Autry had many girl friends, and "quite a way with women." Autry insisted that he was innocent and said that he would take a lie detector test—such tests being much in the headlines since the Refoule case. Autry stated he would cooperate with the police in every way.

On Monday, July 7, Autry was allowed to call his wife and attorney. Since the previous Thursday he had been held virtually incommunicado while the police tried desperately to tie him with the murder. On Tuesday, the press was allowed to interview Autry. This was the same day that Paul Refoule filed his suit in federal court against the Fulton County police. The effects that the Refoule case would have upon police procedures, for the present and in the future, were beginning to be felt.

Autry stated to the press that he had done absolutely nothing wrong and was innocent of the murder charge. He said that the police had treated him all right and that he had not been abused physically. But he complained he could not call his wife or attorney until today and had not been allowed to shave. Autry said that he was born near Covington, Georgia, and had been in Atlanta working as a cook and a baker for the past 27 years—except for the time he spent in the army, seven months during World War II. He stated that he used to work near the police station, and some of the policemen had been very nice to him. He said that he had nothing on his conscience and that he was worried about his wife and mother. Autry's attorney stated to the press that he was filing a writ of habeas corpus to get Autry released. Autry's wife said she and her husband had just returned from a four-day honeymoon trip to Asheville, North Carolina, when the police picked up her husband. During the honeymoon, Mrs. Autry recalled there was no mention by her husband of the Reyman case and that he was not nervous on the trip, did not read the Atlanta newspapers, and slept well. He did not act like a man with something on his conscience. Mrs. Autry had her own ideas about why her husband was being held on suspicion of murder. She said there was another man who wanted to marry her before she married Autry, and she was positive this was the man who phoned the tip to police which first implicated her husband in the murder. It was just jealousy. Mrs. Autry developed this theory when she realized that nobody charged her husband with the slaying or with suspicion of murder until Autry married her.

Detectives checked and rechecked the information that caused them to detain Autry in the first place. There was absolutely no firm evidence linking Autry with the case, and in the face of a writ of habeas corpus filed by Autry's attorney, the police released Autry from custody. He was never charged with the murder.

On July 17, 1947, detectives Sikes and Mullen, who had been assigned to the investigation of the Reyman case the week before, took into custody a 29-year-old taxicab driver named Glenn Robinson. The detectives learned that Robinson had formerly been a resident of Athens, where he worked as a carpenter. He had been employed by the Reymans some months before in helping in the building of the motor court and restaurant at Bogart. In that week, the officers made five different trips to Athens and Bogart, interviewing witnesses who knew both Robinson and the Reymans. In these trips they felt they had learned enough about Robinson to book him for suspicion in the Reyman murder. The cab driver had long been a suspect in the case, but he gave the police a good alibi for the afternoon of June 25, the day of the slaying. By hard work detectives Sikes and Mullen had broken the alibi and determined that Robinson was not driving his taxicab that day between the hours of 1 and 5:30 p.m. as he stated to the police the first time he was questioned. The inability to substantiate his alibi was the most damning evidence against Robinson and would remain so throughout the investigation of the murder.

INDICTMENT

On July 25, 1947, Glenn Robinson was indicted by the Fulton County grand jury for murder in connection with the death June 25 of Mrs. Jeanette Reyman. Robinson had spent a week in jail before the indictment was issued. The formal charge of murder was lodged against him just minutes before a scheduled habeas corpus hearing demanding Robinson's release was to be held. Immediately after the murder charge was made the habeas corpus hearing was dismissed, and Robinson was held in Fulton Tower jail without bond.

Detectives Sikes and Mullen stated that there were three major breaks that led to the action. The first of these was the apparent breaking of an alibi which had purported to show Robinson was on duty in his cab on the afternoon of the slaying. Originally a cab company official had stated that Robinson had been working during that period; however, a signed statement from the owner of the cab company stated that company records showed that Robinson was off duty from noon the day of the murder until 5:30 p.m, which would have allowed him time to kill Mrs. Reyman.

The second break in the case was the discovery of blood-stained khaki pants in the Robinson home. The detectives stated that the suspect had previously denied owning a pair of khaki trousers. On a second search of Robinson's home the officers found a pair which had just been returned from the cleaners. Stains on the waistband of the pants were analyzed by Dr. Herman Jones, head of the Fulton County Crime Laboratory, and declared to be human blood stains.

The third and most dramatic break was the identification of Robinson by a person who said he saw the man with Mrs. Reyman the day of the slaying. This was the clerk at the Sears store who waited upon Mrs. Reyman and sold her two kitchen knives. The clerk picked Robinson out of a lineup as the man who accompanied her to the store that day. In actual fact, the investigation of Robinson was far from complete, but the action of Robinson's attorneys in seeking a writ of habeas corpus had forced the police to either indict him or release him as a suspect.

When confronted with the evidence, Robinson admitted to the police that he did not drive his taxicab the day of the murder, as he had previously told police. He refused to say where he was during this time. In fact, during all the interrogation of Robinson, he behaved exactly the opposite from Paul Refoule. He answered most questions put to him by the police with a curt yes or no and volunteered no other information; to some he replied, "I don't know."

TRIAL

On September 15, 1947, Glenn Robinson went on trial for murder. The defense asked for a change of venue in the case. Robinson's lawyers claimed that their client could not possibly get a fair trial because of all the unfavorable newspaper accounts of the case. The motion for a change of venue was denied by Judge Frank Hooper. The first bitter exchange in the trial between Solicitor General Paul Webb and Defense Attorney Al Henson came over the testimony of G. D. Hawks of Bogart. Mr. Hawks was a witness for the state. He had worked with Robinson on construction of the motor court. He testified that Robinson said on three occasions that he liked Mrs. Reyman and sure would like to have sexual relations with her. Henson objected to this testimony, but Judge Hooper allowed it when Webb stated that the state would prove that the slaying of Mrs. Reyman was a sex crime.

The husband of the murder victim was the second witness for the state. He testified that Robinson was employed by him in building the tourist court for a period of sixty days. He testified that Robinson knew his wife and that Robinson drove him (Mr. Reyman) to Winchester, Indiana, upon two occasions. Mr. Reyman said he had never had any trouble with Robinson and that he quit working for him voluntarily—Robinson just did not show up for work one morning and Reyman did not hear from him again. Mrs. Reyman's brother testified upon cross-examination by the defense, that he never noticed any undue attention paid to Mrs. Reyman by Robinson. Mr. Reyman had testified to the same thing earlier. Mrs. Robinson, wife of the defendant, and their three small children were in the courtroom at all times. The children were attractive and well behaved. The jury could not help but notice. The Robinsons were also expecting a fourth child, as Mrs. Robinson was obviously pregnant.

When the trial was resumed after the luncheon recess, the clerk at the Sears store identified Robinson as the man he saw with Mrs. Reyman in the housewares department between 2 and 2:30 p.m. on June 25. He testified that he sold Mrs. Reyman two kitchen knives. He noticed her companion because he discussed with her the good qualities of hollow ground knives. He said they were in the department about five minutes. The Marietta businessman testified that he noticed the pickup truck in which Mrs. Reyman's body was found because it was similar to one he himself had owned. He said he only caught a glimpse of the driver and picked out Robinson as the driver. On cross-examination Defense Attorney Henson confronted the Mariettan with the testimony at a coroner's inquest when he identified William Autry as driver of the death truck. The Mariettan said that he had picked Autry out of the police lineup and was never positive that he was the driver. He further admitted he could not be positive Robinson had been the driver.

As the trial of Robinson entered its second day in Fulton superior court, the courtroom was jammed by the largest crowd ever to try and get into a murder trial. Robinson was accompanied again in court by his wife and three small daughters.

Dr. Herman Jones identified a pair of trousers which the state claimed were worn by the taxi driver as having been stained by human blood. Dr. Jones stated that the victim had been sexually assaulted. Then, Detective Sikes took the witness stand. His appearance provoked a lively exchange between defense counsel and Solicitor Webb. Judge Hooper instructed both lawyers not to exchange words directly. Detective Sikes was on the witness stand for one hour. Most of the time was spent in replying to the defense counsel's charge that he had arrested Robinson to get his name in the newspapers. Sikes denied this. He stated that he questioned Robinson as to whether the latter owned a pair of khaki pants, which the Sears clerk Monday had said were worn by a male companion of Mrs. Reyman. Robinson denied owning such a pair of pants. He further testified that he then returned to Robinson's home and found Mrs. Robinson packing a trunk. Mrs. Robinson voluntarily started through the trunk, looking for khaki clothing, and there was discovered a pair of khaki pants, which Dr. Jones identified as bearing human bloodstains.

Cross-examined by Defense Counsel Henson, Sikes denied

that he had grilled Robinson severely without giving him an opportunity to see his counsel or his wife. Sikes stated that Mrs. Robinson visited her husband a day before he had been placed in jail.

The trial of Robinson took its most sensational turn on the third day when a defense witness identified another man in the courtroom as being the person who parked the death truck in front of the Standard Coffee Company on Moreland Avenue. M. A. Manus was testifying to the court that he had identified a former suspect as the driver of the truck in which Mrs. Reyman's body was found. Defense Counsel Henson asked: "And when is the last time you saw this man?" Mr. Manus replied: "I reckon it was in the courtroom this morning." The audience murmured in surprise. Defense counsel then asked that a man he identified as William Autry, the same man who was questioned by police for several days in the Reyman case, be brought into the courtroom. A tall man wearing a blue suit was brought to the railing and stood uncomfortably as the crowd in the courtroom gaped at him. It was Autry.

"Is this the man you saw leave the truck?" defense counsel demanded.

"Yes sir, that is the man," Mr. Manus replied positively. Autry was then led from the stunned courtroom. It was a typical "Perry Mason" maneuver and the crowd enjoyed the stunt. The judge rapped for order. Defense counsel then made a motion for a direct verdict of acquittal. He said that all the evidence presented by the state thus far was purely circumstantial and that it was insufficient to convict Robinson of the brutal crime, even had he accompanied Mrs. Reyman to the Sears store on the afternoon of her death. Judge Hooper overruled the motion.

The state rested its case. The defense immediately called three Sears clerks to the stand and they all testified they had seen Mrs. Reyman around noon on the day she was slain and that she was alone. Lt. Coppenger, head of the homicide bureau, told the jury that three persons identified Mr. Autry as the man who parked the bloody death truck.

A woman dressed in black appeared in the crowded courtroom carrying a loaded pistol in a cellophane bag and demanded that she be allowed to testify. She claimed to have seen two men in the Reyman truck and stated she had to carry a pistol because the two men had made threats against her. She had followed the trial avidly, but the judge told her sternly that if she made any further disturbance, he would have her permanently ejected. No effort was made to relieve her of her weapon!

J. D. Farlow, official of the taxicab company which employed Robinson, testified he left Robinson shortly after 1 p.m. on June 25 near the Kimball House Hotel. He stated he saw Robinson again about 5:30 p.m. the same day, and then cruised about in a cab with Robinson until about 9:30 p.m. Robinson showed no signs of emotional strain, he testified.

Robinson then took the stand in his own behalf. He denied emphatically that he knew anything about the slaying of Jeanette Reyman. "I am not guilty," he said. "I have a wife and kids and have no time for other women. I worked that day until 2:30 p.m. and then got another man to work for me while I went to the Kimball House and took a bath. I then went to Crump's Restaurant where I met my nephew and his wife. I spent an hour with them, talking about going into the army. I left Crump's about 4:15. I knew nothing about the murder until the next day. I had worked for the Reymans and liked them." Defense Counsel Henson then closed the case for the defense.

Solicitor General Webb, although he had closed for the state earlier, asked to be allowed to offer another witness. His request was granted and he put Roy Chandler, a clothier, on the stand. Chandler surprised the defense by testifying Robinson called for his new cab driver's uniform close to 6 p.m. on June 25, the day of the murder. Chandler said Robinson, dressed in a khaki uniform and apparently in a hurry, came into his shop and took the uniform off the rack, went to the rear of the shop, put on the new uniform, and walked out.

On the following day, the state asked for the death penalty without a recommendation for mercy for Glenn Robinson. The state asked the jury to show Robinson the same mercy that was shown Mrs. Reyman when she was brutally slain.

The defense had a lengthy summation. Robinson's attorney declared that the precipitant test for blood could not be relied upon after such stains had been submitted to dry cleaning and steam pressing, and that the trousers in question had been cleaned twice before they were examined. Defense counsel attacked the testimony of Dr. Herman Jones to the effect that the Fulton County Crime Laboratory was several years behind—but quickly apologized upon receiving a frown from the bench and an objection from the state. Robinson sat impassively throughout the entire trial, his face a mask. When witnesses gave damaging testimony, he showed not the slightest emotion. His wife and three young daughters sat in the courtroom every day.

The murder case went to the jury at 9:40 a.m. on Friday, following a full week of testimony. At 3:30 p.m. the panel came out and the foreman told the court that the vote stood eight for guilty with recommendation for mercy and four for outright acquittal. The four who stood for acquittal, the foreman declared, had said they would not change their minds until a certain place froze over. The judge then sent the jury back to continue its deliberations and strive to reach an accord, and at this time the defense moved for a mistrial. The motion was denied.

Two hours later the court summoned the panel to the courtroom again and found the jurors still divided. Judge Hooper then declared a mistrial and dismissed the jury. As the jury stood, eight of the twelve men who heard the cab driver tried for the murder of Jeanette Reyman favored conviction with a life sentence. Such a sentence would have been mandatory on the court on a verdict of guilty with a recommendation for mercy. The other four jurors held out for acquittal.

ORDEAL PROLONGED

On October 21, 1947, Glenn Robinson went on trial the second time for the murder of Jeanette Reyman. Judge Frank Hooper, who presided at the initial trial, was again presiding. Detective Sikes was the first witness for the state. He testified that Robinson had been picked out of the police lineup as the man seen with Mrs. Reyman when she was at the Sears store. Sikes stated that a Sears clerk had identified Robinson and that Robinson turned pale but kept silent when the clerk put his hand on Robinson's arm and said: "That is the man."

Defense Attorney Henson cross-examined Sikes and asked him if he had ever seen anybody accused of murder who did not turn pale. Sikes said he thought he had not but insisted that accused prisoners generally made immediate denials.

Henson then brought out that Sikes began the investigation which resulted in Robinson's arrest 20 days after the crime—after other detectives had made other investigations.

The second witness to take the stand was Raleigh Reyman. He gave essentially the same testimony he gave at the first trial. The second trial got off to a late start when defense attorneys sought to have Judge Hooper issue a subpoena requiring the police to produce statements allegedly incriminating other defendants besides Robinson with the murder. Henson charged the police possessed sufficient evidence to bring four persons to trial. Judge Hooper took the request under advisement. Start of the trial was also delayed when a surprising number of prospective jurors declared themselves opposed to capital punishment. Whether or not this was because of moral conviction or the desire to escape from jury duty would be hard to say.

Two carpenters who had worked with Robinson in the construction of the tourist court at Bogart testified Robinson had lusted after Mrs. Reyman. The witnesses were J. D. Hawks (who testified at the first trial) and Leonard Roberts. They said Robinson had expressed a desire for Jeanette Reyman as she passed them while they were at work. At the second trial Robinson was again accompanied by his wife and three daughters.

On the second day of the trial attorneys for Robinson made a motion asking for a direct acquittal in the case, claiming the state had failed to establish in what county the crime actually had been committed. Medical examination of the body had shown the victim had been criminally assaulted more than once. Physicians said that she had died from three heavy blows on the head, probably inflicted by a wrench or some similar instrument. Now obviously all this did not occur in front of the Standard Coffee Company. But where? Twigs, leaves, and honeysuckle vines found on the victim's body and clothing indicated to investigators she died in a swampy area. This posed a puzzle that the police, in spite of Herculean efforts, had been unable to solve. The description of the crime scene fit at least a dozen places around the Atlanta area. But the exact murder site could not be located. To add to the confusion, police officers discovered the truck Mrs. Reyman drove to Atlanta from Bogart had been filled with gasoline when Mrs. Reyman left Bogart. When found on Moreland Avenue, the gas tank was empty, indicating it had been driven considerably farther than she would have gone on the shopping tour. Nevertheless, Judge Hooper overruled defense counsel's motion for a mistrial.

After four days of testimony the case went to the jury at two in the afternoon. After seven hours of deliberation the jury reported to the court that they were hopelessly deadlocked. Judge Hooper dismissed the jury and declared a mistrial. The jury foreman stated that after many ballots the vote never varied from the 7 to 5 vote from the beginning of the deliberations. Judge Hooper, in his charge to the jury, stressed the necessity of the state's proving beyond a shadow of a doubt the guilt of Robinson before they could return a verdict of guilty. Since much of the evidence was circumstantial, Judge Hooper said if there was doubt in the juror's minds they must bring in a verdict of innocent. Seven jurors thought that Robinson was guilty, one less than in the previous trial.

On December 3, 1947, Glenn Robinson went on trial a third time for the slaying of Jeanette Reyman. The case was much like the other two trials. One new development emerged in the strategy of the defense. After stating that he could prove that Mrs. Reyman had been previously married to a man named Poole and she had resided in Atlanta in 1942, Defense Counsel Henson cross-examined the slain woman's husband, Raleigh Reyman, about his wife's life prior to her marriage to him. Reyman denied his wife had at any time lived in Atlanta. He insisted that the fatal journey here June 25 was the first time she had ever been in Atlanta alone. She had come to Atlanta with him several times to purchase supplies for the Bogart tourist establishment, however. The state contended Robinson was the only person in Atlanta Mrs. Reyman would have allowed in her truck. Henson was trying to prove that she knew others in Atlanta who might have killed her.

Judge Virlyn Moore presided at the trial. He decided to hold night sessions because opposing counsel were unable to agree on releasing the jury nights. Another reason was the scarcity of hotel rooms, for the jury had to spend Tuesday night on cots on the mezzanine at the Robert Fulton Hotel. By holding night sessions, the judge expected to complete the trial the following day. The jurors could not endure many nights on those cots.

Witnesses at the night session included Dr. Herman Jones, who said he found blood spots on Robinson's trousers. He admitted, however, that the same spots could have been as much as seven years old. Another witness was a storekeeper, who stated that the day the truck was found, Robinson came into her store, nervous and excited, and bought a package of cigarettes. She said that several days later he returned and wanted to know if anyone had seen the driver of the murder truck.

Other witnesses were D. N. Stephens, who saw the murder truck on Forrest Avenue the day of the murder but could not positively identify the driver; M. E. Van Sant, Moreland Avenue clerk, who saw a man park the truck in front of his store and walk up the street; and L. W. Clyburn, investigator, who described a wooded area near Sears where the state contended the crime was committed. Solicitor Paul Webb placed Detective E. O. Mullen on the stand, and Mullen testified how he and Detective Sikes had found a pair of khaki trousers in Robinson's apartment which Robinson refused to identify as his own until shown his initials on them. E. D. Carden, a clerk at the Sears store, testified he had sold Mrs. Reyman a paring knife and a butcher knife around noon the day she was murdered. He said Robinson was with her at the time. He later identified Robinson in a police lineup. G. D. Hawks and Leonard Roberts, carpenters, who worked with Robinson at one time building the Reymans' tourist court at Bogart, testified that Robinson had made remarks to them about how much he wanted Mrs. Reyman.

On the following day the jury, after spending another bad night on cots, heard the summation from the opposing lawyers. Solicitor Webb, in his final closing argument, said that there was a chain of evidence which linked Robinson with the death of Mrs. Reyman. Webb said that Mrs. Reyman was a stranger in Atlanta; two witnesses testified Robinson had expressed an "unholy desire" to have her, and other witnesses had identified Robinson as being with the murdered woman, had identified the truck, and had destroyed his alibi. Webb attacked Defense Attorney Henson's effort to convince the jury that if it did not think Robinson deserved the electric chair, it should not convict him. If the jury in a circumstantial case does not recommend mercy, the judge can sentence a man

convicted of murder to life imprisonment. Webb made it clear
that he felt that the jury should give Robinson the electric
chair or, if not that, life imprisonment.

Robinson again took the stand in his own defense. "I am not
guilty of this charge. All I know about the murder is what I
read in the newspaper." Robinson spoke in the same quiet,
lifeless fashion which had marked his appearance at all three
trials. He gave a detailed account of his actions the day Mrs.
Reyman was slain. He said he went to work about 6 a.m. that
day, drove a cab in company with J. D. Farlow from 8 to 11
a.m., went to get uniforms at 11 a.m., and was told he would
have to wait 30 minutes until they were ready. He said he
waited for the uniforms and then went to the Kimball House
Hotel, where he shaved and took a bath. About 3 p.m. Robinson said he joined his nephew and niece at Crump's Restaurant after which he went to the cab office where he stayed
from 5 to 5:30 p.m. He said he spent the evening until 9:30
p.m. driving with Farlow, ate at Crump's, then returned to the
Kimball House for the night.

"Gentlemen, I am looking for my wife to be confined any
minute. I have three kids and I have spent five months in jail
for something I am not guilty of and I would appreciate it if
you gentlemen come back with a verdict of not guilty," Robinson concluded.

The defendant took the stand shortly before the defense had
rested its case. Several rebuttal witnesses were placed on the
stand in an effort to impeach Robinson's alibi. The state ar-
gued that although the actual murder scene of the crime was
in doubt, the fact that the slain woman's body was found in
Fulton County made it proper for the trial to be held in the
county. Webb told of Mrs. Reyman's moving to Bogart last
January from her home in Indiana and said it was the state's
contention that she was the type of woman who would not
have picked up a man unless she knew him as she did Robinson. Webb said that it was reasonable to assume that Robinson joined Mrs. Reyman on pretext of getting a ride back to
Bogart to his wife and children.

Defense counsel insisted the jury could have more than a
reasonable doubt as to Robinson's guilt. Henson described testimony of some of the state witnesses as being "highly ques-
tionable, to say the least." Despite the lateness of the hour,
the courtroom remained crowded, spectators on the edge of

their seats. One elderly woman on the front row removed her shoes to rest her bare feet.

THE VERDICT

Late that night the case went to the jury. After some two hours of deliberation the jury returned its verdict in the case. The jury acquitted Glenn Robinson of the charge of murdering Jeanette Reyman. After five months and three trials, Glenn Robinson was a free man.

A monumental effort was made to convict Glenn Robinson for the death of Jeanette Reyman. Three juries remained unconvinced. One of the factors that influenced the jurors was: Why should they convict Glenn Robinson for the death of Jeanette Reyman when Paul Refoule was going free? To many people of the time, this was logical thinking. What appears today to be somewhat more logical is that the Atlanta police probably made the same mistake in the Reyman case as the Fulton County police made in the Refoule case. One person who thought so at the time was the head of the homicide squad, Lt. Coppenger. He did not believe that Robinson was guilty of murder. Detective Mullen, who arrested Robinson, was convinced that the taxi-cab driver was the culprit. In fact, detectives do not always agree on the guilt or innocence of a suspect in a homicide case, and unlike fictional murder mysteries, some homicides appear to be void of any rational solution. We should point out, however, that while no professional investigators now feel that Refoule was guilty of the murder of his wife, there is a rather evenly divided opinion among them concerning Robinson and Jeanette Reyman. Some think he was innocent. Many believe he was guilty.

What is interesting is how the two murder cases were tied so closely together. Robinson was able to take advantage of the way the police abused Refoule and use it to his own advantage. The courts were beginning to hand down decisions that restricted the way the police had investigated murders in the past. And it was a time of change and social upheaval. The defense counsel who represented Robinson in all three trials stated that he felt that Peggy Refoule and Jeanette Reyman were probably killed by the same man, and this would certainly exclude both Refoule and Robinson.

In 1947 the city of Atlanta had 91 homicides—the year of the Refoule and Reyman murders. In contrast, Milwaukee, a city of comparable size, had only four murders. But in this era Southern cities often had more homicides than Northern cities. The poverty, the racism, the heat—these were factors that made murder more likely.

Of the 91 homicides in Atlanta in 1947 nine victims were white persons and 82 were blacks. Black murders led because at the time the South refused to face the fact of treating black murder seriously and still followed the ancient custom of treating such homicides as "just another Negro killing." This caused the South to reap an inevitable crop of black homicides in the period following World War II, and was one of the contributing factors to the rise in the number of homicides in this turbulent era. Because in this period white juries almost invariably treated more or less lightly the crime of murder when it was confined to the Negro race, the homicide rate in this type of crime remained high.

During the same months of the investigation into the Refoule and Reyman murders, the grand jury indicted Frank Bryant, a black man, for the slayings of three other blacks. Bryant quarreled with John Jackson, a man living at Bryant's address on Farrington Avenue, and then shot him to death. When Louise Jackson, John Jackson's wife, attempted to come to the victim's aid with a butcher knife, Bryant shot and killed her. Then, Nancy Barnes, mother of Louise Jackson, arrived on the scene and she in turn was killed by Bryant. Bryant next started up a nearby street where he met Willie Barnes, husband of Nancy Barnes, and started shooting at him. Barnes ran but turned and shot back at Bryant. One shot broke Bryant's arm. When police arrived on the scene, Bryant was in the act of picking up his pistol with the other hand. There were several eyewitnesses to the killings and there was no doubt that Bryant was guilty of the murder of three people. The case was never tried. The charge was reduced to manslaughter and Bryant received six months probation. Whether or not the person committing this particular crime received the punishment commensurate with the crime, which of course he did not, is beside the point. The fact is that a dual society looked upon homicides within those separate societies in quite a different manner.

During this same period, James Ward Sims, a black male, aged 17, was accused of assaulting a white nurse in her home on Richardson Street. Sims had previously entered guilty pleas on two indictments charging him with larceny of an automobile and burglary from a house. He received a total of 25–30 years on those charges, but he refused to enter a guilty plea on the criminal assault charge of the white nurse. He maintained he was innocent. He was placed on trial on this charge, and the trial lasted one afternoon. He was found guilty by a jury after a half hour's deliberation of criminal assault and sentenced to die in the electric chair!

The aftermath of World War II, economic instability, boom times, a growing population that was on the move, and racism—all these factors contributed to a rise in the homicide rate in Atlanta and in the nation in the years 1946 to 1947. There was a growing awareness among police officials that ancient approaches of handling homicides would no longer suffice in the future.

5

Opera Singer John Garris

In the late 1940s Atlanta turned out to be a jinx town for the Metropolitan Opera Company. On the 1948 tour, a train wreck outside the city marooned most of the company's property effects, and the curtain went up on *Carmen* with the stars wearing makeshift costumes. In 1949, Patrice Munsel was shaken up and badly bruised in a traffic accident on her way into the city from the airport.

A sense of impending doom hung over the entire company when the opera season opened in Atlanta on April 18, 1949, but the cast was in top form when it sang *Otello* at the Fox Theater on that Monday night. John Garris sang the role of Cassio. In the last act when Cassio is stabbed by Iago, he cries out as he falls:

> *I am maimed forever—*
> *Help, ho! Murder!*
> *Murder!!*

On Tuesday night, Garris sang the part of Laerte in *Mignon*. His masterful performance in the first act brought accolades from the audience and rave reviews from the press.

John Garris was noted particularly for his Wagnerian roles and had won wide acclaim for his rendition in *Die Meistersinger*. He had sung with the San Francisco Opera Company for several seasons before joining the Met.

Garris was regarded as one of the Met's most promising new tenors. The husky, six-feet-tall singer was thirty-six years old and was a native of Frankfurt-on-Main, Germany. His German name was Hans J.K. Gareis, but when he came to America, he adopted the Anglicized version and became John Garris. It was by the latter name that he was known throughout the music world as a man with a great deal of talent and a promising future.

When the 1949 season concluded with a performance of *L'Elisir d'Amour* on Wednesday evening, Garris was present as a member of the audience instead of as a featured singer. At 7:45 on the following morning, a workman on his way to work in downtown Atlanta discovered the singer's body in a dismal, rain-soaked alley at the rear of 305 Marietta Street.

John Garris had been shot in the region of his heart by a single bullet which entered directly below the left underarm. His body lay straightened out on its back, the legs almost carefully crossed at the ankles. It was attired in dark flannel trousers and a white shirt. Very little blood was noted in the vicinity where the body was found, which led police to theorize that the handsome tenor had been shot elsewhere and that his body had been taken to the alley.

Later, Garris' coat was found about two blocks away, carelessly thrown on the top of a garbage can. Police theorized that Garris had been killed somewhere else and the body was dumped in the alley; then as the car sped away the coat was thrown from the car. There was no bullet hole in the coat. None of the slain singer's valuables was touched by the killer or killers. His wallet, which contained twenty dollars and jewelry and personal papers, was found intact. An alien registration receipt bore the Germanic identification "Hans J.K. Gareis."

Atlanta police telegraphed Memphis police to hold all passengers on the special opera train when it reached Memphis. The train had been scheduled to leave Terminal Station at 3 a.m., but it did not get underway until after 5 a.m. It was reported that Garris boarded the train before midnight, but then got off again. He never returned, but when the train departed no one on board noticed his absence.

HIS LAST DAY

On his last day in Atlanta Garris had lunch at the Biltmore Hotel. Although the stars of the opera troupe stayed there, many of the lesser performers stayed at the YMCA. At 2:30 p.m. on Wednesday, Garris placed a call from the Biltmore to a member of the troupe at the Y. He placed no more calls that day from the hotel and received none. At 3 p.m. Garris was supposed to meet Miss Herta Glatz, a contralto with the Met cast, to attend a tea in the hotel for some of the members of the cast. At the last moment he called Miss Glatz at her room and begged off, explaining that he had a headache. When he met Miss Glatz before that evening's performance, he told her he had napped and slept well, and he seemed to be in very good spirits. The two singers were joined for dinner by a local opera buff, Mrs. Rosalie Mayer, after which the three of them attended the opera together. A member of the opera troupe saw Garris at the theater and talked with him. He followed the performance with great interest and was in a good mood. Miss Glatz and Garris left the Fox Theater together right after the last curtain at about 11 p.m. and went by the Biltmore to pick up their luggage. Mrs. Mayer drove them to the Terminal Station, where they arrived around 11:45 p.m. Garris went in search of a red cap while Miss Glatz sat in the car with Mrs. Mayer. Garris soon returned with a porter, obtained his and Miss Glatz's luggage, thanked Mrs. Mayer for her kindness, and left.

The two members of the opera troupe went to their separate cars, Miss Glatz to Car 12, Garris to Car 13. Garris had told Miss Glatz that he intended to write a letter to a friend in Los Angeles, with regard to a German-English translation which he wanted to send to a New York agency. Garris and Miss Glatz were planning a concert tour together after the Met season, and the New York agency was pressing both to submit certain translations for the tour. Miss Glatz went to her car and wrote a letter concerning the matter.

According to the porter of Car 13, John Garris seemed to be in a hurry, and he gave the porter his luggage stubs and the money for the red cap, saying that he was going to the rear car to play cards. No member of the troupe recalled seeing Garris playing cards. Miss Glatz said he did not mention it to her, and she stated that he never played cards. The porter took care of Garris' two suitcases and topcoat, putting the larger suitcase in the men's room, the smaller one on the lower berth assigned to Garris. The porter did not see Garris again after that. He noticed during the night that the berth was not occupied, but assumed that Garris was in another car still playing cards.

When Miss Glatz had finished her letter she went upstairs to the main concourse of the station to mail it. On her way back to the train she met Garris, who showed her his letter which he was on his way to mail. He went upstairs to the station and Miss Glatz returned to her car. She did not see John Garris again.

In Memphis, Lt. M.M. Coppenger and other detectives from

the Atlanta homicide bureau were interviewing members of the Met chorus and ballet and the stage hands. They interviewed several members of the company who stated the last time they saw Garris was about 12:55 a.m., Thursday, in the parking lot in front of the train station, where several members of the cast were getting into an automobile to go for sandwiches, when Garris approached the car and wanted to go along. Since there were already six people in the car, it was decided after some conversation that Garris could not be squeezed in and so the car drove off and Garris was last seen walking away from the station toward downtown. Edwin Johnson, the Met's general manager, and Max Rudolph advised Lt. Coppenger that they were on the platform at the train station at 3:30 a.m. and that they did not see Garris anywhere in or around the station, and that he had not attended a party given for the artists of the opera company following the last performance.

One of the assistant stage managers stated that he was walking toward town after midnight looking for a place to eat, when Garris overtook him and they discussed the best place to eat at that time of night. As they passed the Western Union office Garris told him that he had to send a telegram, and the two separated. The stage man stated that he walked on and found a restuarant and that after eating he retraced his route to the railroad station. He did not see Garris again.

Garris went into the telegraph office and sent a wire to his agent in New York, assuring her that all texts and translations of songs for the concert tour would reach her by Friday. The person on duty later remembered Garris because he asked him how to spell some of the words in the telegram. He said that Garris was in a very normal condition and that he appeared neat and was wearing a sport coat but no top coat and had his hat pushed back on his head. He seemed to be perfectly calm. The man stated that Garris was in the office about fifteen minutes and that the telegram went out a few minutes before 2 a.m. He was the last person known to have seen John Garris alive.

When news of the slaying broke, many theories were discussed throughout Atlanta. The case quickly revived memories of the Refoule and Reyman cases. People were betting that this one also would go unsolved. The Atlanta police were determined to solve the case, and probably spent more man-hours working on it than on any other single homicide which had ever been committed in the city. Pressure built quickly for an early solution.

Opening night of the Met in Memphis found white-socked Atlanta homicide detectives mingling with the black-tie audience. While Jerome Hines sang on stage:

> *Do not murder! For thus is writ:*
> *"He who sheds another's lifeblood,*
> *Such shall be his doom!"*

detectives backstage circulated behind props and curtains in the hope of picking up a clue to the murder. Members of the company were being questioned behind the backdrops and in the dressing rooms to find out what they knew about Garris' movements in Atlanta and what possible motive there might be for someone to take his life. During the intermission the audience talked more about John Garris than they did about the night's performance of *Lucia di Lammermoor*. The backstage police work was not done quietly, and several performers threatened not to continue unless the police got out. When a confrontation developed between the singers and the cops, it appeared for a while that there would be no second act that evening, at least with the curtain up. Edwin Johnson rushed around backstage soothing ruffled feelings and requesting the police to please work more quietly.

Following the performance, the police concluded their questioning of the members of the opera company. Lt. Coppenger and his men returned to Atlanta and the Met went on to its next stop on the tour. The Memphis interrogations gave the police some information concerning Garris' movements that proved helpful; however, no vital clues were unearthed.

John Garris had no relatives in the United States. News of the singer's death reached his parents in Frankfurt while they were attending a performance of the opera *Gotterdammerung*. The stunned parents, Josef Gareis, 73, and his wife, Maria, 70, asked to have the body cremated and the ashes returned to Germany.

BACKGROUND

Police learned that Garris' career had been a stormy one. After studying at the Frankfurt Conservatory of Music, he made his debut as a conductor at age 19. When Hitler came to power Garris fled to Greece, where he stayed until 1941. He earned a living by singing over the radio. Ultimately he worked his way to the United States and succeeded in arranging an audition at the Met, but was unable to obtain a post as a conductor. Although he had never studied voice, nor knew a singing operatic role, he tried out and was accepted eventually at the Met as a singer. Out of his salary he paid for singing lessons, soon winning wide acclaim as a recitalist for his perfect intrepretation of German *Leider*. The singer lived at 362 West 57th Street in New York City, where he shared an apartment with Lutz Peter, a drama coach. The latter, born Uhnfelder, was also from Frankfurt.

Lutz Peter was in Los Angeles at the time of Garris' death, but he returned to New York when he was informed of the murder. Detectives from Atlanta flew to New York and questioned him closely, but they learned little of value.

In New York music circles many persons recalled Garris as a debonair, charming man on the stage. When the curtain fell, however, it screened his private life. Tenants in the building where he lived described Garris as an unassuming and quiet neighbor. The woman who lived in the apartment directly above his said that she and other tenants frequently turned off their radios so they could enjoy the singing of Garris and his guests.

Lutz Peter told investigators that Garris was a modest person with a quiet disposition and that he had no enemies. Peter said that he had last seen Garris on Sunday just before the Met tour began. He said he was to have met Garris in Los Angeles when the Met tour reached there. Peter said that when Garris reached the United States in 1941 he had seventy-five cents in his pocket. Garris went to live with Peter, who coached him in all of his opera roles and advised him on his career. The coach added that Garris had been engaged to his sister, Lottie Uhnfelder, but that she had died in a concentration camp during the war. Peter had no idea who could have killed Garris, and he felt that jealousy or envy as a motive for the killing was not likely because Garris was such a likeable person.

Meanwhile, Atlanta detectives established an interesting lead. They learned that a hotel reservation had been made in the name of John Garris for Thursday night in Dallas, Texas. This indicated that Garris had changed his original plan to accompany the cast to Memphis, where he had no roles to sing, and instead planned to go directly to Dallas, the next stop on the tour where he was slated to sing. If this were the case, then why did Garris place his luggage aboard the Memphis train? And why did he tell no one of his plans to skip Memphis? It was not unusual for members of the company, when they were not scheduled to sing, to skip certain cities of the tour. If Garris had decided at the last minute not to go to Memphis, he still could have planned to send part of his luggage on with the opera special after returning to the train and retrieving his small overnight bag. But if he were planning to go directly to Dallas, he had not made any train or plane reservations.

BEAUTIFUL AND RICH

As soon as Lt. Coppenger returned from Memphis, he boarded another plane for Dallas. There he drove to an exclusive residential neighborhood and stopped at an impressive, Spanish-style mansion. This was the home of the young woman who claimed Garris had wired her to meet him at a Dallas hotel on Thursday night. The girl lived with her parents. She was 21 years old and a striking beauty with green eyes and red hair. She was very rich. She told Lt. Coppenger that she was madly in love with John Garris and had fallen for him when she was studying voice in New York the year before. She had seen him at the Met and had gone backstage to meet him and ask for his autograph. She said that after they got to know each other, he asked her for a date. They continued to see each other until she returned to Dallas, and thereafter she wrote him almost every day. A month before, she had received a letter from Garris telling her he would be in Dallas in April. Two weeks later she got a long distance call from the singer saying that he would be in Dallas on Thursday, April 21st. The young woman said she waited all that day to hear from Garris, but the hours passed without a call or a message from him. She was worried but did not know what to do. She turned on the radio and heard the news of Garris' murder.

Coppenger questioned the young beauty for three hours. She stated that during the time she knew Garris in New York, she had encountered no one who might have had reason to harm him. He had been attractive to women of all ages, she reported, and his feminine fan mail had been huge. Although girls had swarmed around him for autographs, he apparently had never become entangled with any of his feminine admirers. It began to appear more and more that the entire scenario of the murder—including culprit, motive and actual commission—centered on Atlanta.

Meanwhile in Atlanta, detectives continued to search for a late model green Buick sedan which had been seen circling the area near Marietta and Thurmond streets, N.W., during the early morning hours on the day of the murder. A man and a woman were reported riding in the car, which returned to the scene after daybreak. A warehouse watchman told detectives he overheard a shot near the entrance to the alley at around 3:30 a.m. Thursday—four hours before the body of the singer was discovered. Another night watchman and a taxicab driver reported to police that they saw the green automobile circling the area at that time. Detectives also were checking on reports of a restaurant operator in the area who stated that a man answering Garris' description came into his restaurant with several other persons early Thursday and left a short time later.

Dewey Wrenn, who lived only a short distance from the alley where Garris' body was found, told police that he heard a pistol shot sometime Thursday morning. He said that he remembered switching off a light and going to bed at 12:30 a.m. but could not recall how much time elapsed before he heard the shot. Wrenn stated to detectives that on the Monday or Tuesday before the slaying he had seen an automobile pull up to the curb near his house. He remembered the car because of its smart appearance and because it bore an out-of-state license plate. In the car was a man and a very attractive woman. The car remained there for awhile and then drove off. Detectives expressed doubt that Garris was in an automobile when he was shot, since there were no visible powder burns on the clothing or body. They pointed out that an automatic pistol fired at such close range would have left powder burns.

Atlanta police next got their first big break in the case. South Carolina authorities arrested a suspect driving a gray sedan with no license plates. The suspect was identified as Grover "Tojo" Pulley, a white male, aged 44, a parole-jumping convict from North Carolina who once had been convicted for murder. The pistol in Pulley's possession was a 9-millimeter automatic of Belgian make. Police in Clinton, South Carolina, found in Pulley's car a stained pair of trousers, an army blanket splotched with dark spots, and a $10 bill with dark brown smears.

Dr. Herman Jones of the Fulton County crime laboratory drove to Clinton to make ballistics tests of the gun. Police learned that Pulley was in Atlanta the night Garris was slain with a 9-millimeter bullet apparently identical to the bullet found in Pulley's pistol. Earlier in the investigation Dr. Jones had announced that the death slug came from a .38-caliber pistol—almost exactly the size of a 9-millimeter bullet. Dr. Jones fired six bullets from Pulley's pistol in Clinton and then left immediately for Atlanta to make a microscopic comparison of those slugs with the bullet which had been removed from the body of John Garris. A quick, superficial comparison of the test bullets with the bullet removed from the body of the slain tenor indicated that they bore a strong resemblance, but a more thorough examination would be necessary.

PRESTIGE OF MET

Meanwhile, Clinton authorities held "Tojo" Pulley on open charges after he admitted having served 17 years in a North Carolina penitentary for murder. North Carolina authorities confirmed that Pulley had jumped parole a year earlier. The patrolman who arrested Pulley in Clinton stated that the Belgian automatic found on Pulley was rather unusual, and he reported that he had found one cartridge in its chamber, two more in Pulley's pocket, and a full clip of 15 cartridges in his car.

Police learned that John Garris was not highly paid by the Metropolitan Opera Company and that up to the time of his death his greatest recompense was the glamour and prestige which surrounded his singing career. Officials of the Met were not sure that there was enough money in the slain singer's bank account to defray his funeral expenses. His friend Lutz Peter was making arrangements to travel to Atlanta to claim the body. The singer had requested that in the event of his death his body be cremated.

Atlanta police could not determine positively if the bullet which killed Garris had been fired from the gun of "Tojo" Pulley. The bullet taken from the body of the murder victim and the test bullets fired by Dr. Jones were forwarded to the FBI in Washington for analysis. An Atlanta man notified police that he knew Pulley as "Harvey Perkins" and that Pulley visited his home in Atlanta on Saturday, April 16, 1947 and remain there until 7 p.m., Wednesday, April 20th. The man told police that Pulley told him that he was going to North Carolina. The man stated that he did not know Pulley's background or his real name until he saw his picture and read a story in a local newspaper.

At this point in their investigation of the slaying, police conjectured that John Garris was killed as he strolled along the railroad tracks before the opera special pulled out of the train station Thursday morning. The probable motive, they believed, was that he had unwittingly surprised burglars attempting to break into a printing establishment near where his body was later found. Police records showed that burglar alarm calls sounded twice Thursday morning to the Montag Printing Company building on Marietta Street at the approximate time the singer was killed. Night watchmen in the area reported hearing a shot about 3:30 a.m.

Police found an assortment of burglary tools in Pulley's car. The case against him was building. But up until this point it was all circumstantial. The one piece of evidence that could really incriminate Pulley was the pistol. If the test bullets were the same as the death bullet, the police would then have a good case against Pulley. However, it was their opinion that he had not acted alone. Detectives felt that at least two men were involved in carrying the husky 175-pound opera singer from the place he was killed into the rough, rain-drenched alley. The ground under Garris' body was dry, indicating that it had been placed there before the pre-dawn rain started.

On April 25, 1949, the autopsy on the body of John Garris was completed. The results of the autopsy led police to believe that the victim died trying to defend himself against his killer, for the completed autopsy revealed Garris was fatally shot as he crouched on his knee in a defensive position. The evidence clearly indicated that Garris was shot as he rested on his right knee holding his left arm up in what could have been an attempt to fend off his attacker. Scores of tiny cinder fragments were embedded in the singer's right knee. This meant that the shooting could have occurred near the special train on which Garris was scheduled to leave Atlanta. It certainly meant that Garris was killed in the vicinity of the railroad tracks. The only area in the vicinity of the alley where

Garris' body was discovered in which cinders were found in profusion was the railroad right-of-way on which the special train was parked. The autopsy revealed that the body had abrasions on the left hand. It was also noted that Garris' right trouser leg was ripped and torn in the area of the right knee. An analysis of the contents of Garris' stomach confirmed that he had eaten shortly before he was murdered.

Governor Herman Talmadge announced that the State of Georgia would offer a reward of $1500 for the conviction of Garris' slayer. The police had asked the governor to post the reward after they found themselves in a maze of false leads and unfounded rumors. Admitting that the investigation of the case was at a standstill, they asked the governor for assistance.

Atlanta was abuzz with conversation concerning the slaying of John Garris. Everybody had a theory. The police were waiting for the report from the FBI in Washington concerning the bullets from Pulley's gun. Garris' body was still in the morgue awaiting the arrival of Lutz Peter from New York. In the interim, the case was the major topic of conversation. People wanted to know if, as some theorized, Garris was fatally wounded in the railroad yards, how did he manage to thread his way in the dark through a confusing network of railroad tracks to the alley area several hundred yards away where his body was found? And how did the supposedly dead or dying man's sport coat come to be placed on a garbage can several hundred yards farther to the north?

The FBI reported that the bullets fired from the Pulley gun by Dr. Jones did *not* match the bullet removed from the body of John Garris. The big break the police had hoped for did not materialize, for without the incriminating bullet they had no case against Pulley.

Chief Herbert T. Jenkins of the Atlanta Police Department, who was personally overseeing the investigation, paid a call upon his friend Ralph McGill, editor of *The Atlanta Constitution*. As a result, McGill wrote the following editorial for the next morning's edition of the paper.

> Atlanta police are under an uneasy national spotlight as they endeavor to solve the slaying of Metropolitan opera tenor John Garris. Already one major theory has collapsed and police are now working on other but less tangible leads. We trust they will continue their efforts without letup until the mystery kill-

ing is solved. We do not have many unsolved murders in Atlanta and Fulton County, but those remaining in that category
seem invariably to be the ones which attract the widest attention. There are reports that certain information which might
be of value in solving the Garris slaying has not been made
available to the police. Persons who possess information about
the crime or information concerning the movements of the
slain man prior to his death owe it to the community to divulge
their knowledge to authorities. And they should not await a
formal request. Delay simply gives the killer or killers a
greater chance of escape. Every new report appears to increase
the mysterious circumstances surrounding the slaying. Police
need help, the help of anyone having information which might
shed light on the numerous dark spots of the case . . .

This editorial appeal for help produced scant results.

On April 27, Lutz Peter arrived in Atlanta to claim the
body and make arrangements for returning it to New York. In
an emotional statement to the press he commented that it was
his belief that his friend had been murdered by someone who
was known to Garris. Peter said Atlanta police had not questioned him or asked his opinion about the case. The small,
slightly-built dramatics coach added he was anxious to meet
detectives and give them his views of the case. Peter cited the
pleasant expression on Garris' face and the carefully laid-out
position of the body as his reasons for believing this. He added
that perhaps an hysterical admirer or fan had killed his
friend.

THEORIES AND SPECULATION

Lutz Peter arrived in Atlanta by automobile with his
brother, Alfred Uhnfelder, of Richmond, Virginia, and Miss
Marie Wier, of New York. The latter was an old friend of Garris. Peter said that an admirer of Garris had offered a burial
spot in a New Hampshire cemetery for the body, but that the
singer's parents had requested the body be returned to Germany. The following day the body of John Garris was taken to
Macon, Georgia, and cremated.

Following six days of extensive investigation, Lt. Coppenger announced that police had been able to account for the
tenor's movements up until shortly after midnight of the past
Wednesday. Coppenger assigned detectives to comb all-night
restaurants in the hope of finding someone who observed Gar-

ris between midnight and the time the first of the opera specials pulled out for Memphis at 4:18 a.m. Detectives carried
pictures of Garris as well as of Pulley on the rounds of restaurants. Coppenger also ordered pictures of the two men to be
shown employees of the train station and night watchmen in
the area. He said police still had a considerable amount of
investigating to do and that detectives were running down
other clues in the mysterious slaying.

Lutz Peter was questioned by Lt. Coppenger for three
hours. He told Coppenger that he had no idea who could have
killed Garris. His comments to the press about Garris being
killed by someone known to him had been mere theorizing, he
explained.

Police then received an anonymous telephone call placed
locally from a man who would not identify himself. He said
the police should check out a Virginia divorcée who was a
close friend of Garris and had followed him to Atlanta.

Upon checking, police discovered that Mrs. Frances Tyler of
Middleburg, Virginia, had been a friend of Garris for several
years. She denied that there had ever been any romantic interest between herself and Garris, adding that she had met
Garris in New York some years ago and they had become
friends. She had last seen Garris in Washington, D.C., during
the Easter season, and she said on Palm Sunday she had gone
to the National Cathedral where Garris was among singers
on a special Holy Week program. She insisted however that
she had never been in Atlanta, and could throw no light on
the mysterious slaying. She stated that she had been shocked
to read of the tragic death of her friend.

Next, detectives located the restaurant where Garris ate
his last meal. They learned also that Garris had eaten at this
same restaurant on Monday and Tuesday. Garris talked with
the wife of the manager about leaving an autographed picture
of himself to be hung in the restaurant. She had talked to
Garris on Monday and Tuesday but she had not worked on
Wednesday or Thursday; other employees, however, stated
that Garris was in the restaurant sometime after 2:30 on
Thursday morning. No one could remember whether Garris
was with someone or alone. Tipsters frequenting all-night restaurants, hotels, and the like thought Garris "met the wrong
man" during or immediately after going to the restaurant.
Persons with criminal records were known to frequent certain

late-hours restaurants. Coppenger felt that had Garris left the restaurant with a local person, other local persons would have seen them, and at least one of them, to get in good with the police, would have come forward to identify Garris' companion. Coppenger felt it was all conjecture, and he did not think much of this theory.

Atlanta police next learned that about 36 hours after John Garris' death a women whose maiden name was Jean G. R. Gareis was shot to death in upper New York state. A startling and fascinating similarity existed between the two murders. Both victims had formerly used their full first names, two middle initials, and the same surname. The name "Gareis" was certainly not a common one in the United States, and for a person with a lively imagination it could appear as if someone bore a grudge against members of the Gareis family or their survivors. Jean G. R. Gareis, the 25-year-old wife of the Reverend George Hetenyl, an Episcopal priest, had been killed by a single pistol shot. The victim in the slaying had fled Nazi Germany just before World War II. The murder was unsolved. Was there some connection between the two murders or just a weird coincidence? There was no hard evidence either way, but the police thought it was simply that, a weird coincidence.

Ten days after the slaying the Garris case had bogged down. To the dismay of the police all the effort generated in an attempt to find the slayer seemed to be getting nowhere. Tojo Pulley was still considered a prime suspect, but the police had yet to locate anything that definitely tied him to the homicide.

Lt. Coppenger was checking out-of-state automobiles reportedly in Atlanta the morning of April 21st. Reports of a green sedan circling the area at Marietta and Thurmond streets, near where the body was found, produced no definite information. Other similar reports led detectives up blind alleys.

Coppenger flew to Los Angeles to interview various members of the opera company. He took a statement from Ramon Vinay, a member of the Met company who had sung the title role in *Otello* in Atlanta. Police had discovered that Vinay had checked out of the Biltmore Hotel at 7 a.m. the day that the body was found. Vinay was one of the few Met members who did not accompany the troupe to Memphis. When interviewed by Coppenger, Vinay stated that he did not go to Mem-

phis because he was not scheduled to sing there and that he
and his wife went by train directly to Dallas. Vinay insisted
that he had no knowledge of Garris' plans. As far as he knew,
Garris was planning to go on to Memphis with the cast. The
last time he saw Garris was at the opera performance
Wednesday night in Atlanta.

Coppenger also questioned the members of the company
who stayed at the YMCA during the opera company's stay. He
located the individual whom Garris had called early Wednesday afternoon from the hotel. The man told Coppenger that
Garris wanted some technical data concerning his forthcom-
ing concert tour, and he said the singer had made no reference
to any plans for going directly to Dallas. Lutz Peter was now
staying in Los Angeles and Coppenger checked him out with
people there. He interviewed people who had written letters
from Los Angeles to the Atlanta police saying the police
should check on the activities of Lutz Peter. It appeared that
Peter, in direct contrast to Garris, was the type of person who
made many enemies, and these enemies were very anxious to
cast suspicion on him for the murder of Garris. Was it possible
that someone had a grudge against Peter and vented it by
murdering Garris? Several people whom Coppenger interviewed implied this, but it was all theory. No one had any
hard evidence.

Washington, D.C., police notified Atlanta police that they
had a man in jail who insisted that he knew a certain person
who had threatened Garris' life, and that this individual was
the type of person who carried out his threats. An Atlanta
detective flew to Washington and interviewed the man. It developed that he knew nothing about the slaying or about Garris except what he had read in the newspapers. He was an
artful liar, however, and it took relentless questioning to
break down his story and uncover that it was all just a hoax,
a device he hoped might help him get out of jail.

NEW LEADS

On May 19, 1949, the probe in the slaying of John Garris
took a sensational turn. A nineteen-year-old girl from Richmond, Virginia, named Alma Johnson, *alias* Mary Smith, was
taken into custody by Atlanta police for suspicion of involvement with narcotics. She was arrested following a tip to police
that she knew something about the Garris case. Alma John-

son claimed that she had met Garris three years earlier in Charlotte, North Carolina, and she named him as the father of her baby. She identified pictures of Grover "Tojo" Pulley as her escort in Atlanta the night of April 20, 1949. Miss Johnson said she and Pulley and another couple arranged a meeting with Garris near the railroad tracks shortly before the opera specials left for Memphis. The object of the meeting, Miss Johnson maintained, was to persuade Garris to help care for the child. A fight ensued, during which Garris removed his coat. During the fight, Pulley shot Garris. After Garris was shot, Miss Johnson said, the first thought was to carry him to the hospital. Then, realizing that he was dead, they placed him in the alley. She stated to police that she crossed his legs and attempted to fold his arms.

It made an interesting story and was hailed by some as a break in the Garris case. Very careful checking by police, however, revealed that the story Miss Johnson told was imaginary. Police ascertained that her real name was something else and that she lived in Gainesville, Georgia. Authorities in Gainesville were looking for her on a lunacy warrant. She had previously been in a mental institution. During the time she was held by police and was telling her story, she was also undergoing withdrawal from drug use.

Lt. Coppenger then interrogated Pulley concerning the woman's story. He readily admitted going with her when he was in Atlanta, but said that her story concerning Garris was merely an attempt on her part to get back at him for leaving her in Atlanta. He stated her story was a pipe dream and that she was a "hophead."

On July 8, 1949, a Fulton County coroner's jury was empaneled and heard all the evidence thus far amassed in the Garris case. There was strong testimony at the hearing concerning the bullet. Dr. Herman Jones insisted that the bullet removed from the body of Garris came from Pulley's gun, and although the FBI did not agree with him, Jones had brought in three other experts who did agree that the bullet and comparison bullets were from the same weapon. Mainly on the basis of Dr. Jones testimony, the jury recommended that Pulley be returned to Fulton County and held for further investigation on the charge of murder. But because of the conflicting testimony and the fact that the experts could not agree about the bullets, Pulley was never brought to trial for the murder of John Garris. Lt. Coppenger, whose knowledge of the case was the most extensive, firmly believed that Pulley did not kill Garris. Dr. Jones felt strongly that Pulley was the culprit.

The Atlanta Police Department received a great deal of mail concerning the John Garris case. Many tips and leads came to the police over the telephone. All of this information was carefully checked by Lt. Coppenger and his men. And it all led nowhere.

On April 24, 1950, the Met came to Atlanta for the spring season. But the murder of John Garris the year before hung over the opera season like a dark cloud. Lt. Coppenger once again talked with members of the company but learned nothing new. In the past year Coppenger had worked on the Garris case relentlessly and had finally determined to his own satisfaction the singer's whereabouts in the hours preceding the murder.

Lt. Coppenger felt that Garris, returning to the train station, by chance happened upon something and/or saw something that he should not have seen, and was killed for this reason. Coppenger thought it quite possible that Garris was mistaken for someone else and the slaying could have been a mistaken-identity slaying. In order not to have the homicide associated with whatever was happening there, the murderers carried Garris' body several blocks and then left it where it was found. If Garris had been murdered by an individual whom he met in or around the restaurant, then the singer would have been robbed and the body left where the murder was committed.

There was much speculation that Garris had arranged to meet someone beforehand and left the train in order to do so. But testimony of several members of the opera troupe put holes in this theory. Garris would have gone with other members of the company in the automobile, had there been room, when he left the train to go out for a late meal.

The big speculation in the Garris case centered around the assumption that someone followed Garris to Atlanta for the purpose of killing him. If this were true, then why did the killer wait until the last moment and how did he know where to find Garris unless he was stalking him?

If before his death, John Garris called out the lines from *Otello*:

Help ho! Murder! Murder!!
there is no one who has come forward to say he heard it.

Lt. Coppenger interviewed and had detectives in other cities interview many people who had much to say concerning
John Garris. He was highly thought of and well regarded as
an artist and musician, and the fact that he could sing in five
languages made him a valuable asset to the Met.

One of the most productive interviews was with Mrs. Herta
Adler, wife of Dr. Justin Adler, of Memphis, Tennessee. It revealed information about John Garris which, in the context of
the times, was shocking and sensational. In the long run,
however, although it brought into focus possible new motives
for the murder, it did not effect a solution.

Official police notes of the interview record that Mrs. Adler
stated that she was originally from Frankfurt and that she
had known John Garris in Germany for fifteen years. At that
time he and Peter Uhnfelder (Lutz Peter) were "sweethearts,"
and they were together constantly. John Garris had an automobile upon which he had the initials *L. U.* painted on a door.
It was commonly known, she said, about the conduct of Peter
Uhnfelder and John Garris, and even in those days Garris did
not care anything for the female sex because he was "madly
in love" with Uhnfelder. She said the stories which had appeared in newspapers about Garris being engaged to Uhnfelder's sister were all wrong; they were, she claimed, an attempt by the latter man to "put up a phony front." Mrs. Adler
went on to say that Uhnfelder left Germany first, followed by
Garris, and that their departure resulted both from a dislike
of Nazism and a frantic desire to avoid the rounding-up of
"undesirables" which was then underway.

Mrs. Adler added that in 1946 when John Garris was in
Memphis with the Met tour he stayed at her home. In talking
about Uhnfelder, the singer mentioned how very much he
missed him since he had been on the road. She asked him why
Uhnfelder was not traveling with him, and Garris replied
that the Met would not give outsiders permission to travel
with the tour.

Statements given to the police by other German emigres
contained essentially the same information. The police had
received tips from anonymous sources from the time of the
slaying that there was a sexual aspect of John Garris' nature
which could have been a factor in his murder.

As late as 1955, the Atlanta Police Department continued to get tips concerning the murder of John Garris. These anonymous phone calls implied that a taxi driver with a certain cab company knew something about the murder, but they did not identify the individual by name. Detectives interviewed a number of people but could come up with nothing concrete. Again, in 1963, the Atlanta Police Department received an anonymous call from a man who refused to identify himself. This informer stated that he had overheard a conversation indicating that a particular cab company employee had certain information concerning the murder of John Garris. Extensive investigation led police to several individuals who provided information, but nothing of a conclusive nature was established.

The murder of John Garris remains unsolved.

The Refoule case had a profound bearing on the investigation into the murder of John Garris. Many more elements were present in the latter case to make it even more sensational than the Refoule investigation, but this time both the authorities and the press scrupulously avoided any "Gestapo-like tactics and yellow journalism" in the investigation into the tenor's death. The Garris investigation could have been quite a show had the police and the press wished to make it so. Indeed, the investigation into the murder makes it a case of classic dimensions because it illustrates how improved police methods and practices had become in the short, two-year period from 1947 to 1949. In retrospect the opera singer's murder is most significant because of what *did not* occur in the course of the investigation and reporting of the case.

The Garris case brought to an end the series of unsolved murders which plagued Atlanta in the era following World War II. It is interesting, and probably significant, that the bizarre murders of Peggy Refoule, Jeanette Reyman, and John Garris made them victims not only of homicide, but victims too of the unsettled and changing times in which they lived. All had been intimately affected by World War II, and the people closest to them had been affected by the war. It is quite likely that the lives of the murderers themselves had also been altered in some manner by World War II. While this of course is not the entire explanation for the slayings, it is most certainly an important factor, for if there had been no war the Refoules would probably never have left France or the Reymans their native Indiana, nor would John Garris have fled the Nazis in Germany. Their lives were changed by the events of the time in which they lived, and this contributed to their untimely deaths.

It is unlikely that a lone homicide would ever again arouse in Atlanta the interest which the Refoule, Reyman, and Garris cases provoked. The reasons for this are varied. The Garris case, coming two years later, did not arouse the intensity of interest of the other two cases. Times were changing.

Of course the primary concern of people about these cases was because the crimes were never solved. Even had they been solved ultimately to the satisfaction of everyone, which is highly unlikely, given the trend of the times, interest still would have been intense. In the absence of a confession or eyewitness, it is very doubtful that these cases could ever be solved to the satisfaction of everyone. There were too many elements involved that were a part of society at the time. These cases were not just homicides. They were a part of the social fabric, and are now a part of the social history, of everyone who lived through that era. Housewives read about the death of Peggy Refoule after finishing their ironing and thought: "That could be me!" Small-time crooks read about "Tojo" Pulley and thought the police might next try to pin a murder rap on them. Leaders of the community thought that these unsolved murders were certainly giving the community a bad name. The newspapers and radio brought the news close to everybody. The crimes, in some way and manner, appeared to touch everyone.

6

28 Young Blacks

The murder of children is the most heinous crime imaginable. The multiple murder of more than two-dozen young blacks in Atlanta in the years from 1979 to 1981 rocked the city, made the nation quickly aware of Atlanta's plight, and focused worldwide attention upon the missing and murdered children's cases. Almost simultaneously with the disappearance of the victims or the discovery of their bodies, the cases were catapulted into instant prominence. The unsolved murder cases which had occurred in Atlanta in the years following World War II had absorbed the minds and emotions of the people of Atlanta, and to a lesser extent of the people of the state and region. But the cases of the missing and murdered black children and young adults which occurred following two decades of profound social change in the country, and especially within the city which more than any other had orchestrated that change, gained immediate international notoriety. Certain complex homicides of the past occurred in social environments undergoing ardent social alterations, and in effect acted as harbingers of more that was to come. Perhaps it is no happenstance, then, that the multiple murders of young blacks took place in Atlanta and that at that point in time they most likely would not have occurred anywhere else.

In the last week of July 1979, the bodies of Edward Smith, aged 14, and Alfred Evans, aged 13, were discovered less than 150 feet apart in a dumping area in southwest Atlanta. Smith had died from a single gunshot wound, and the bullet had passed through his body and was not recovered. Investigators believed that he had been shot at another location and his body dumped where it was later found. Medical examiners assumed that Evans died from asphyxiation, but the body was too decomposed for the cause of death to be determined.

In any year, Atlanta will have from six to a dozen homicides of black children. These cases are normally solved and a relative is most often charged with the murder. These are domestic homicides in which the killer is known to the victim, and the victim is nearly always related in some manner to the killer. It is the type of homicide that began with Cain and Abel and is the kind of homicide that, as we have said a number of times before in this survey, police investigators have to deal with daily. There was no reason for the police to assume that the murders of Edward Smith and Alfred Evans, whose bodies were discovered in the hot and humid July heat of an otherwise tranquil Atlanta summer, would in time become the first and second names of murdered Atlanta children on a seemingly endless list.

On October 21, 1979, nine-year-old Yusef Bell left his apartment in downtown Atlanta near the stadium to go on an errand for a neighbor. On November 8 his body was discovered in an abandoned elementary school near his home. He had been strangled. Three days before the discovery of Bell's body the skeletal remains of 14-year-old Milton Harvey were discovered in East Point. Harvey had last been seen a month earlier riding his bicycle near his northwest Atlanta home.

Atlanta police then had in their files four unsolved murder cases of black children. For a period of four months no other cases were added, but in March of 1980 black children again began being reported either missing or murdered. By July, 12 black children had been found murdered, and none of the cases had been solved.

In this period of time, among the families of middle and low-income blacks living in the predominately or all-black neighborhoods of southeast and southwest Atlanta, it came to be believed that some evil and sinister force loose in their communities was "snatching" and murdering their children. Their children were the hope of the future. Now some person or some thing was threatening and taking them away. The black communities of Atlanta became rife with fear, suspicion, and paranoia. The people were up in arms. They were further frustrated in their plight because they had no leadership. The civil rights groups in the city that had in the past always represented black aspirations had been unable to foresee what was happening in Atlanta and to Atlanta's children.

In June, Camille Bell, the mother of Yusef Bell, gathered the mothers of seven other black children who had been slain and called a press conference. She stated that a person or persons unknown were killing Atlanta's children and the elected officials and law enforcement officers were doing nothing to stop it. The mothers demanded some action on the part of the police department. The mothers organized themselves into a Committee to Stop Children's Murders. The guiding force behind the committee was Camille Bell. Out of the frustration and despair of the neighborhoods where the murdered children lived was created an organization dedicated to doing something to stop the killings. Like other groups before it, Camille Bell's organization was born on the wings of helplessness and the sure conviction that there was nothing else that could aid black people threatened by this new and bewildering phenomenon.

Commissioner Lee Brown and the other top personnel within the Atlanta Bureau of Police Services were severely stung by Camille Bell's charges. Most of them did not believe that a sinister killer force was murdering black children. They thought it was the "usual" pattern of homicides with which the city always had to contend. But Camille Bell was stirring things up and others were feeling the heat. Mayor Maynard Jackson voiced confidence in the police department, but he promised to step up the murder investigations.

But all of the cases remained unsolved. The consensus in most black neighborhoods was that the Atlanta police couldn't catch a bad cold. Confidence in the police department in Atlanta, which had always been high, was fast eroding. This was an intolerable situation for a black city administration and police force whose two top commanders were black. The people within the community who in the past had been most supportive of the black leadership of city government were openly criticizing that government and holding it up to ridicule. This was a situation which white-led governments had had to deal with for years—this aspect of the political process which eventually falls upon those who exercise political and police powers within a democracy.

SPECIAL TASK FORCE

On July 17, 1980, Commissioner Lee Brown ordered the creation of a Special Task Force on Murdered and Missing Children. Its sole responsibility was to find out who was killing young black Atlantans. Eventually the task force would have its own separate building on West Peachtree Street in the shadow of downtown Atlanta's most impressive skyscrapers. It originally consisted of four members but a year later it had 175 members, including state investigators and representatives from other metro-area police departments. Assisting the group was a 40-member FBI team.

Whether the Special Task Force was originally set up to handle what the police deemed to be a stymied murder investigation problem or to deal with a political problem will no doubt be debated for years to come. The evidence for now would appear to indicate that the task force was set up to handle what was perceived to be a political problem. The first commander of the task force and the personnel working there were not seasoned investigators nor even detectives, but personnel from the police department's crime-prevention unit. Shortly after the formation of the task force a number of investigators who had worked on murder cases in other cities were invited in to assist.

A number of psychics, some invited and some not invited, also came to Atlanta to assist the police. It is not exactly clear why the task force thought it necessary to bring them in except as a gesture to try to give the impression to the public that the police were on the job. It is a pretty well-believed myth on the part of the public that psychics in the past have helped the police catch killers. Their dismal failure to do so in Atlanta will perhaps prod the public into not believing in their inviolability in future cases.

To understand why the task force thought it necessary to bring in outside investigators is more complex. There was no doubt some thought that the case might be a classic jack-the-ripper type and that any police officers who had dealt with a case like that would be helpful. However, it would seem that there was a more overriding political consideration.

In the beginning it was suggested here that one way to understand the entire phenomenon of the missing and murdered children's cases is to view it in the afterwash of years of segregation—upon the public, the police, and the murdered victims.

It takes years of training to develop a good homicide detective. It means serving a number of years in the uniform division and then more years of work in vice and larceny—some twenty years of police preparation for a detective to accu rately size up murder scenes and develop the contact with informers to supply him with meaningful information. As the Atlanta Police Department was segregated until the early 1960s, only a small number of blacks were beginning to attain this status in 1979, and some of them had left the department to join the Fulton County Police Department when it was formed in 1975. Many of the white detectives who had worked on complex murder investigations in the past had retired by 1979. Generally speaking, the homicide division, like the entire police department, was a young department; neither had experience in dealing with a case of this magnitude. Thus the need for outside assistance. Police officials who would fly into town for a few days and offer advice and then depart were probably more helpful to the police working on the cases than it appeared at the time. We have to constantly keep in mind that cases of this magnitude occur only about every 25 or 30 years, so they in fact become a learning experience for the police as well as for the public.

Whether or not the task force was formed as a public relations arm of the police department, the police certainly had a difficult political problem on their hands. The black public, just emerging from years of segregation, had never experienced anything like this. Following World War II the white public of Atlanta had never experienced anything like the murders and investigations that then stormed across the scene. Much of the black community of Atlanta in 1979 was about where the Atlanta white community had been in 1947–'49 in dealing with this kind of murder investigation. The main similarity is that both had to deal with developments at different points in time with something that was an entirely new experience. The times were different and the aspects of the cases were not the same, but the reaction of both communities in both periods of time was one of fear—fear of the unknown, fear of what was happening to them.

REWARD MONEY

Public and police officials decided that the best way to deal with the political problem was to make some sort of headway in solving the cases. Mayor Maynard Jackson made a public plea for reward money to be offered. Various businesses and individuals immediately came forth with a $100,000 reward to anyone giving information leading to the apprehension of the killer or killers. Mayor Jackson went on television with the hundred thousand dollars in front of him. The idea was that somebody had to know something about some of these murders and the lure of money would smoke out the culprit.

Whatever the intent, the result was disastrous. The task force was flooded with thousands of calls. Everybody who had caught a glimpse of the $100,000 had also, they were sure, caught sight of the culprit. Many investigators feel that the rush to try to collect the reward money on the part of the public so inundated the police with irrelevant information that any hope of finding the murderer at that point was lost.

In spite of the efforts of an ever-expanding task force, by the time of the 1980 presidential election 17 black children had disappeared and 13 of them had been found murdered. With the election out of the way, national media interest became intense. Camille Bell was being interviewed by reporters from everywhere.

With the release of American hostages by Iran and the inauguration of a new president, the full focus of the nation's attention was turned upon the murders in Atlanta. Atlantans felt, like the former American hostages in Iran, that they were being held hostage by the killing of their children. Everyone hoped and prayed for a quick solution to the murders.

The winter and early spring of 1981 in Atlanta had to be among the worst that any community had ever endured. Assistant Chief Morris Redding, a seasoned police investigator, had been placed in charge of the Special Task Force. The Georgia Bureau of Investigation and the Federal Bureau of Investigation had entered the case. The FBI's presence was an unprecedented action because the FBI lacked jurisdiction. This renewed activity, while not immediately productive, coincided with the finding of ten more bodies. Several of those victims had been missing since 1980; consequently, the bodies were in very bad condition, some to such an extent that the cause of death could not be determined. The bodies turned up in rivers, in wooded areas, and in vacant lots. Whereas the first bodies had been discovered within the Atlanta city limits, later bodies turned up in Fulton, DeKalb, Cobb, and Douglas counties. By the first of June, 26 black males and two black females ranging in ages from seven to 27 years of age had been added to the task force list. Since the end of March five bodies had been found, and these individuals were considerably older than the first victims. Practically no investigators working on the cases thought that they were all related. A majority of the younger children on the list were from poor and broken homes; they were street-wise and were accustomed to doing all kinds of odd jobs to earn a dollar. Generally, they were small for their ages, as were the few adults on the list; in some cases the latter were also mentally slow. None of those on the list appeared to have resisted their attacker or to have been given drugs or alcohol prior to their deaths. None had been sexually assaulted. The police were severely hampered in investigating the cases because there was no apparent motive for the killings.

In 1973 police in Houston, Texas, had dug up a number of bodies of young white boys who had been murdered and buried by Elmer Wayne Henley. In 1978 John W. Gacy, Jr., murdered 33 boys and young adults and buried them in the walls of a house in Illinois. Twisted and thwarted sexual desire appeared to have been the motive for those killings. In Birmingham, Michigan, in 1977, mysterious killings claimed the lives of seven white children. No one was ever arrested for any of the Michigan killings, but at least four and maybe more were thought by police officials to be related. Many investigators believed that the Atlanta murders most resembled the cases in Birmingham, Michigan.

POSSIBLE MOTIVES

From the very beginning it was felt by many blacks and by some whites that the killings in Atlanta were racially motivated. Blacks were being assaulted in Buffalo, New York, and Vernon Jordan of the Urban League, who was a native Atlantan, had been shot in an ambush attack. It was natural to assume that these killings could be of a racial nature. Black parents warned their children to be aware of strangers in general and of whites in particular. Young blacks were on guard so as not to be snatched by white vigilantes. Many thoughtful persons, considering the "unreconstructed" people they knew and pondering the vaunted resurgence of the Ku Klux Klan, realized there were certainly some people who were so warped as to murder the objects of their hatred. But as more victims kept turning up it became evident to nearly everyone that the motive was not racial and that the killer very likely was not white.

When the Center For Research In Social Change began to function in the late sixties, one of its first conclusions was that the police needed to place more reliance on scientific analysis. Certainly no one can accuse Commissioner Brown or anyone else on the police investigative team for not relying on the latest up-to-date scientific methods available. Some 150,000 individuals in selected Atlanta neighborhoods were reached by computerized telephone messages from Brown and mothers of the victims. The calls asked for clues in the cases and gave the persons contacted the opportunity to tell what, if anything, they knew about the cases. Computers were used to make electronic searches for links between cases and to match certain data with particular cases. The FBI attempted to lift fingerprints from the bodies, a very difficult procedure that local police departments are unable to execute. Samples of the soil and of fibrous material at the crime scene were painstakingly gathered and sent to the state crime lab for analysis. More than 1,300 tips were sent out for further analysis. Police and volunteer firemen carried pictures door-to-door throughout the city of missing and slain children. Police took pictures of persons attending funerals of the children on the chance that the killer might derive some ghoulish pleasure out of that aspect of the tragedy. A number of persons were brought in for questioning by the police task force and other metro police departments.

All of which cost a great deal of money. Money to pay for police overtime, money to pay for electronic surveillance, and money to pay for a host of other expenses incurred by the Special Task Force. Besides the money spent by Atlanta and by Fulton and DeKalb counties, as well as the cost to the federal government of keeping a 40-man FBI team in the city, the federal government made available $3,300,000 for the investigation and for mental health treatment of children who had suffered emotional problems stemming from the slayings. The involvement of the federal government to such an extent was unprecedented in what theretofore had always been regarded as a purely local matter. The city was grateful for the assistance, and it is not unrealistic to suppose that considerable violence or other upheavels would have occurred without it.

Not only public money but private money was an essential

part of the investigation. Money from businesses and individuals was received from all over the country. Charity benefits by Frank Sinatra, Aretha Franklin, and Sammy Davis, Junior, and an increase in the reward fund from $100,000 to $500,000 by a gift from former boxing champ Muhammad Ali were but a part of vast sums of money contributed or raised by well-known personalities, school children, big corporations and ordinary citizens. Money poured into City Hall, the Southern Christian Leadership Conference, and the Committee to Stop Children's Murders. The money was used to pay funeral expenses for the victims, to contribute financial assistance to the families of victims, and to provide for recreational activities for Atlanta children during the summer of 1981.

There was almost as much talk and speculation about the money raised as there was about the murder investigation. Certainly no other investigation had ever before in history brought forth such an outpouring of money. People wanted to know if the money was being spent wisely and for the proper purposes. This is another question that will be debated for years to come, if for no other reason than that nobody really knew how much money was actually contributed. Camille Bell's Committee to Stop Children's Murders was severely criticized by many for the way it handled donations. It appeared, however, that if mistakes were made, they came about primarily because the committee had grown so much faster than anyone had anticipated and because the members were unprepared for handling the responsibilities thrust upon them.

"HELPERS"

Money, psychics, dog-trackers, detectives who worked on other renowned murder cases, famous persons, and reporters from all over the world flowed into Atlanta. The Atlanta Bureau of Police Services was chastised for not having a press officer to handle the flood of media folk. The department's response was that it had barely enough resources to handle the unprecedented demands of the investigation and the media would have to fend for itself. A spokesperson eventually was designated to handle press inquiries, but much of the official word from the department continued to come from Commissioner Brown.

On the heels of the press followed a band of young people

from New York who called themselves the Guardian Angels. They were an unofficial group organized to protect users of New York's crime-plagued subway system. Their presence in Atlanta was not welcomed by Atlanta police or by the residents of Atlanta's inner-city neighborhoods. The Guardian Angels came and went, but their coming to the city sparked the formation of a citizen-defender organization in the low-income Techwood Homes area. One would-be leader of the latter group announced plans to arm volunteer vigilantes with baseball bats. In response, the police insisted that no person or group would be permitted to arrogate unto itself any portion of the police function.

Members of the task force and FBI agents interviewed hundreds of people who in some way had aroused suspicion. A number of suspects looked good, but in time further investigation caused the leads to fizzle.

Many ordinary residents of Atlanta were working either to solve the children's murders or to prevent future slayings. Every Saturday morning groups of citizens gathered at various checkpoints throughout the city to search for clues to the missing children. Other people became block parents and members of parent patrol groups and kept an eye out for all neighborhood children. These groups operated separately from the Committee to Stop Children's Murders. Some were under the auspices of city government; some were merely community-wide efforts to help protect the city's children.

The outpouring of money, offers of assistance, and expressions of sympathy continued to be received from around the world. One of the more tangible results, and one which did an inestimable amount of good, was a cost-free week on the Caribbean island of Guadeloupe, which was made possible by Club-Med Inc. The international resorts firm flew several groups of 20 black children to the resort of the privileged. The week of sun, swimming and frolic—a totally new experience for most of the youngsters—caused them to return home with sparkling eyes and only vague reminders of the series of horrors which had caused the hot school-free summer months to loom portentiously over their parents and Atlanta's officials.

NEW DEVELOPMENTS

The tenseness which had gripped Atlanta into the late spring of 1981 was momentarily alleviated on June 4 when

police officials announced with great fanfare that a suspect
had been questioned in connection with the death of 27-year
old Nathaniel Cater, whose body had been fished from the
Chattahoochee River a few days earlier. In an unusual departure from established procedure, Public Safety Commissioner
Lee Brown identified the suspect as Wayne B. Williams, a 23-
year-old black man. Attention had been focused upon him
since early on the morning of May 22, when a police stakeout
under a bridge over the Chattahoochee had heard a loud
splash nearby. Calling to a colleague on the road leading to
the bridge above, he asked whether a car could be seen. The
latter ascertained that one was moving slowly in his direction; when it was stopped a few minutes later the driver identified himself as Williams. FBI agents and police interrogated
him, but had no basis for placing charges. It was not until two
days later that the body of Cater, the city's 28th black murder
victim, was recovered from the river.

A police recruit recalled later that a pile of clothing was in
the back of Williams' car when he was stopped near the
bridge, but no attention was paid to it at the time. Subse-
quently neighbors reported that the next day the suspect was
seen removing several boxes from his home. Williams was
questioned by the FBI, but after several hours he was again
released. He remained under constant surveillance, however,
a circumstance of which he seemed to be aware but which did
not keep him from leading police on several high-speed chases
around Atlanta.

Finally, on June 14, Wayne Williams was arrested and
charged with the murder of Nathaniel Cater. Police stated
that evidence in the form of hairs and carpet fibers collected
from Williams' home and car showed "no significant microscopic differences" from evidence found on Cater's body *and
also on the bodies or from the sites where the bodies of other
victims had been discovered.*

Soon Williams was charged also with the death of Jimmy
Ray Payne, whose body had been found in the Chattahoochee
on April 27. In that case, as in others, the cause of death was
determined to be asphyxiation by means unknown.

A possible clue to the puzzling fact that no evidence had
been uncovered to indicate that any of the victims had
struggled to save their lives was found in one of many newspaper stories dealing with the tragedies. In it the reporter

quoted a member of an emergency rescue crew with whom the suspect often hung out as saying that Williams sometimes sprayed his playful companions with Mace, an aerosol compound with temporarily-disabling qualities.

As the evidence against him continued to mount, there appeared to be more than a passing chance that the accused man would be charged with several more of the young blacks' murders.

Who was Wayne Williams? The answer is not easy, for police and local newspapers reported that he appeared to be many things: a brilliant high school student who became a college drop-out, a radio station operator and free-lance photographer, a procurer of talented young blacks for supposed television appearances, a preparer of his own inflated resumés who delighted in proximity to the powerful and famous, a hustler who created illusory successes upon a foundation of disguised failures, and a man who found the limelight in which he gloried only in the pitiless and destructive publicity which could lead to the permanent loss of his freedom—or even of his life.

The unprofessional, even frivolous, manner in which police officials handled the headlong rush to identify Williams even before he was charged with a crime caused them to be severely criticized. *The Atlanta Constitution* joined the chorus on June 24 with a stinging rebuke captioned "Let The Circus End."

> Wayne B. Williams has been arrested and charged with the slaying of one of the 28 young blacks whose deaths have plunged this city into the depths of fear and tragedy. Even with Williams behind bars, the investigation goes on.
>
> The slayings and the investigation have occurred in a circus-like atmosphere that has given our city an international black eye. The investigation and arrest of Williams also were carried out under the most bizarre of conditions. Around-the-clock open surveillance of the suspect, law suits, press conferences, high level meetings with the governor—all these things have given the investigation a kind of surreal movie-like aura.
>
> It is time now to end the movie spectacular. It is time to let the wheels of justice grind without an attendant carnival. Wayne Williams is behind bars. But in the American tradition, he is presumed innocent until and unless he is proven guilty.
>
> It is time for law enforcement officials to end leaks about evidence in the case. It may also be time to stop worrying about

who pressured whom to initiate the arrest and set the prose-
cutorial system in motion.

Let the show-biz atmosphere dissipate. Let the kooks and
cranks clear out. Let the official press conference (in which no
announcements are made and no questions are answered) come
to an end. Let the criminal justice system take over, and without further hindrance, let justice be done.

Mayor Maynard Jackson attempted to calm the general agi-
tation by noting that "We must be ready to turn *to* each other
and not *on* each other." He agreed with an official of Atlanta's
Coca-Cola Co. who said "The sorrow has been unparalleled,
but the unity has been unprecedented." The mayor went on to
say that despite the tragic killings, Atlanta was still a boom
town. "The impact of the killings on the economy," he added,
"has been negligible."

Atlanta, despite such soothing words, must have been perceived by many millions of persons around the world as having suffered a notable diminution of its once-proud image. The
sparkling New South city of towering skyscrapers and feverish growth, the inheritor of the steel-and-magnolia tradition
of the Old South, was undoubtedly scarred from two years of
trauma, but its staunchest admirers believed its wounds
would not be fatal. Eventually, when justice had taken its
ponderous course, it would again be hailed as "The city too
busy to hate" and "The world's next great city." Until then
Atlantans could be grateful that, for whatever reason, the
shocking series of black murders seemed to have stopped.

If the tragedy of Atlanta in the 1980s can awaken people
everywhere to an awareness of the harsh realities of life in
the closing years of the twentieth century, and also equip
them to cope more effectively with the challenges thus confronted, the victims of the senseless series of murders will not
have given up their young lives entirely in vain. Already it is
apparent that no murder or murder investigation has ever
before touched the lives of so many people. In an age of instant communication, each new development in the seem-
ingly-endless stream of murders was carried via satellite
throughout the world. Eventually a shocked and impatient
public reluctantly realized that cases of this type do not lend
themselves to quick and speedy solutions.

7

The Aftermath

The Heinz, Refoule, Reyman and Garris murders had a profound impact upon police practices in regard to homicides because they were never solved to the satisfaction of everyone, if solved at all. Since these murders involved prominent victims who led unusual lives, and the cases received wide publicity, and because television did not exist at the time, they provided a certain interest, even entertainment, for everyone. These murders occurred in a period of upheaval that led to changes which affected everybody. However, this was not the only backdrop. There was also the background of a rising incidence of homicides within the community, and these four murders were used by the press to highlight the rising number of homicides. These murders made compelling reading and the general public became aware, for the first time, of changing conditions within the city insofar as the homicide rate was concerned.

The public would never have become aroused had not prominent people been killed, and as long as murder was largely confined to the inner-city, mostly-black population of the community, there were few demands that something be done to bring the homicide rate down. But the murder of important people made people *aware*. Once people were made aware, then, they began to realize that the high homicide rate was due mainly to generations of segregation, poverty, and police and public neglect. Therefore, these particular murders became more than just mere homicides; they became the basis of social awareness and, ultimately, police change. Had these murders never occurred, it is very doubtful that the larger community would have become as exercised as it did over the number of homicides within the city. But people who were never aware of a knife-killing within an upstairs room off a back alley across from the downtown railroad tracks were touched by the murder of Henry Heinz in Druid Hills and

Peggy Refoule in Buckhead. The complacency of the very private, untouched worlds of these two havens had been forever disturbed. The people who lived in these neighborhoods were galvanized into taking action which would prevent further intrusions into their private refuge. But once aroused, the people of the community would go on and insist that the police and press work for a more civilized community. The deaths of Henry Heinz, Peggy Refoule, Jeanette Reyman, and John Garris became the impetus which led to public concern which in turn led to startling changes in police practices in regard to homicides.

The following figures indicate the number of homicides, the number of these homicides which were solved, and the number of victims who were black and white in a given period of years. The chart, in some years, indicates more cases solved than homicides for the year. This is because some crimes solved in a particular year were murders of a previous year.

HOMICIDES IN ATLANTA

Year	No. Of Homicides	No. Solved	VICTIMS	
			No. of Whites	No. of Blacks
1944	69	88	13	56
1945	91	87	15	76
1946	97	82	10	87
1947	91	83	9	82
1948	76	78	2	74
1949	88	87	9	79
1950	101	106	15	86
1951	83	83	9	74
1952	102	96	15	87
1953	74	75	4	70
1954	85	79	10	75
1955	79	81	14	65
TOTAL	1036	1025	125	911

These figures cover the period from the end of World War II up until the mid-fifties. It indicates a rising homicide rate during the latter war years. A chart from the Depression years and just afterwards would indicate a similar pattern—

a rising homicide rate during the Depression and reaching a peak in the years immediately following.

In the peak year of 1946, 97 homicides occurred in Atlanta. Afterwards, for the following two years, there is a drop each year until 1949 when the rate goes up slightly, and in 1950 when it jumps, way up, and then goes down again in 1951. A probable explanation for the rise in the years 1949–'50 is the recession and outbreak of war in Korea, but of course the homicide rate will reflect many factors and this is only conjecture. It is interesting that it shows a rise in the 1949–'50 period. After 1950 the homicide rate in Atlanta dropped steadily throughout the early 1950s and then leveled off at an average of about 86. Remarkably, the number of homicides in Atlanta never again went over 100 until 1964. The year 1952 shows a jump. This is misleading. On January 1, 1952, the city of Atlanta extended its limits and took in a large area that practically doubled the size of the city's boundaries. Therefore, the figures for 1952 include statistics for an area twice the size of previous years. What is surprising about this chart which indicates the number of homicides in this period is that even after the city of Atlanta doubled its size and increased its population by addition (*not* including growth) by some fifty thousand people, the homicide rate declined considerably from what it had been in the 'thirties and 'forties.

There are two reasons which have already been mentioned that partially explain this phenomenon: In the first place, the several sensational murders in the 1940s (and there were others besides those mentioned) led to public awareness and support for the press and police to do something about the problem. Secondly, the 1940s were a time of war and social upheaval which contrasted sharply with the period of the rather placid and serene 1950s. And, thirdly, there were profound and far-reaching changes in police procedure.

The courts began to take a stern look at the methods employed by the police in homicide investigations, and cases based upon station-house confessions and continuous grilling of suspects began to fall apart in the courtroom. In order to secure convictions the police had to find other means of establishing guilt in murder cases. Mainly the police had to establish a strong case against a suspect before they arrested him. This led to new procedures. It also meant hard work and longer hours on the part of police detectives.

The national press had been very critical of police procedure in both the Refoule and Reyman murders. It concluded that the Fulton County force made no real effort to find the true killer in the Refoule case, and that detectives merely asked workmen known to have been in the area prior to the murder: "Did you murder Mrs. Refoule? Well . . . No? Do you know anyone who might have?" etc. etc., and *Newsweek* stated that Atlanta police "stumbled over each other" in investigating the Reyman case.

This criticism led to further changes and innovations. The detective division of the Atlanta police force was further upgraded and divided into specialized squads to deal with all types of violent crimes. But no matter how good the organization or the physical set-up, nothing can be done about homicides unless competent men providing outstanding leadership are doing their jobs. In Atlanta, under Mayor Hartsfield and Chief Jenkins, and most importantly Detective Superintendent Glynn Cowan, the Atlanta Police Department developed in the 1950s one of the finest homicide divisions of any police department in the world.

With the implementation of the Plan of Improvement in 1952 the old Fulton County Police Department was merged with the Atlanta force. Residents outside the city limits were impressed with the way Atlanta police were now handling homicides, and were keenly observant that the homicide rate in Atlanta was declining. The bitterness of the Refoule case lingered, and Buckhead residents were only too glad to come under the protection of a police department dedicated to do something about homicides.

The Heinz, Refoule, and Reyman cases mark the end of an era in homicide investigations. Social changes occurred in our society which altered the nature of homicides and the quest for their solution.

We cannot hope to abolish homicides. Murder has been going on since Cain and Abel. It is not likely to cease anytime soon. The problem which faces society today is an attempt to control homicides as much as possible.

We now live in a world very different from Cain and Abel. We live in a world very different from the America of the 1930s, 1940s, and 1950s. Our lives no longer follow the patterns of the past, nor do our homicides. The only thing that is the same is that the killing continues.

The homicide rate in America today is on the increase, not only in our cities but in the suburbs and smaller towns and hamlets. Homicides which in the past were mostly committed in the inner city now occur everywhere. Events have made people knowledgeable. As the Heinz and Refoule murders touched people of another era, widespread coverage of murder by the media has alerted everyone to the increasing number of killings occurring in our society today. As Atlanta in another time learned, today everybody knows what is going on. The reaction, thus far, has led primarily to an increase in weaponry. People fear the increasing violence of our times. We are told and read constantly of people being murdered in the course of a stick-up or robbery. People do not feel safe. The idea has flowered that people will kill you for no reason. People purchase guns because they do not feel safe.

Since the latter 1960s, an increase in the purchase of guns parallels an increase in homicides. While purchasing a gun makes an individual feel he is less likely to be assaulted and murdered, statistics do not bear this out. As the number of guns in private hands climbs, the homicide rate soars.

It is obvious that the elimination of handguns by itself would not abolish homicides. The 1930s were a time of economic depression. For the poor, firearms, unless stolen, were hard to come by: They simply did not have the money to buy guns. But in the 'thirties the homicide rate was inordinately high. As you go back and read through case after case from this period the one striking common denominator that comes across on the fading crumpled pages of the police reports is that, even without guns, if a person is determined to kill, he will find the means of doing so. People were stabbed to death with ice picks, but technological advance has virtually eliminated this weapon. Victims were hacked to death with axes. Household and pocket knives were favorite murder weapons. They severed jugular veins, penetrated hearts, ruptured kidneys, ripped out intestines, and partially succeeded in hacking away heads in an orgy of blood and guts that often made crime scenes look like meat processing plants. A hunk of concrete, bricks, and a variety of rocks of varying size, weight, and design were bashed over people's heads and crushed their skulls and converted the human body into a bloody pulp. We think of murder in the 'thirties being committed by tough talking crooks firing handguns. It was this way on the screen, but not often in real life. In the era of hunger and want and fear and lynchings and electric chairs, homicides were committed by whatever means handy and had about them an aura of intensity that surpasses even the killings of the present day.

The violence of the period was vented upon the police as well as the ordinary citizenry. While making a routine drunk arrest at a downtown tavern, an Atlanta policeman was murdered when a man stabbed him with a knife. The assailant was ultimately arrested and died in the electric chair. A policeman tried to arrest a Negro man who was assaulting a Negro woman with a knife. While making the arrest the black prisoner slashed the officer and nearly severed the jugular vein and cut him severely on the shoulder. The officer was off-duty and on his way home and walking from the police station when he happened upon the situation in the street. The woman was screaming and called out to the policeman for help. He rushed toward her and took hold of his assailant and jerked him away from her. When the assailant cut him, the officer knocked the man down with his pistol, putting the gun out of commission. The man continued to fight with him and the officer beat him over the head with the pistol until he was subdued. Although badly wounded, he walked the man two blocks to the police station and locked him up before seeking medical attention.

But citizens suffered even more. Atlanta police were called to investigate a homicide. They viewed the body at the funeral home, for the police had not been called to the scene when the murder was committed. This happened often in those times. The victim had a cut under his left eye and his face appeared as if it had been hit with an iron pipe or battered with brass knuckles. The victim also had a 1½ inch hole in the back of his head and neck. After much checking, the police managed to locate the crime scene and several witnesses. Everybody stated to the police that the victim fell off the porch during an argument. The police interviewed the individual who was having an argument with the victim and were told that the man just fell off the porch. The eyewitnesses backed up the man's story. The police calculated that the victim fell about 10 feet from the porch to the ground. The ground was free of sticks and stones and could not have made the hole in the victim's head. It was obvious that the man had been brutally murdered. The police talked with numbers of people. No one would incriminate anyone else, for whatever reason. No relatives came forward with any information or demands that the police "do something." The homicide did not make the newspapers. The people concerned had no interest in finding the culprit. The police lost interest. No one was indicted for murder.

This was a typical homicide of the time. They nearly always occurred for no good reason, over nothing; they still do. A quarrel among persons is ended when one of the individuals is murdered. It begins as a case of assault which ends in homicide.

In a case of simple assault, there is even more indifference on the part of the people involved. There was a case of the period when two men got into a quarrel at the factory where they both were employed. At the end of the day tempers had not abated and the two men went outside to settle the argument. A fight ensued and one man pulled a gun. He shot the other man in the abdomen and when the man turned to run away from the gun, the man shot him again in the backside. Both bullets were fired at close range. The bullet which hit the man in the abdomen went clear through the man's body, fortunately by-passing all vital organs on the journey. The second bullet did not go all the way through, but miraculously it also did not penetrate any vital parts of the body. The injured man was given first aid and sent to the hospital. He quickly recovered and was back at work. The man who shot him was not off the job even for a day. Why? The man who was shot said it was just an argument and he was not mad anymore. No, the man who was shot did not wish to press charges or prosecute. Besides, he had sold the gun to his assailant in the first place—on credit! But it was a case where, had either of the bullets varied in the slightest, the man would have been a homicide statistic. Was it not probable that, having used his weapon once, the man would use it again? But there was nothing that could be done. It takes a corpse to arouse people, and, as we have seen in this era, even that often did not excite people very much.

The way homicides are occurring in the present day reminds us of the bloody 'thirties and 'forties all over again. The main difference now appears to be in a change of attitude and in the choice of weaponry. It is now handguns that commit the most homicides and while other means are still employed, none are as much used as firearms. The same cavalier disregard for human life exists, however. Just recently in Atlanta a young expectant mother closed her eyes and fatally wounded her husband after he handed her a cocked .22-caliber pistol and dared her to shoot him. When the police arrived on the scene the young woman told them that she and her husband had an argument over his going down to the Tenth Street area and that during the argument the man kept hitting her and when she began crying and saying that he had hurt her, he became really angry; when he handed his wife the gun and dared her to shoot him, she closed her eyes and pulled the trigger. Her husband, shot in the chest, died in a hospital operating room. There were no witnesses to the murder, but police tended to believe the wife's story. In the old days if a wife had shot her husband she would have told the police it was an accident, that the gun just happened to fire accidentally as her husband approached threateningly. But a new generation has developed a new approach to homicides. They no longer devise elaborate ruses denying guilt—at least in homicides which are the result of a domestic argument. Homicides which are the result of assault and/or robbery are quite a different matter. But an argument between husband and wife which results in the murder of one or the other is all very casual nowadays. Premeditation, planning, intense hatred are all definitely a thing of the past. The police, by talking to the individual, usually determine quickly the facts in the case. The young mother-to-be in the above-mentioned case was routinely indicted for murder. The story attracted scant attention from the media. It was all very matter-of-fact.

A really vicious murder of the 1940s type occurred in the Atlanta metro area a few years ago. A young businesswoman vanished from a shopping center parking lot without a trace. Five days later her bound and gagged body was found covered with leaves in an adjoining county. The killer was traced to Texas. Previously he had tried to use the victim's credit cards and to cash one of her personal checks. When apprehended by the police the killer admitted his guilt. He said that he did not intend to kill her; he had intended only to steal her automobile and credit cards. He stated further that he was on heroin and morphine at the time it all happened. In the 'thirties killers often told police they murdered because they were drinking and did not remember. Harsh and Gallogly pleaded this line. Horace Blalock robbed and murdered to play the "bug." Nowadays all the murderers are on drugs and don't plan to kill and don't remember if they do kill. This aspect of the homicide story has not changed; there is merely a shift of emphasis on what the individual states is his reason or excuse for committing murder. It is doubtful that alcohol, playing the "bug," or drugs are often the cause of homicides, regardless of what the murderers say.

The killer of the young businesswoman was returned to Cobb County to be tried for the murder. The case had received wide publicity and at the time the young woman's body had been found, sight-seers had rushed to the scene in ways reminiscent of the now-legendary Refoule murder. One would expect the murder trial to draw a large crowd. But before the case-followers could even gather up their sewing work and brown-bag lunches, the most sensational would-be murder trial in Atlanta in years was concluded. In a dramatic courtroom scene the 27-year-old murderer entered guilty pleas to charges of murder, kidnap, rape and armed robbery. He was sentenced to four consecutive life terms plus three more years for stealing the victim's car. He would be eligible for parole in seven years, but considering the charges against him, gaining parole in that length of time seemed unlikely, but not impossible. No one had been sentenced to the electric chair in Georgia in a number of years, but it was no doubt still possible and since only a jury could sentence a person to the electric chair, the defendant in this case decided to take his chances with the judge.

In the old days nobody ever copped out in a case like this. The more guilty a person was in a homicide case, the more determined he was to try and beat the rap with a jury. But for a variety of reasons the sensational, headline-grabbing murder trials appear to be a vanishing spectacle.

The homicide rate at present is going up, not down. Three factors, and no doubt many others, are basic to the general upswing in murder. One is the cheap, readily-available handgun. The second is technological advance. Improvements in the field of communication, especially the advent of television, have changed everyone's life, and television has probably played a villain's role in causing the murder rate to accelerate. The third reason is social revolution and war.

The first of these factors concerns firearms. Although we live in an era of generally rising prices, the overall cost of a handgun is less now than it was in the thirties. Guns are in great supply and available at relatively low cost. Every time a national figure becomes a homicide victim, there is a movement to restrict the manufacture and sale of handguns, a movement which wanes in momentum rather quickly. Even though there was great demand for a ban on the sale of guns following the assassinations of national figures in the 1960s, there are many more guns sold to private individuals now than there were then.

Approximately 80% of some type of firearm is responsible for all homicides. Virtually all homicides which are the result of assault and/or robbery are committed with a handgun. Few robberies are carried out by the robber demanding the money from the cash register at the point of a knife. It is always a gun, or the *threat* of a gun which is a factor in hold-ups. Without the presence or the threat of the presence of a gun, there would be far fewer deaths as a result of robbery. The person who is a homicide victim as a result of a robbery is far more likely to be innocent of any wrong-doing than the person who is killed as a result of a quarrel in a domestic situation.

The latter situation is the traditional or Cain-Abel type homicide wherein the victim is a relative or friend of the assailant. In our society today, robbery resulting in a murder is armed robbery. It is doubtful that the would-be thief without his firearm would be nearly so bold and audacious. And even in street crime when the victim is robbed, if the robber is armed with a knife and the victim is slashed, the victim's chances of recovery are far greater than if his assailant had been armed with a revolver and had used it. There is little rationality for the continuing widespread availability of firearms. Yet there are more guns available for killing people than ever before. How can such a situation exist in a supposedly civilized society and, because of the guns and killing, are we becoming less civilized day by day?

Nothing is done about all these lethal weapons in our midst because there is no public pressure for action. If the press and the police had widespread public support, the gun problem could be solved. People say that a law outlawing guns would be of no use because it would not be enforceable. But if the police had the support and a law, then guns could be removed from the hands of those most likely to use them to commit homicides. There is no demand to do away with firearms. Everybody who has a gun is determined to keep it. Indeed, people are paranoid on the subject of guns, and the killing continues. Even in the wild west things always got so bad that a sheriff would get elected to office with strong support of the community to "do something." The first thing the new sheriff did to make the community more civilized was to have everybody do away with their gun belts. Today we have returned to the wild west mentality, and things may have to get worse before they can get better. A society which is fearful of violence and places its trust in guns becomes more violent and then more fearful—a dizzying merry-go-round of guns and death.

If we take an historical view of homicides, things do not appear quite as bleak. Since the time of Cain and Abel, people have become more civilized and are less prone to kill one another. We are much superior to medieval times, when people were hacked to death at random. Literally nobody was safe. But comparing our society with past times is not entirely flattering. Most other aspects of medieval times are no longer prevalent in our present-day society. Certainly we face many problems in our world today, but they are mostly the problems of modern times created by modern man. Homicides are a rather ancient link with our medieval ancestors. We should have disposed of them long ago, but have not.

Technological innovations, in direct contrast with our medieval links, also contribute to the high homicide rate. The coming of the automobile brought an upsurge of ride-rob types of homicides in the 1930s. Probably the most significant technological advance which touches everyone and contributes to an increase in homicides is television.

Television begins to look like a possible culprit or suspect when one takes a very close look at the individual homicides of the present time. Eliminating homicides which occur incidental to a robbery and concentrating solely on the Cain-Abel type of killing, one is immediately struck with an emerging pattern. There is in these murders a certain flipness, one might say cuteness, wherein the perpetrators of these crimes appear to be acting out something which to them lacks little semblance to reality, and their bravado and their posing appear to be an imitation of what they may have seen on tele-

vision. There is a very strong indication nowadays that when
one person shoots another he does not really believe the bullet
is going to fire and kill the person. He has seen so much killing on the screen, he is so attached to his handgun—for reasons that neither he nor society fully understands—that
when pushed so far he takes the gun and kills. Afterwards the
killer does not say anything. People used to plead and carry
on afterwards and say over and over again that they did not
mean to do it. Today most likely they will not say anything.
Or if they do say anything they will very carefully give accurate details and facts about everything that had happened.
The closest they come nowadays to the old "I didn't mean to
kill him" routine is a quiet and rather rueful "I didn't 'know'
that it would kill him." From the actual killing, through the
time of interrogation, even to the appearance in court, the accused of today very often acts as he has seen others act—as if
he is giving some kind of performance which is expected.
Maybe it is not correct to blame television for a more casual
attitude toward homicide. It could merely be the trend of the
times. But what has affected more the times in which we live
than this marvelous technological development?

Maybe social revolution and war. In times of social unrest
and war, the homicide rate always goes up. In the 1960s the
homicide rate began going up as civil rights demonstrations
and anti-war protests accelerated. The period of the Depression saw an increase in homicides, as did the turbulent years
after World War II. There seems to be a similarity between
the period of the late 1940s and the 1970s. The rise and pattern of homicides in both periods is similar. If they were similar, then we should have seen a leveling-off of homicides in
the latter 1970s. But we live in more complex times and
things never repeat themselves exactly, especially homicides.
With all the guns in circulation and the continuing changes
in the way people live, it is doubtful the homicide rate will
decline very much in the 1980s unless concerted action is
taken at a governmental level.

One area that is of particular importance is the field of scientific advancement in police investigative procedures. There
has not been enough advancement in the field of detective
work in recent years. A great deal of money has come into
police work lately, but most of the new resources have been
spent on sophisticated weaponry—from Mace to helicopters—

but very little has been spent on basic research. And this is critical in detective work. When homicides began to increase in the thirties, scientific analysis, for the first time, came to be used in the investigation of murders. The two major developments in chasing culprits came with the perfection of ballistics tests and fingerprints. The development of technology to the point where it could be determined if a certain bullet was fired from a particular gun has had an enormous impact on police work. When a person is shot, the bullet becomes a vital piece of evidence; it cannot be retrieved by the perpetrator. Conversely, if a person is stabbed to death it is far more difficult to link the murderer with the crime unless the weapon is recovered. Thus, bullets have become a vital piece of police procedure and have been used as strong evidence to bring guilty persons to justice.

Fingerprints are probably the best scientific advancement thus far in the field of detective work. It is still quite often the major means of linking a particular suspect at a certain crime scene. One would imagine that, considering all the publicity and knowledge of fingerprints among the general population and especially the criminal society, that would-be murderers would take precautions not to leave fingerprints behind. But, as we have seen, most murders today are not planned. The perpetrator does not intend to kill, and if he does kill he does so as a by-product of some quarrel or disagreement. The murderer is shocked as much by the killing as the victim. He does not think about fingerprints, or, perhaps with the emerging flipness in regard to murders, does not even care.

Some criminal investigators feel that the fingerprinting method should be extended to cover the entire population, and that the FBI should have everyone's fingerprints on file. This raises cries of restrictions on the non-criminal population that should not be placed upon them. More than likely, however, it will inevitably be necessary.

Scientific investigation desperately needs to go beyond ballistics and fingerprinting. Murders, as we have seen, often become very difficult to solve unless the individual is caught in the act, or unless there are eyewitnesses. It is almost impossible to conceive of the number of police man-hours spent upon investigating the Refoule and Reyman cases. Or of calculating the cost to the tax payer. In those days the police would drop everything else to work on a sensational murder case, but because of crime in other areas and of the varied demands made upon police today, this is no longer possible. There are not enough man-hours. The investigation of a homicide today is severely restricted because of the time element and the press of other cases. The police are burdened with other duties. No one any longer has the time to reflect about a homicide because one case is constantly interrupted by additional killings. It is, too often, an emergency room procedure. There is no time to think about or work out the jigsaw pieces of the latest homicide puzzle. Thus the police need improved scientific means to help speed up the investigation of murders.

The time of day, the day of the week, and the month of the year have a distinct relationship to homicides. The most popular hour for killing is Saturday night between 8 and 12 midnight. These same hours on Friday night are almost as dangerous. The next most likely day to be killed is Sunday, but this includes, of course, the Saturday night carry-over. There are three times more homicides on Friday, Saturday, and Sunday than on the other five days of the week. Monday is a slow day for murder, and Tuesday the least deadly day of the week. If couples need to have heated arguments, they should always plan them for early Tuesday afternoon. Wednesday and Thursday, in the past, were rather slow days but are picking up considerably, and as the work week continues to contract it is quite possible that Thursday will become as deadly a day as Friday. In Atlanta and other Southern towns in the 'forties and through the early 'fifties, it became a common practice for all the stores to close around noon on Wednesday in order for employees to have a half-day off. The homicide rate in this era rose somewhat on Wednesday afternoon and evening. Is it only a coincidence that the Refoule and Reyman murders occurred on Wednesday afternoon?

So much for being murdered Monday through Sunday. How about January through December? The following figures list the number of murders, by months, which occurred in Atlanta in the period from 1944 to 1956.

Month of the Year	Number of Murders in that Month from 1944–1956
JANUARY	77
FEBRUARY	71

MARCH	92
APRIL	101
MAY	76
JUNE	101
JULY	107
AUGUST	117
SEPTEMBER	111
OCTOBER	85
NOVEMBER	74
DECEMBER	106
TOTAL	1118

The figures indicate that from a medium rate in January, the incidence of murder drops in February to its lowest point of the year, begins to rise slightly in March and higher in April, and then dips downward in May. This indicates a slightly higher rate of murder in the spring months over wintertime. But it is nothing compared to what happens in the summer months. The murder rate begins climbing in June and peaks at the hot point of the year in July and August. Even the advent of air conditioning has had little impact on the murder rate. Quite obviously, people most inclined toward murder do not live in air-conditioned apartments and houses. In September the murder rate goes down once again, but the rate in September is still higher than in June. From October through February the murder rate is generally downward but does take a spurt upward in December. In recent years, there has been an increase in murders in late November. As the length of the Christmas season expands, the murder rate climbs upward.

A community which is experiencing a higher murder rate in January and February over past years might as well resign itself to a whopper year of killings because it is almost certain that if the rate is climbing over past years in the slow months, in all likelihood it is going even higher by mid-summer.

Where a person is killed remains a pretty stable statistic. People have always been more likely to be murdered in their homes than at a place of business or on the street. Nearly always when a person is killed in the home, he was killed by a relative or a friend.

Cain-Abel killings occur in the home. That is why murders

which deviate from this pattern become so difficult to solve.
People could not believe that Henry Heinz was killed in his
home by someone unknown to him. The Reyman murder did
not occur in the home. This is a possible reason for believing
that the person who murdered her was not known to the victim. We still do not know whether Peggy Refoule was murdered in her home, but in any case it was in the vicinity. This,
in the eyes of the police, made the husband suspect.

Contrary to popular belief, being murdered on the street is
no more likely than in the past. The jump in the number of
homicides is very real, but this increase is a reflection of
people being murdered in their residences, rather than on the
street. People murdered at their place of business shows only
a slight increase. More cash registers are being robbed than
ever before, but a murder seldom occurs as a result, and when
it does it is more likely to be an accident than anything
planned.

In Atlanta, during the period of 1930 through 1960, a black
person was five times more likely to become a murder victim
than a white person. This did not change much in the 1970s.
There is in the 1980s an increase in white victims but also an
increase in black victims. The rate is pretty much—with perhaps a slight increase among the percentage of blacks—what
it was in the past. Therefore, all past efforts to do something
about black killings have accomplished little.

Insofar as murder and level of income are concerned, there
again appears only very slight changes over the years. Homicides committed in high-income areas and involving prominent people still get the most attention and publicity, although they occur very seldom. There is a decrease in
homicides in high-income groups and a very sharp decline in
Cain-Abel killings within this group. Well-off people are not
murdered with the frequency that they once were. It would
appear to be bad news for the mystery writers.

Of course, the largest number of murders, those which receive the least attention and least publicity, are those involving people in the lowest income group. Poor people have always been the most prone to get killed, and their rate of
increase is still the highest. There is an increase of murders
among people of the middle-income group. The increase is not
as great as among the poor, but when we consider that murders in the high-income group are declining, even the small

rise in murders in the middle class should be considered significant. Practically all of these killings are of the Cain-Abel type.

If a person is concerned about being murdered, the safest place for him to be is on the street on a Tuesday afternoon in February. The time and place most likely for a person to be murdered is in his second-floor walk-up home on a Friday and Saturday night in late summer. Unfortunately, pinpointing the location of homicides does not lessen their occurrence. It does provide some interesting sidelights of changing patterns of homicides.

The murders of President Kennedy, Martin Luther King, Jr., and Robert Kennedy in the decade of the 1960s somehow ripped away the veils of mystery and intrigue that have hovered over homicides of the past. The television medium made everyone feel what it was like to be a part of a murder. Before, it had always been the family and friends of the victim who suffered, but television allowed everybody to suffer. For the first time society experienced what the families of Henry Heinz and Peggy Refoule and countless other families had experienced. We then realized what the relatives of these people could have told us long before—murders are not much fun.

Any police detective who has spent years investigating homicides would agree. The one thing that any police detective has a hard time understanding is the public's fascination with murders. To them, investigating murders is a grueling, unpleasant job. A police detective learns very quickly the lack of value placed upon human life. He wonders as he examines blood-drenched bodies, interviews stony-faced or hysterical relatives, and follows an often haphazard court procedure if there will ever be any end to all the killing.

Police detectives who work every day at the job of solving homicides are greatly concerned at the increasing frequency with which they are committed. They feel generally that people who murder are nowadays let off too lightly. In many instances, those who are convicted of murder get off with light sentences or even probation, whereas in the past they would have gotten twenty years or life. Some investigators firmly believe that the re-institution of capital punishment is the only solution to making a dent in the rising murder rate. Others believe that even the chair, if it were revived, would not be the deterrent that it once was. People who commit murder, they argue, are nowadays totally unaware of or unconcerned about the consequences of their acts. However, practically all detectives are united on one point: They firmly favor a stiff gun-control law. It is interesting that the day-in and day-out viewing of what guns can do to the human body makes this rather hardened group become appalled at the continued increase in the number of guns in the hands of citizens.

Some detectives say that if you were to eliminate all cops, judges, parole officers, and courts, it would have a highly negligible effect upon the homicide rate. As one seasoned Atlanta detective put it: "People were being murdered before I came on the job, people are being murdered now, and people will be murdered after I am gone."

In Atlanta, in another era, because of a variety of factors, the homicide rate was reduced. We have covered the events and factors which brought this about. We will add quickly that even then murder was not abolished, but the homicide rate was brought lower than it had ever been before and was stabilized for a rather lengthy period. It is therefore a fact of the past that when the public is aroused, the press is alert, and the police vigilant, society can reduce the number of killings occurring in a given locality at a particular time.

Many people feel that an increase in homicides can be dealt with only by harsh measures and a return to capital punishment. But more than likely this would lead only to more taking of lives and would make our society more violent and less civilized. A look at how one community, Atlanta, responded to an increase in homicides in a past era of upheaval and social change can be instructive to the problem of the present day. The response of the police and public to the Refoule killing was not exemplary, but the police and the community learned from that experience and as a result went on to do something about future investigations of homicides. Police effort should be toward newer methods and a turning away from, and not a return to, past methods. If we are willing and determined to make the effort, we can do something about the problem without a resort to violence. If we do not make the effort, murders in growing numbers will continue to plague all of our lives.

Credits for Illustrations

The author acknowledges his indebtedness and his appreciation to the following sources for the illustrations indicated:

Skyline of Atlanta—Atlanta Chamber of Commerce.

Fox Theatre, Fulton Tower, Ansley Hotel, Mrs. Henry Heinz, Rainbow Terrace, and Terminal Station—Atlanta Historical Society.

Henry Heinz and Mayor William B. Hartsfield, Horace Blalock—*Atlanta Weekly*.

Judge and Mrs. Robert Refoule, Refoule home—*The Atlanta Journal-Constitution*.